Jim Tolpin's
Table Saw
Magic

POPULAR WOODWORKING BOOKS
CINCINNATI, OHIO
www.popularwoodworking.com

READ THIS IMPORTANT SAFETY NOTICE

To prevent accidents, keep safety in mind while you work. Use the safety guards installed on power equipment; they are for your protection. When working on power equipment, keep fingers away from saw blades, wear safety goggles to prevent injuries from flying wood chips and sawdust, wear headphones to protect your hearing, and consider installing a dust vacuum to reduce the amount of airborne sawdust in your woodshop. Don't wear loose clothing, such as neckties or shirts with loose sleeves, or jewelry, such as rings, necklaces or bracelets, when working on power equipment. Tie back long hair to prevent it from getting caught in your equipment. People who are sensitive to certain chemicals should check the chemical content of any product before using it. The author and editors who compiled this book have tried to make the contents as accurate and correct as possible. Plans, illustrations, photographs and text have been carefully checked. All instructions, plans and projects should be carefully read, studied and understood before beginning construction. Due to the variability of local conditions, construction materials, skill levels, etc., neither the author nor Popular Woodworking Books assumes any responsibility for any accidents, injuries, damages or other losses incurred resulting from the material presented in this book.

Jim Tolpin's Table Saw Magic. Copyright © 1999 by Jim Tolpin. Printed and bound in the United States of America. All rights reserved. No part of this book may be reproduced in any form or by any electronic or mechanical means including information storage and retrieval systems without permission in writing from the publisher, except by a reviewer, who may quote brief passages in a review. Published by Popular Woodworking Books, an imprint of F&W Publications, Inc., 1507 Dana Avenue, Cincinnati, Ohio, 45207. First edition.

Visit our Web site at www.popularwoodworking.com for information on more resources for woodworkers.

Other fine Popular Woodworking Books are available from your local bookstore or direct from the publisher.

03   02   01   00   5   4   3   2

Library of Congress Cataloging-in-Publication Data

Tolpin, Jim.
    Jim Tolpin's table saw magic / by Jim Tolpin -- 1st ed.
        p.   cm.
    Includes index.
    ISBN 1-55870-512-0 (alk. paper)
    1. Woodworking tools.   2. Circular saws.   3. Woodwork.   I. Title.
TT186.T64   1999   99-13009
684'.083--dc21   CIP

Edited by Michael Berger, Mark Thompson
Designed by Brian Roeth
Production coordinated by Erin Boggs
Production art by Lisa D. Fryxell
Computer illustrations by Settingpace and Joseph W. Bradley

Dedication

This book, the summation of all I have
learned on and about the tool that for
years put the bread and butter on our
table, I dedicate to my son Yuri.

METRIC CONVERSION CHART

TO CONVERT	TO	MULTIPLY BY
Inches	Centimeters	2.54
Centimeters	Inches	0.4
Feet	Centimeters	30.5
Centimeters	Feet	0.03
Yards	Meters	0.9
Meters	Yards	1.1
Sq. Inches	Sq. Centimeters	6.45
Sq. Centimeters	Sq. Inches	0.16
Sq. Feet	Sq. Meters	0.09
Sq. Meters	Sq. Feet	10.8
Sq. Yards	Sq. Meters	0.8
Sq. Meters	Sq. Yards	1.2
Pounds	Kilograms	0.45
Kilograms	Pounds	2.2
Ounces	Grams	28.4
Grams	Ounces	0.04

About the Author

Jim Tolpin has worked professionally in woodworking as a custom cabinetmaker for nearly 25 years. In the last ten years, he has turned his attention to writing about general woodworking, cabinetmaking, finish carpentry and, more recently, architectural design. He has written articles for most of the major woodworking magazines and maintains a regular column for both *CabinetMaker* and *Woodshop News* magazines. His other books include *Working at Woodworking; Finish Carpenter's Manual; Measure Twice, Cut Once* and *Building Traditional Kitchen Cabinets*. He can be reached through his Web site at www.cottagehome.net.

Acknowledgments

I must first of all acknowledge a certain 9" Rockwell-Delta table saw, long ago given over to another woodworker's hands: My first power saw, bought with a month's worth of paychecks, and the Trojan horse in which I rode into jobs that were well over my apprenticemanship-level head. I have much to owe to this small but sturdy tool. For without its help I would never have pulled off those challenging jobs so I could learn and go on to bigger and better projects. Even though it has long since been replaced by a much larger and more modern machine, I still remember that little 9" Delta with much fondness.

And then, of course, there are the people to thank whose contributions were essential to the creation and production of this book:

• Kevin Ireland for talking me into writing a book about the table saw in the first place.

• Bob Moran for his extensive and insightful technical and editorial contributions.

• Editor Adam Blake for turning my pictures, drawings and reams of words into a readable and worthwhile book.

• Woodworker Jim Bringham for his astute suggestions on safety and Nathaniel Smelser for some fixture suggestions.

• Engineer John Jory—creator of AngleWright tools—for his considerable expertise on setting up miter angles.

• Engineer and woodworker Mark Duginske for technical advice about his eminently useful Minitrack system.

• Jacob Middleton for giving me a hand (literally) during the photo shoots.

• Craig Wester for his photographic work.

• These suppliers and manufacturers who loaned me tools—and advice—over the course of producing this book: Airware America (Racal); AngleWright Tool Co.; Delta International Machinery Corp.; Forrest Manufacturing Co., Inc.; HTC Products; Industrial Safety Co.; In-Line Industries; JDS Company (Accu-Miter); Jesada Tools; Jet Equipment and Tools, Inc.; Frank Klausz (of Klausz-Tech); Lie Nielsen Tools; Mesa Vista Design; Record Tools, Inc.; Modulus 2000 Machinery, Inc.; Rei Tech; Taylor Design Group, Inc. (Incra); Woodhaven; and Woodworker's Supply, Inc.

And last but not least:

• Cabinetmaker extraordinaire John Marckworth for his help with fixture development and for other technical contributions since this book's inception.

TABLE OF CONTENTS

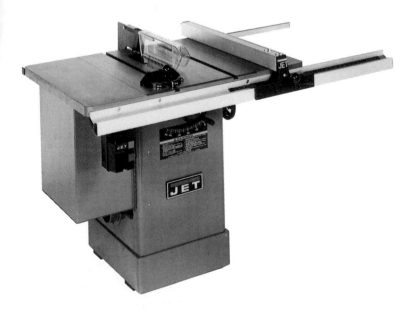

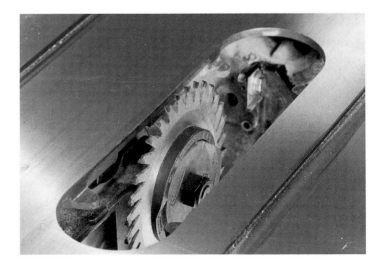

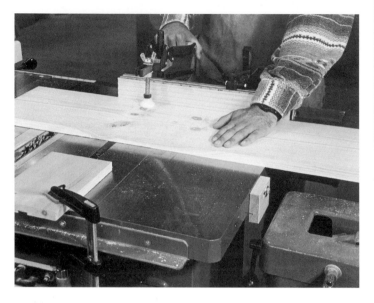

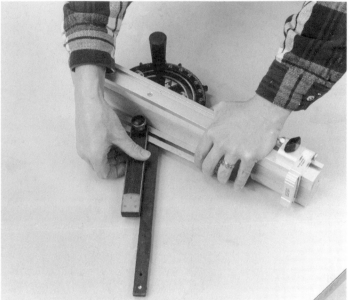

INTRODUCTION

If you, a seafaring carpenter, were shipwrecked on a deserted tropical island and could choose only one power tool to take with you, which one would it be? (We'll assume there is a magical source of electricity, of course.) The stock answer is the band saw, for with this tool you could easily create the curved components of a boat—and thus your ticket back to civilization.

But that wouldn't be my first choice. If I found myself shipwrecked on some tropical island after living for nearly two decades here in the soggy Pacific Northwest, I doubt I'd much want to leave. And since I intend to hang around, I'd want the one best tool with which I could create many of the essential parts of my dwelling such as siding, windows, doors and trimwork. With a roof over my head, I'd then eagerly go on to make cabinetwork and furnishings, using the tool to quickly create the most complex furniture components.

That tool would be (as if you haven't already guessed) the table saw. For it is this machine—of all the power tools at a woodworker's disposal—that most quickly produces straight cuts (not to mention grooves, dadoes and rabbets) with unfailing accuracy. With the help of shop-made stock supports, it's a cinch to handle long boards or wide panels—even without my man Friday. And, with the aid of certain fixtures, which I will show you how to build, I can cut the tiniest workpieces with accuracy and safety. I will also introduce you to the basic procedures and fixture systems that allow you to produce any number of identical pieces with speed and precision.

And it doesn't stop there. I will also show you how to create my "Universal Fence Fixture"—the heart of my table saw system to which an entire galaxy of accessories and sliding fixtures can be attached. With this system you can use the table saw to create a wide variety of joints with speed and precision: from mortise-and-tenon joints to tongue-in-groove and spline joints, to box and cross-lap joints. Other innovative fixtures will help you produce moldings of every description (including cove profiles wider than those produced by industrial-strength shapers) and reproduce complex shapes. I'll even show you how to use the table saw as a sanding machine.

At this point, I doubt you'll be surprised when I go on to present fixtures you can build that will allow you to cut curves and circles. Which reminds me. Maybe I would eventually build that boat with its curvaceous components after all. Till then, you'll find this shipwrecked carpenter working away on his table saw—not to mention his tan.

CHAPTER one

The Table Saw

The table saw is a magnificently simple machine—little more than a table through which a spinning blade partially protrudes. A rip fence set parallel to the blade guides a piece of wood through the blade lengthwise, while the miter gauge guides the wood crosswise. That would be the end of this story if all you could do with this tool was rip or crosscut boards.

The table saw is capable of performing an incredibly wide range of cutting tasks. That's because the table saw—even my grandfather's funky homemade version with the white oak top—is highly adjustable. It boasts two rack and worm-gear assemblies that allow you to raise and lower the blade and to tilt it up to 45° from vertical. It has guide rails to ensure that the rip fence sits parallel to the blade at a selected distance. The miter gauge allows you to lock its guide fence at an angle to the blade. Adjustability, in combination with the jigs and fixtures I'll be showing you, makes the table saw one of the most versatile and essential machines in your woodshop.

TYPES OF TABLE SAWS

There are four basic types of table saws: benchtop, contractor's, stationary and combination. Each offers a particular set of attributes, capabilities and recommended applications. If you are looking for a new table saw, remember that saws vary in quality. Being well-informed will ensure that you get the saw that best suits your wallet and your woodworking needs.

Benchtop Saws

A benchtop saw, though light enough for one person to heft onto a bench or into the back of a truck, is capable of performing most of the operations of a full-size saw—though on a smaller scale.

A lithograph showing an early table saw.

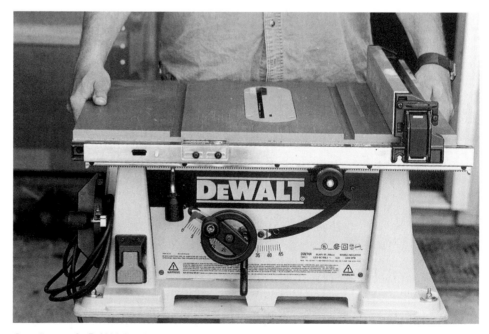

Overall view of a DeWalt benchtop saw—light enough to carry.

This Ryobi benchtop saw is tricked out with options: stand, extension tables, sliding crosscut table, router support and integral vacuum system. It now approaches the weight and appearance of a contractor's saw, but it is still at heart a lightweight benchtop.

Benchtop saws are legless table saws that you can clamp to a workbench for use. When not in use, they can be stored completely out of the way. Benchtop saws, like all other table saws, are measured by the maximum diameter of blade they can accept: in this case, either 8" or 10". Of course, the larger the blade, the deeper the cut you can make. On most benchtop machines, an 8" blade cuts 2¼" deep at 90° and 1⅝" deep when the blade is tilted to its maximum angle of 45°. A 10" saw cuts 3" deep at 90° and 2¼" deep at 45°. Be aware, though, that benchtop saws have modest power, and you may have to make two or more passes to accomplish a full-depth cut, especially in hardwoods.

Most models of benchtop saws have nearly all the blade-adjustment features and guide systems of the larger saws. They are thus capable of making the same types of cuts and employing many of the same blades and accessories. It's important, however, when choosing a benchtop saw, to check that its arbor—the threaded

driveshaft to which the blade is bolted—is ⅝" in diameter. The ½"-diameter arbors on some saws not only require special blades but tend to wobble under load. Also, check that the arbor has enough length to allow you to install dado sets for cutting grooves and rabbets.

There is a price to pay for the diminutive size and relatively low cost of these machines. The arbor of a benchtop saw is often "motorized"—attached directly to the motor—instead of belt driven like the arbors of saws in other categories. While this cuts down on weight, not to mention the cost of production, this drive system lacks the torque gained by a speed-reducing belt drive and may bog down or even stall under heavy load. Motorized benchtop saws usually have universal motors, like those in routers, so they're significantly louder than saws with induction motors. In fact, benchtop saws are screamers.

Still, if you are working in a small shop with stock that is seldom more than 4' long and no more than 1" thick, the

benchtop saw may prove to be the only saw you will ever need. I wouldn't have said this several years ago. Until recently, due to ubiquitous poor quality in table surfaces and guide attachments (i.e., the rip fence and miter gauge), precision cuts with benchtop saws were nearly impossible. But newer models are very much improved, featuring precision-cast aluminum table surfaces that are much flatter than the old stamped-steel versions, and fence systems that lock down securely and accurately.

One model, shown above, even offers an optional sliding table for precision crosscutting, extension tables, a router-mounting system and an integral vacuum system. This machine can perform most of the same tasks as its larger brethren as long as you work with small-scale projects, don't treat the lightly made components too roughly and don't push the motor.

Finally, consider this: The money you save purchasing a benchtop machine can be put toward high-quality carbide

Heavier, larger and more powerful than the bench-top saw, the contractor's saw is, for the money, the best all-around saw for both construction work and home woodshop projects.

blades—the number one way to improve the speed and precision of any table saw. I'll have a lot more to say about choosing saw blades in chapter four.

Contractor's Saws

Contractor's saws are the next step up from benchtop saws. Designed for more rugged work than the benchtop variety, these saws are still light enough, at roughly 300 pounds, to move around with help from a friend. Contractor's saws spin a 9"- or 10"-diameter blade, sit on an open steel stand, and usually feature tough, cast iron tables. Their rip fences can be positioned 24" away from the right side of the blade, sometimes more. Extension fence sys-

tems that expand the capacity to 48" or more are a typical option. If you have the shop space and intend to frequently cut plywood to size, these extensions may be well worth having.

The arbor of a contractor's saw will accept a variety of accessories, including dado cutters and molding heads. These saws are usually belt driven by a 1½ hp induction motor that mounts at the back of the saw. With the saw well tuned and driving a sharp blade, this is enough power to rip 2"-thick oak if it's free of internal stresses. Furthermore, because the motor is held with a universal mounting bracket, it's an easy matter to upgrade to a more powerful motor. If you rip a lot of dense

hardwood or green construction lumber, ask your saw dealer to recommend a suitable motor for your particular saw.

While the saw's open stand helps portability, it can also be one of its drawbacks. The stand's potential for racking, coupled with its light weight, translates into a lack of stability and inertia. This can mean a saw that tends to tip over when you're handling large, heavy workpieces. Better saws of this type feature a stand made of heavy sheet metal with wide cross braces and well-bolted joint intersections. A tendency to tip can be solved by throwing a sandbag across the frame's bottom supports. Nevertheless, a lightly made, poorly designed stand can wobble

JET 10" STATIONARY SAW
The stationary saw is a much heavier and more stable machine than a contractor's saw. Its precision-machined and balanced parts are the key to its ability to produce cuts with unwavering accuracy in a production environment.

and rack dangerously, and there's little you can do about it short of modifying it or building your own.

The contractor's saw is portable, upgradeable and has a full range of features. It is therefore a perfect choice for on-site construction work and for the home workshop. If you have room for a full-size saw, can spend a little more money than you might for a benchtop variety, but aren't ready for the major investment of a stationary saw, this is the saw for you.

Stationary Saws

A stationary saw can cost twice as much as a contractor's saw. I wasn't exaggerating when I said it's a major investment. And a stationary saw is still a 10" table saw, so what makes it worth that kind of money? Not much, if you have no intention of using it for anything but carpentry

ROBLAND X-31 COMBINATION MACHINE
Though not much bigger than a dedicated stationary table saw, a combination machine will, with several minutes of setup time, turn into a planer, jointer, shaper or mortiser. It is an ideal solution for a woodworker willing to spend money on quality machinery but with limited room in which to house it.

HOW FLAT IS YOUR TABLE SAW'S TOP?

To check how flat a table saw top is, you'll need a reliable straightedge. Before you start, lower the blade all the way down and then remove the throat plate and rip fence. If the table has extension wings, be sure they are not projecting above the surface of the main table—the straightedge will inform you of this right away. If they do project, you'll have to loosen their attachment bolts, nudge them flush using a rubber mallet (or a hammer and a block of wood) and then retighten the bolts.

Begin the check with the straightedge, sweeping it across the table. If there are high spots, the edge will rock on them. Low spots show up as gaps under the edge. A spotlight directed across the table at eye level, opposite from where you are standing, may help you see these gaps. Mark the spots with a crayon so you don't "discover" the same spot several times and get a wrong impression.

Even if a table is free of humps and hollows, it may be warped. To detect warp with the straightedge, first check that there are no gaps or humps along the four edges. Then check both diagonals. If the straightedge reveals no gap along one diagonal but reveals gap along the other diagonal, the table is warped.

You can also check for warp with a pair of winding sticks (straight sticks ¾"x1" and a little longer than the width of the table saw). Place one stick across the front of the table and the other across the back. Hunker down and sight across the tops of the sticks. Your eye is an amazing instrument: You will be able to see if the top edges of the sticks are out of parallel by as little as .1°.

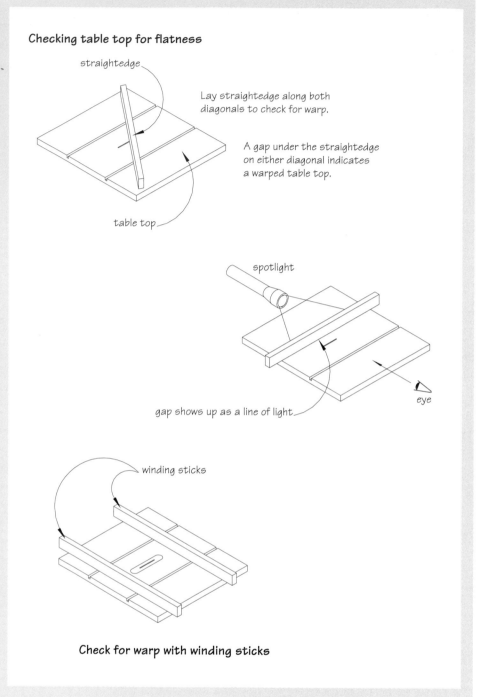

Checking table top for flatness

straightedge

Lay straightedge along both diagonals to check for warp.

A gap under the straightedge on either diagonal indicates a warped table top.

table top

spotlight

gap shows up as a line of light

eye

winding sticks

Check for warp with winding sticks

work and occasional small cabinets and furniture.

But if you were to build lots of kitchen cabinets or fine, intricately joined furniture on a contractor's saw, you would probably want to replace its standard fence system to gain width capacity and precision. You might also increase the size of the motor to improve cutting speed, single-pass depth capacity and motor service life. You might enclose the stand to prevent racking and to keep the sawdust from spreading throughout the shop. At

this point, you would have spent almost as much on your contractor's saw as you would have spent buying a stationary saw, and you still wouldn't have as good a saw.

There are some good reasons why a typical 10" stationary saw weighs 200 pounds more than a 10" contractor's saw and costs at least $200 more than that tricked out one. The additional weight of thicker steel, heftier castings and the enclosed stand make the stationary saw an absolutely stable work platform. The heaviest workpiece I can lift and push

across the table will not slide or tip my stationary saw.

Much of the additional weight comes from heavy castings—not just in the massive table but throughout the innards of the machine. The more massive components aren't there just for the sake of stability. The beefier arbor-support assembly ensures rigidity of the arbor under load, reducing blade drift in the cut. The extra mass helps dampen vibrations, reducing blade wobble. The net result for the cabinetmaker is significant-

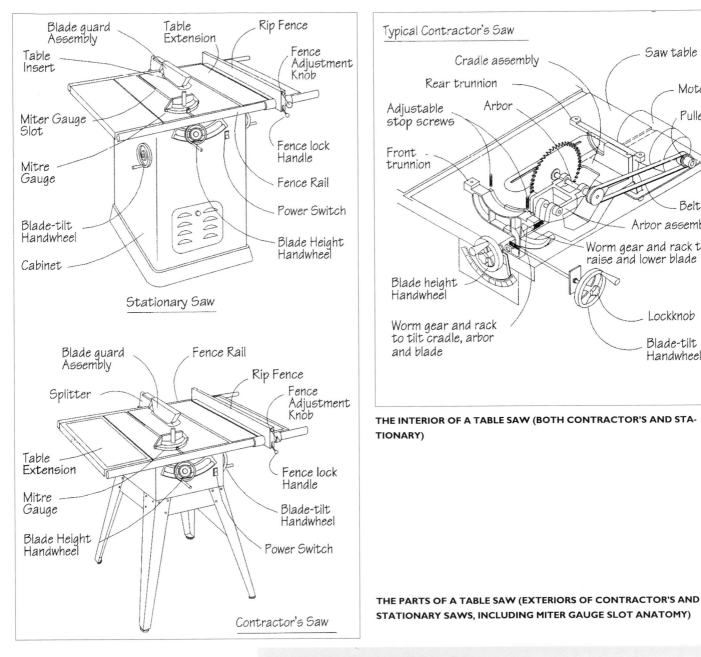

THE PARTS OF A TABLE SAW (EXTERIORS OF CONTRACTOR'S AND STATIONARY SAWS, INCLUDING MITER GAUGE SLOT ANATOMY)

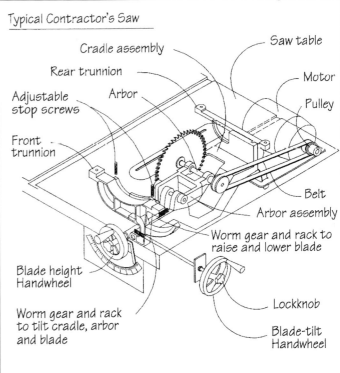

THE INTERIOR OF A TABLE SAW (BOTH CONTRACTOR'S AND STATIONARY)

ly increased precision.

The additional cost of the stationary saw isn't all for cast iron. It also goes into more precise machining. The arbor and the drive pulleys, for example, are turned and balanced to closer tolerances than those of a contractor's saw. Large-diameter adjustment wheels (7" vs. the typical 5" on a contractor's saw) make it faster and easier to tilt and to raise and lower the blade. The precision-made devices that lock the adjustments offer more security against blade creep under load.

There are important differences between the motor and drive of a stationary saw and those of a contractor's saw. Most stationary saws feature a 3 hp fan-

THE RIGHT TOOL FOR THE JOB

For more years than I care to admit, I made my living with a 9" contractor's table saw. There was nothing wrong with the saw, but I was asking too much of it. Having evolved from finish carpentry to cabinetmaking, I found myself wrestling 4'x8' sheets across its diminutive table and ripping miles of hardwood with its begrudging motor. The volume of work overwhelmed the saw's fence system, arbor controls and motor.

So with great anticipation I dreamed of a 3 hp, enclosed-base stationary saw. When it finally came, I was like a child at Christmas. I no longer worried that 75-pound sheets of panel stock might tip the saw over or that

ripping hard maple would blow up the motor. With a machine designed to do the work I demanded of it, I could focus on the work itself: I could concentrate on adjusting the fence to the correct position instead of on making sure it would stay there during the cut. Instead of second-guessing how deeply I could cut in a single pass, I could concentrate on setting the tilt and height of the blade for raising a panel. And I knew that if I needed to spend eight hours ripping lumber to width, I wouldn't have to do it in half-hour sessions separated by half-hour breaks for the motor to cool.

cooled motor. Often, 12" stationary saws are equipped with 5 hp motors. The motor is totally enclosed to keep dust out, reducing wear and extending service life. Unlike the long, single belt of the contractor's saw, the stationary saw uses multiple short belts. This increases power transfer by reducing vibration and slippage and makes for a quieter running saw. Perhaps no single difference between a stationary saw and a contractor's saw warrants the added cost, but all the differences taken together add up to a whole new experience in woodworking—a saw that you fully trust to do its job, letting you concentrate on the wood and how you want to cut it.

Combination Machines

European-style combination machines group a table saw with several other stationary power tools into a compact cluster of machinery that can perform most cutting and milling tasks. A typical machine has a 10" table saw with the power, capacity and precision of a 10" stationary saw. It also includes a 12" jointer, a 12" thickness planer, a shaper and a slot mortiser, all on a footprint not much larger than that of a 12" stationary saw and all built to stand up to full-time professional use.

In a high-production setting, cabinetmakers generally shy away from combination machines primarily because of the time required to switch from one function to another—even though most changes can be accomplished in just a few minutes. Operations like jointing and ripping can require constant switching of fence positions, so the time consumed over the course of a project can become considerable. For a pro, this time is money off the profit line.

But if your woodworking is not production oriented, you are cursed with limited shop space and are looking for the complete woodworker's dream machine menagerie, a combination machine may be an ideal solution. The high prices they command, even used, seem reasonable after adding up the costs of individual machines of comparable quality.

ASSESSING QUALITY

Most table saws in today's marketplace are of good quality. But like any other

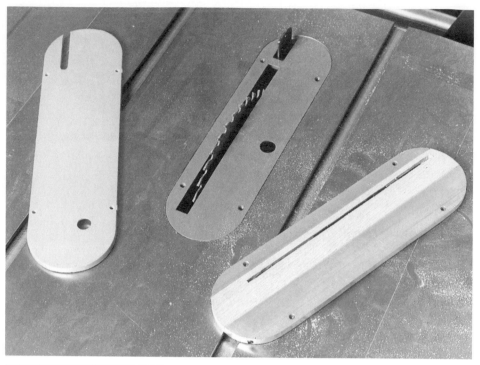

AFTERMARKET THROAT PLATES
The aftermarket throat plates flanking the standard plate offer better performance by allowing a custom fit to a particular blade. The plate on the left is high-impact plastic, ribbed on the underside to prevent flexing. It's blank—you cut the opening with the blade at the angle you intend to use it. The aluminum plate on the right features a replaceable, slide-in oak batten.

type of product, you can run across a poor quality brand that looks good at first glance and an exceptional quality unit that may not look much better without an in-depth inspection. Price is often a good indicator of quality, but you really need to see the machines to make your judgments. If you can't visit a distributor's showroom or attend a woodworking machine fair, ask the manufacturer to send not only detailed specs but also a list of local owners. Any reputable outfit will be happy to provide you with one.

Only in person can you, for example, read the motor plate information, see the quality of castings up close, press on the throat plate to check for flimsiness, crank on the adjustment wheels and slide the rip fence to check for speed and smoothness. The rest of this chapter outlines the things I look for to gauge what I'm getting for my money.

Mass

One of the first things I look for, or rather "sense," in a table saw is its mass. In general, a massive saw runs more smoothly than a lightly made model because vibrations are dampened and absorbed by the machine itself. Sturdier individual components tend to indicate higher-quality materials and manufacturing—meaning that the tool will perform with greater accuracy and last longer. The extra mass provides stability, making the machine more resistant to sliding or tipping when heavy stock is pushed across the table. Mass, however, is not the only factor preventing vibration. Many benchtop saws and some European stationary machines successfully rely on precision-made aluminum castings and carefully balanced drive mechanisms to ensure vibration-free performance in spite of their light weight.

Table Surface

The table is the part of the saw where weight and quality of construction are most immediately visible. Traditionally made of cast iron, it is machined dead flat and polished to a smooth finish. Sheet steel is rarely used except for extension wings; it tends to warp, making precision cuts impossible. The castings must be allowed to age a year or so to release internal stresses before machining, or they will not stay flat. Unfortunately, there is no way to know by inspection if

MAKING A THROAT PLATE

It's surprisingly easy to make your own throat plate. After all, the plate that came with the saw can be a pattern that you trace onto a piece of flat hardwood, smooth-faced plywood or melamine-covered MDF. Then saw to the line with a band saw or jigsaw. Plane, rasp or sand away any rough or over-size edges.

An even faster way to cut out the plates is to use the original insert, or one you just made following the method above, as a router template. After tracing the original on the stock and rough sawing to within ⅛" of the line, use double-stick tape to attach the original to the stock. Install a flush trim bit in a table-mounted router, and trim the new plate to the exact shape of the original. Make a bunch while you're at it—you'll eventually use them all.

Cut a ¾" hole near one or both ends for a finger grip and then, with the blade lowered and the saw unplugged, try the fit in the throat opening. It should be snug. If it's too loose, glue a strip of sandpaper along one edge—the coarser the grit, the thicker the strip. Screw a fender washer to the underside of the back edge of the plate to prevent it from lifting during use.

Check that the top of the plate is flush with the table surface. If you made the plate in solid hardwood, you have the opportunity to plane it to the exact thickness required. Otherwise, lower the plate by carving recesses where the plate is supported on the underside, or build it up with strips of veneer. You can fine-tune the height of the insert with a strip of sandpaper on each supporting ledge.

To cut the blade slot in the blank throat

plate, first install the blade you wish to use with the plate. Lower the blade all the way down, and then install the blank plate. If the blade catches on the underside of the plate, rout out a recess just deep enough to clear the teeth. Now hold the plate down by sliding the rip fence over it, and make sure the fence isn't positioned directly above where the blade will come up, for obvious reasons. If the bottom of the rip fence is not tight to the plate, insert some thin wood wedges between the fence and the plate. Turn on the saw and slowly raise the blade through the plate.

Label the plate to indicate which blade it is used with. If the plate is made from wood, coat both sides with shellac to help keep it stable and to provide a slick surface.

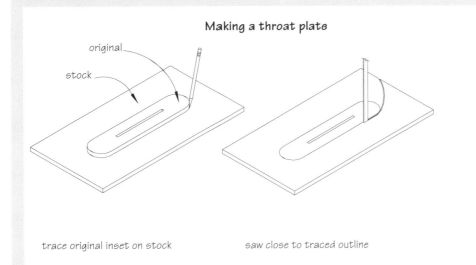

Making a throat plate

original

stock

trace original inset on stock

saw close to traced outline

Router made plate

original throat plate

new plate

bearing

bit

flush trim bit in table-mounted router

cast iron has been properly processed; here you must rely on the experiences of past buyers.

Some lightweight saws—mostly bench-top varieties—are equipped with precision-machined aluminum tables that are deeply ribbed on the underside to prevent flexing under load. There is nothing wrong with aluminum tables, especially for lighter-duty work where table weight is not needed for stability and the easily gouged aluminum will be treated kindly. Whatever type of material makes up the table, examine the surface carefully: Look for cracks, pitting, uneven machining and rough edges. Extension wings should sit

flat and flush with the table. Make sure there are easily accessible bolts running through slotted holes that will allow you to adjust the wings so they're flush with the table.

If the table is warped or uneven, notify the manufacturer. If the unevenness is outside the company's tolerances, you'll likely get a free replacement table. Be forewarned that tolerances vary from manufacturer to manufacturer. If the saw is used, find a machine shop that has a Blanchard grinder—a machine designed to surface large areas quickly—to see the cost of regrinding the table. You can remove small humps yourself with a belt

sander set up with a medium-grit belt or a coarse diamond sharpening stone. Work slowly, and constantly check your progress with a straightedge.

There are no widely accepted standards for saw table flatness. A table is flat enough if you find that cuts made on the saw are acceptably flat, straight and smooth. But that depends on what you try to do with it and how fussy you are. If you can't find any humps, hollows or twist, then you know that your skills can grow without being limited by a mis-shapen saw table.

Look closely at the miter gauge slots. They may be shaped either like a U or an inverted T. Saws with a T-slot come with a miter gauge that engages the slot, preventing it from falling if you pull the gauge out past the near edge of the table. However, as I explain in chapter five, if the stock is so wide that you have to pull the gauge out that far then you should use a sled rather than a miter gauge to make the cut. For me, the T-slot is useful as a convenient and secure way to attach featherboards and other fixtures.

Throat Plate

Take a close look at the throat plate, also called the table insert. It should sit flush with the tabletop and fit snugly in the opening. A sign of good quality is the throat plate's resistance to flexing when you push down on the center. If the plate flexes when the saw is still on the showroom floor, it will be dished not long after you start using it; then you won't be able to accurately measure blade height, and short stock won't be adequately supported. Also, a good plate will have height-adjustment screws so you can make it perfectly flush with the table, and rubber spacers to dampen vibration.

Even the best standard throat plates have a built-in disadvantage, however: The large opening around the blade, which provides clearance for tilting the blade, prevents the plate from supporting the wood right up to the edge of the teeth. This allows splintering on the underside of the cut and can reduce or even eliminate critical support for a workpiece being run on end in a tenoning operation (see chapter ten).

Gaps also invite thin offcuts to lodge between the edge of the opening in the plate and the spinning blade, an annoying and dangerous situation. I invariably replace the throat plate with either an aftermarket plate, like the ones shown, or one of my own making as explained in Making a Throat Plate. To maximize performance and ensure the safest cut, I use different throat plates to accommodate the different kerf widths of each of my blades and plates specifically for dado blades and molding cutters.

Arbor

The arbor is the solid, hardened steel shaft, threaded on one end, that holds the

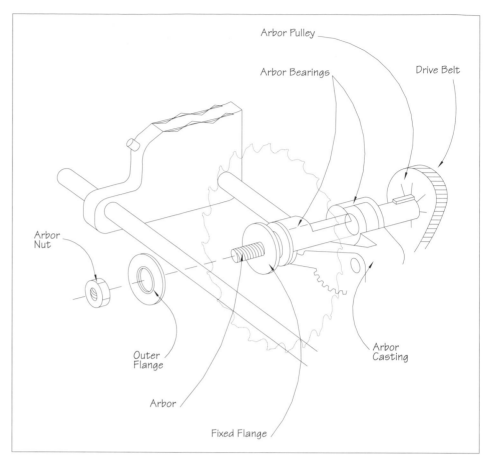

EXPLODED ARBOR ASSEMBLY

IN-LINE INDUSTRIES PERFORMANCE PACKAGE: LINKBELT AND MILLED PULLEYS
By installing machined pulleys and a link-type belt on a contractor's saw, you can reduce the saw's vibration by 90 percent (see Appendix B for sources).

HOW TO GET THE MOST POWER FROM YOUR MOTOR

The best way to keep the table saw up to speed while at the same time ensuring its longevity is to increase its power and efficiency. Here's how.

• First, be sure your table saw is getting adequate electrical power. If it's on an extension cord, it must be of the correct gauge, relative to the cord's length and the amperage demand you're asking of it, to reduce power loss to a minimum.

• Use a dedicated rip blade. For the cleanest and most efficient cut, choose a blade with teeth configured for chisel cutting, that is flat-topped, square across and with a hook angle of about 20°. If your stock is green or reactive, the kerf tends to close up after it exits the blade, so install a blade with coarser teeth (less teeth per inch) and greater set to make a larger kerf. Otherwise, go with a thin-kerf rip blade. With a thin kerf, less wood is being removed and thus less power is required to move the blade through the wood.

• Make sure the blade is clean and free of pitch buildup (see chapter four for blade cleaning techniques). The sharper it is, the easier it can remove material and get through the wood, placing less demand on the motor.

• To prevent binding, use a splitter to keep the kerf open behind the blade. Be sure the splitter is aligned parallel with the face of the blade. If it's out of alignment, it may rub against one side of the kerf, forcing the wood against one side of the blade and increasing resistance, not to mention throwing off the cut if it draws the wood away from the fence.

• To increase the effective power of your saw when cutting denser wood, switch to a smaller-diameter blade. Because of the smaller radius (the distance between the arbor and the cutting teeth), the wood has less leverage on the blade as it's being cut. You do sacrifice some cutting depth, but you'll notice an increase in the speed of the rip.

• Maintain a smooth and steady feed rate. If you go too fast, you're not giving the blade enough time to make the cut, bogging down the motor. If you feed too slowly, you allow the blade to stay too long against the highly heated wood, which can cause the blade plate to warp and possibly bind in its kerf. With practice on your particular saw, you will get to know optimum feed rates for various situations.

---

saw blade. It keeps the blade perfectly aligned while transmitting power from the belts to the blade. The arbor should be ⅝" diameter, except on 12" stationary saws, which require a 1" arbor to handle the larger cutting forces. Some of the older benchtop saws had ½" arbors. Avoid these. They tend to deflect when heavily stressed, and they require special ½" arbor-hole blades. The arbor must extend at least 1¼" past the flange to accept dado blades and molding heads, which not every saw does. Because some brands of accessories are unusually wide, it's a good idea to know the required arbor length of the specific accessories you intend to use with the saw.

If the table saw is to run with minimum vibration and to cut with precision, the arbor must be carefully machined by the manufacturer. The shaft must be turned dead straight and the cast iron flange against which the blade is seated must be machined flat and installed square to the center line of the arbor. The two sealed bearings through which the arbor passes must be precisely aligned or they may introduce friction and unnecessary wear on the bearings.

So how can you tell if the arbor of the saw you want to buy is up to snuff? Some manufacturers make it easy for you: They list the runout specs for the shaft and the flange in the manual. If you don't have access to the manual before purchasing, you can ask to inspect the machine (see chapter two for instructions on how to check for runout). If an inspection isn't possible, you have to trust the reputation of the manufacturer, who should guarantee that the arbor shaft will run out less than .001" and the flange less than .003". You don't want more than that—runout at the edge of a 10" blade will be many times the runout at the edge of the flange. Excessive runout results in a noticeably wider, rougher and less accurate kerf. There's little you can do to fix an out-of-spec arbor except talk the manufacturer into replacing it (and maybe even the entire arbor assembly).

Drive Mechanisms

Most table saws are driven by a V-belt and pulley system connecting the arbor and the motor. The exceptions are direct-drive units found in small benchtop saws and some older contractor's saws—setups that sacrifice some torque for fewer moving parts and less weight. Shorter and more numerous belts transfer power better by reducing belt-induced vibration and slippage. To minimize vibration further, the pulley grooves should be uniformly machined, the bore for the arbor or motor shaft precisely perpendicular to the face of the pulley, and the motor pulley in exactly the same plane as the arbor pulley. These specs are usually well met on stationary machines but are looser on contractor's saws, which use cast rather than machined pulleys.

The long, single-belt drive of the contractor's saw is a primary source of vibration and noise. Proper alignment between the arbor and motor pulleys is helpful, but the standard cast pulleys and the V-belt itself contribute to the problem. (See chapter two for techniques for checking and aligning a contractor's saw's pulley drive system.)

Since the grooves of cast pulleys are rarely uniform, the belt can move slightly up and down along the inside wall. That means the motor will move up and down as well, since it hangs from the belt. This can cause as much as 75 percent of the vibration.

The construction of a conventional V-belt doesn't help either. The fibers that run through the belt to strengthen it also cause it to change shape as it wraps around the pulleys. This prevents smooth and uniform seating of the belt. The strengthening fibers also transmit vibrations rather than dissipate them.

You can improve the drive system of a contractor's saw by installing aftermarket pulleys that are precisely machined from a solid blank of steel, like those on the stationary saw. You can also replace the standard V-belt with a link-type belt as shown in the photo. These new-generation belts produce up to 90 percent less vibration.

Motor

The industry standard for an 8" or 9" belt-driven saw is a 1½ hp motor. If the motor draws at least 16 amps at 115V (volts), it should provide enough power for sawing hardwood up to 2" thick. Direct-drive benchtop saws use somewhat smaller motors that draw 12 to 13 amps. Most 10" saws also come with a 1½ hp motor, but it will often stall and/or trip the circuit breaker if you're ripping green construction lumber or hardwoods more than 2" thick. If you intend to do more than cut dry, small-size stock, install a 2 hp motor, or even 3 hp if you're confident your saw can handle the power and motor weight. On a stationary machine, go to 5 hp if you intend to regularly rip hardwoods or green lumber at maximum capacity. A 5 hp motor is essential on a 12" table saw if you intend to use its greater cutting capacity.

To learn exactly what you're getting in a motor, read the plate attached to the electric motor. Find out if the motor features all-ball bearings (and not sleeves) and a built-in overload protector that can be reset after the motor cools. Be sure the horsepower rating is the "continuous" or "rated" horsepower and not the "peak" or "developed" horsepower of the motor. Be more concerned with the amount of horsepower available to saw the full length of a board without overloading than with the amount of horsepower available during a momentary high-load situation. Be suspicious of small motors with big horsepower listings.

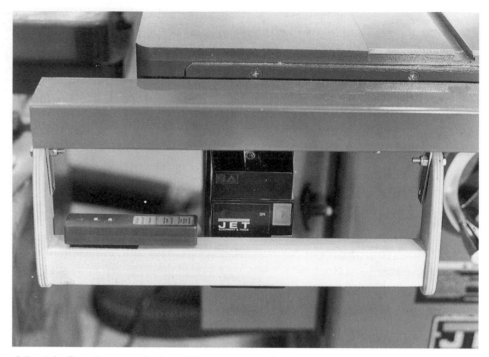

A "panic bar" running across the front of the magnetic switch of my stationary saw allows me to turn off the saw with a bump of my hip—or even a jab with my foot. The small box Velcro-taped to the bar is a remote switch for the dust collection system.

MAKING A SHUTOFF BAR

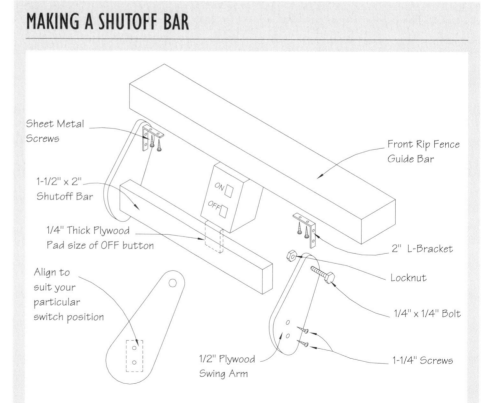

Sheet Metal Screws

1-1/2" x 2" Shutoff Bar

1/4" Thick Plywood Pad size of OFF button

Align to suit your particular switch position

1/2" Plywood Swing Arm

Front Rip Fence Guide Bar

ON / OFF

2" L-Bracket

Locknut

1/4" x 1/4" Bolt

1-1/4" Screws

One of the easiest and most effective ways to increase the safety of your table saw is to install a hands-free shutoff switch. This simply made version consists of a wood bar hinge-mounted to the front of the saw and running across the existing push-button switch. It turns the machine off with a light bump of your knee. Your hands are left free to control the workpiece. What do you do if your machine has an old-fashioned toggle switch? Replace it with a push-button switch, and build this shutoff board to fit.

Instead of building a shutoff bar, you can purchase an aftermarket switch that presents a huge (9"×12") off button. The on button is recessed to reduce the chance of an accidental turn-on. See Sources at the back of this book.

SAFETY *tip*

THE SAFE SAW

How you operate your saw ultimately determines its safety, but here are some aspects of the machine itself that can make some saws safer than others:

- A smoothly operating blade guard. Check that it doesn't tend to jam on the front edge of a board as you feed it into the blade.
- A solid stand with a broad footprint. It should be highly resistant to wobbling and tipping.
- A rip fence that reliably and easily locks down exactly parallel to the blade. Avoid or replace a rip fence that does not. An out-of-parallel fence can cause your work to bind or kick back.
- A lockable on/off switch to prevent unauthorized starts. Check that the switch is designed in such a way that it cannot be turned on inadvertently by being bumped or brushed.
- A rugged guard over the drive belt and pulleys.

Ask if the motor is totally enclosed. Although they cost more, TEFC (totally enclosed fan cooled) motors run longer and stronger because they keep the sawdust out of the innards. While TEFC motors are usually standard equipment on stationary saws, they are a worthwhile upgrade on contractor's saws. Another worthwhile motor feature, standard on some brands, is a built-in electronic blade brake. This safety feature stops the blade within seconds after the power is shut off.

Power Switches

While the power switch may seem like a trivial concern when choosing a saw, keep in mind that you use it twice every time you use the saw and that it can make a difference in how many fingers you carry around. You want to be able to easily turn the saw on and off, especially off, even when you have big and awkward stuff on the saw.

Most contractor's and benchtop saws employ mechanical push-button switches to turn the power on and off. Because they are designed to be much harder to turn on than to turn off, they are a distinct

A magnetic switch, which is simply a trip relay, protects the motor from overload. It also protects you from dangerous restarts when the power comes back on after an interruption.

safety improvement over the old-style toggle switch. Some even have a locking mechanism, usually a removable fitting, that defeats children's potentially disastrous curiosity.

Take careful notice of where the saw's power switch is located. It should be mounted for easy accessibility, even when running large sheets of plywood across the table. But it should not be so accessible that it can be accidentally turned on by brushing up against it. Stand in front of the saw as though you were making a cut and ask yourself which hand you would use if you had to turn the saw off in a hurry. Is that the hand least required to hold the stock? The answer depends on whether you're right or left handed and how you hold the stock.

Also ask yourself if you can turn the saw off without getting in line with the blade and any scrap of wood the blade might throw at you. Not entirely satisfied with factory-supplied switch arrangements, I made and installed a wooden bar system that hangs in front of the switch. I reach through it to start the machine but need only bump the bar or paddle with my knee to shut it down. You can also buy a commercially made shutoff switch that accomplishes the same thing.

Magnetic Switches

Another safety advancement is the magnetic switch, a relay-type switch that turns on and off with just a flick of a finger. When built in a housing that recesses the on button but leaves the off button protruding, you can turn the saw off by slapping your open hand at the switch. Standard equipment on most stationary saws, this relay-type switch not only makes the saw extremely easy to turn off, it also protects against overloads, something mechanical switches can't do, and it trips off if the power source is interrupted. This eliminates the potential for surprise restarts if the power goes off for a few seconds and then comes back on. If you have any doubts at all about the safety or location of the switch on your saw, or if your saw motor doesn't already have overload protection, I recommend that you replace your existing switch with a well-located magnetic switch. If your tool dealer doesn't seem cooperative in

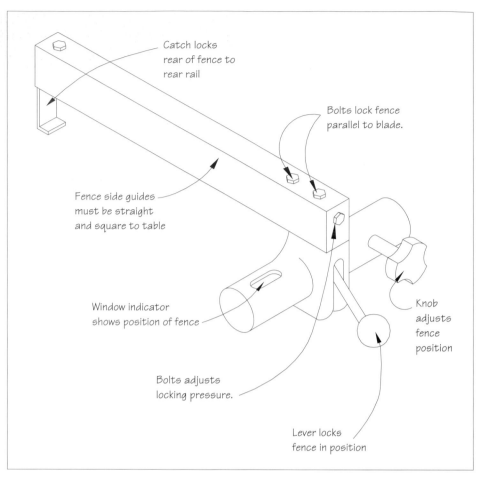

Catch locks rear of fence to rear rail

Bolts lock fence parallel to blade.

Fence side guides must be straight and square to table

Window indicator shows position of fence

Bolts adjusts locking pressure.

Knob adjusts fence position

Lever locks fence in position

PARTS OF A TYPICAL FENCE

making this upgrade, talk to a licensed electrician.

Blade-Adjustment Handwheels

The blade's height-adjustment handwheel, located on the front of the saw, drives a worm gear that engages a rack gear on the arbor assembly and raises or lowers the blade. The angle-adjustment handwheel on the side of the saw drives a worm gear that engages a rack gear on the cradle assembly and sets the blade at a 45° to 90° angle to the table. A locking mechanism, which is engaged by turning a knob at the hub of the handwheel, locks the gears in position. An indicator scale shows the angle of the blade (various interior and exterior parts of a table saw were shown earlier in this chapter).

Your blade-adjustment handwheels should turn easily. This is usually the case with stationary saws, which typically feature 7"-diameter wheels, but not as common with the 5" wheels often found on contractor's saws. You should be able to turn the wheels without skinning the back

of your hand on the underside of the saw. Check the effectiveness of the lock knobs by tightening them down and then testing to see if you can still crank the worm gear. Chances are you can on anything less than a stationary saw. If you find that you can crank the worm gear with little effort, then the lock is too loose and the blade may creep off its setting during heavy cutting processes.

The Rip Fence

The rip fence is yet another reason you should go out of your way to try out a saw before you buy it. Only by working the fence for yourself can you tell how smoothly it runs on its guide rails and how accurately and snugly it locks down. While the alignment of the fence parallel to the blade is usually adjustable (check to be sure), the basic feel of the fence is something you are going to have to live with, or pay to replace.

Check the saw's fence for these specific attributes (refer to the saw's instruction manual if necessary):

- An adjustment that sets the fence parallel to the blade. It should be capable of moving the fence in very small (invisible to the eye) increments.
- An adjustment for locking pressure. You need to be able to increase the pressure of the locking mechanism to ensure that heavy materials and/or feed pressures won't cause the fence to jump or drift out of parallel.
- An indicator that shows the distance from the blade to the fence. It should be easy to read and easy to recalibrate.
- Smooth, accurate operation. The rip fence should slide without binding along the full length of the guide rails. It must also lock down parallel to the blade at any point in its travels. If it doesn't, there is no easy way to make it do so.
- Accurate fence sides. These should be flat and square to the table. If they aren't square, you should be able to adjust them until they are. An effective way to square a fence to the table is to add a wooden auxiliary fence that you can shim to square it to the table.

If the particular saw you are interested in has all the features and qualities you are looking for but you still feel the fence is not up to snuff, you can replace it with a higher-quality fence. You may be able to do this through the saw dealer or through independent suppliers listed in the sources at the end of this book. To learn techniques for setting up and aligning a rip fence to maximize your saw's performance, see chapter two.

Miter Slots and Gauge

In many cases, you'll find that the sliding miter gauge is an indicator of the quality of the saw as a whole. If the gauge is flimsy, with thin castings, small handles and sloppy angle stops, more often than not you will find the same lack of quality, and flimsiness, throughout the rest of the machine.

A well-made miter gauge feels heavy in your hand. The casting of the body is substantial enough not to break if dropped from table saw height. Its guide bar should

This aftermarket miter gauge features an aluminum extrusion fence with two sliding stops and positive angle setting stops. It represents a vast improvement over the basic miter gauge (see Sources).

be made of solid-steel bar stock, not folded sheet steel, and should fit snugly in the miter slot with no slop or binding as you slide it the full length of the table slot. You can contend with a bit of looseness in the slot either by adding an adjustable fitting or by peening the metal (both strategies will be covered in chapter two). But if a miter gauge is sticky, it will take a lot of work with a file to correct. Finally, check that the angle scale is easy to read and that the built-in stops are free of play. If you aren't satisfied with the standard-issue miter gauge, you can upgrade to an aftermarket variety, some of which offer hefty fences and precision sliding stops (see photo).

Blade Guard

The standard blade guard assembly on most machines (see photo) consists of a sheet steel and Plexiglas assembly mounted just behind the blade. It acts as a splitter, an antikickback device and a blade guard. The vertical metal splitter enters the saw-kerf, preventing the wood from closing up, binding on the blade and kicking back at you. The pivoting, tooth-edged "fingers" allow the wood to pass only in the direction away from you, grabbing the wood if it starts to kick back. The clear

plastic hood over the blade keeps your hands away.

Unfortunately, the splitter prevents you from using the guard during a fair number of cutting operations, including rabbets and dadoes. Because many people find the standard guard cumbersome—not only to refit but to use in general—blade guards all too often end up in a dark corner of the shop.

Fortunately, you can get blade guards that not only prevent binding and kickbacks and keep your hands away from the blade, but come with a shield unit that moves in and out of place in seconds (two of these guard systems are described more fully in chapter three). The secret is in their mounting system: the guard hangs from an arm that attaches to the far side of the table. The disadvantages of these guards are that they require a lot of room, only work on saws with sizable side extension tables, and they are expensive, ranging from $200 to $300.

Dust and Dust Collection

It's unfortunate, but sawdust, and lots of it, is an unavoidable byproduct of using the table saw. It can make your shop floor slippery, put a film of dust on your tools and work surfaces, and coat the inside of

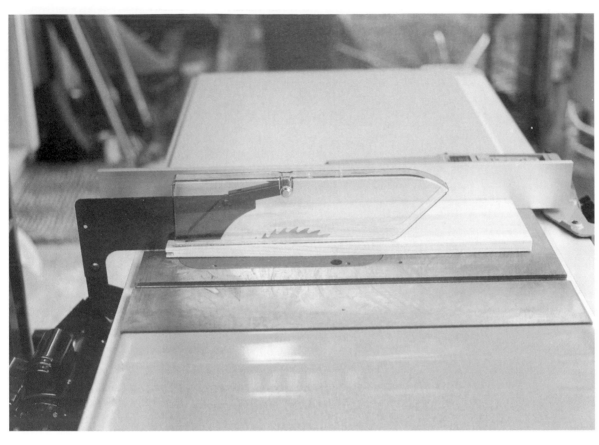

The factory supplied blade guard system works well for basic ripping and crosscutting operations though you must remove it for dadoing, rabbeting and many other common table saw operations.

your sinus passages and lungs with health-threatening particles. None of this is good news, but recent advances in dust collection technology have made these problems a lot easier to keep under control.

It used to be that only stationary saws were designed for dust collection, and even their provision was marginal, consisting only of a dust collection hose outlet near the bottom of the enclosed base. For years, designers of contractor's saws ignored dust collection entirely. Now these saws are often supplied with a dust collection port just below the saw blade, as shown in the photo. While this is an improvement, it is not as effective as it might be because the back of the saw is still open.

To capture the dust generated above the saw table, some aftermarket blade guards incorporate a dust collection fitting in the plastic shield surrounding the blade. This blade guard fitting significantly reduces the amount of dust that the cutting action of the blade throws directly toward you.

Portable dust collectors can be extraordinarily lightweight and compact, and can follow the saw onto the job site or throughout the shop. As long as you keep

A worm's eye view of a dust collection port mounted directly below the blade. This collects much of the sawdust, keeping it from getting dangerously underfoot.

TABLE SAW CHARACTERISTICS

	Benchtop Table Saw	Contractor's Table Saw	Stationary Table Saw
Motor			
Induction vs. Universal	universal	induction	induction
Phase	one	one	one or three
Volts/Amps	115 V/12 to 15 A	115V/13A or 230V/6½A	240V/amps vary
Horsepower	1 to 1½ hp	1 to 2 hp	2 to 5 hp
TEFC/Open	open	either	TEFC
Overload Protection	usually not	some	yes
Blade			
Diameter	8¼" to 10"	9" to 10"	10" to 14"
Cutting Capacity @ 90°	2½" to 3⅛"	2⁷⁄₁₆" to 3"	10" blade/3⅛"
Cutting Capacity @ 45°	1⅝" to 2⁵⁄₁₆"	1¹¹⁄₁₆" to 2⅛"	10" blade/2⅛"
Arbor			
Tilt: Left or Right	usually left	left or right	left or right
Shaft Diameter	⅝"	⅝"	⅝" to 1"
Shaft Usable Length	¼" to ¾"	½" to ¹³⁄₁₆"	minimum ¹³⁄₁₆"
Accessories			
Miter Gauge	yes	yes	yes
Dado Set/Molder Head	some	yes	yes
Dust Collection Capacity	some	some	some
Table Top			
Material	cast aluminum	cast iron	cast iron
Extensions Available	no	some	yes
"T" or "U" Miter Slot	"U"	"U" or "T"	"T"
Miter Slot Size	varies	⅜" x ¾"	⅜" x ¾"
Fence			
Standard Rip Capacity	10" to 25"	24" to 32"	24" to 55"
Opt. Fence Pkg Available	no	some	yes
Weight	30lb to 60lb	125lb to 300lb	275lb to 600lb
Street Price	$200 to $500	$350 to $800	$750 to $4000
Primary Use	portable/home shop	semi-portable or shop	shop

up with emptying their relatively small collection bags, they are surprisingly effective.

Instruction Manual

You've heard the quip, "When all else fails, read the instruction manual." While most modern manuals are clear and easy to read, you'll still run across some that seem to bear no relation to either the saw or to the English language. Read them anyway—and don't throw them away. If you're buying a used saw that's missing the manual, try to order a replacement from the manufacturer. The manual and, usually, an accompanying parts list should contain an exploded view of the machine that shows and lists the name and catalog number of every component. Consider the manual and parts list as important accessories to the saw, as you will need them to order replacement parts.

If you don't understand something in the manual, call the technical support number. Mail in any product registration forms not only to inaugurate the warranty but so the manufacturer can contact you with product information bulletins or a safety recall. File the manual and parts list where you'll be able to find them.

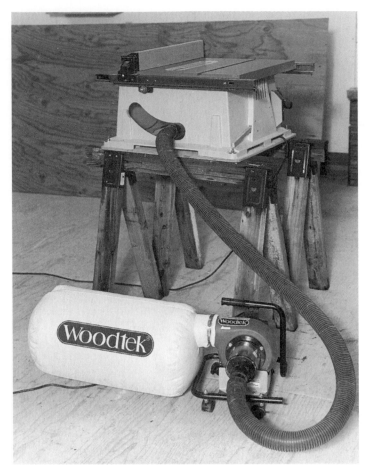

When working away from the shop, I use a miniature dust collection system on my contractor's saw.

Setup, Tune-up and Upkeep

You've figured out what kind of table saw you need, you've found a model you like, you've made your best deal, and now you've brought it home to the shop. You are raring to put it to work, but is your shop ready for it? Have you designated a place that will accommodate the saw while leaving sufficient work room around your other machines and space for the unencumbered flow of materials? Is the area well lit? Are the electrical wiring and circuitry correct for the saw's power requirements? Have you made provisions for dust collection? Consider the saw itself—it may not be ready to give you the best work it is capable of producing. To enjoy a smooth-running, easy-to-adjust saw that makes consistently accurate cuts, take time to perform some careful tune-up work. This applies whether the saw is well used or brand new. So don't go cutting up boards quite yet. Instead, read this chapter and see what you can do to get the best performance out of both your shop and your saw.

SAW PLACEMENT

Before you take the saw out of its shipping carton, give some serious thought to where you are going to set it up. This is important because the table saw will likely be the central workstation of your shop. The best location for other machines and processes will depend, at least in part, on the saw's location. Careful forethought will also expedite the installation of wiring and dust collection ducts.

Think through how the placement of the saw will accommodate the flow of materials within your work space. For me, the stock comes in the door, then gets crosscut to rough length, jointed, and planed before passing on to the table saw.

As you can see in my shop floorplan

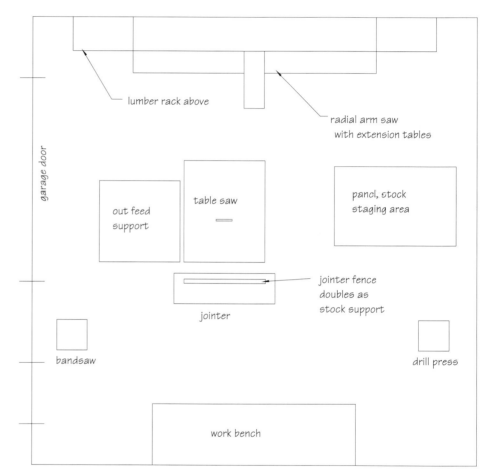

If your shop is small or oddly shaped, it may be quite a challenge to provide clear runs for the stock and still accommodate all your machine stations. You may find it helpful to raise up the table saw so workpieces can pass over the top of your jointer's fence as shown in Space Saving Work Surface Heights on page 30. This will let you place the jointer tight against the saw, creating a compact work station. Later in the book, I'll show you how to make a fixture that you can set on the jointer bed to provide support for panel stock and large sled fixtures. Also, be sure to make any nearby workbenches the same height as the table saw's surface—they can then aid in supporting oversize stock passing through the saw.

(above), materials move unobstructed to, across and away from my table saw. I located the saw just a step away from the shop's permanent lumber storage racks, and just ahead of a temporary staging area where material, especially panel stock, can be organized and stockpiled, ready for cutting. An outfeed roller support captures the stock as it leaves the end of the table. Notice how nearby workbenches and stationary tools are oriented so they don't interfere with the workpieces as they pass through the saw during either ripping or crosscutting operations.

LIGHTING

Once you have chosen the best place for the table saw in your shop layout, the next step is to light it—and to light it well. You can't work quickly, accurately and safely on the table saw unless you have ample light, free of shadows and glare.

To reduce shadows, use fluorescent lighting for the bulk of the light within the shop. You can add incandescent bulbs and halogen shop lights to reduce flicker, to add a warm-colored hue, and to place direct light on the area just ahead of the blade. When hanging the fixtures, be sure they won't get in the way of workpieces flowing from storage areas or being turned end for end near the front of the saw.

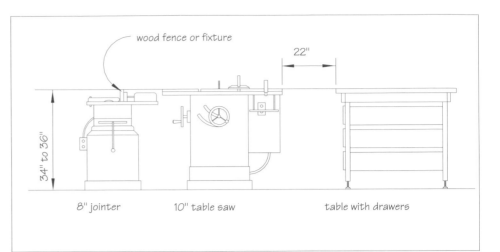

SPACE SAVING WORK SURFACE HEIGHTS

If your space is really tight, consider mobilizing your saw with a rolling base. You can orient a mobile saw to cope with different sized materials within your particular space, and you can park it out of the way when it's not in use. The base shown here incorporates its own fold-down outfeed support, which reduces setup time and provides additional space savings.

LOCKING PLUGS, CONNECTORS & RECEPTACLES

Nothing is more frustrating or potentially dangerous, than having a power tool come unplugged while you're using it. Workshops and job sites present plenty of opportunities for a power cord to hang up and disconnect as you move around, and a standard, straight-blade plug doesn't offer much resistance. A good solution to this problem is a locking plug and receptacle. To make a connection using these devices you must first push the plug's blades into the connector or receptacle and then twist the plug. This locks the plug's blades and prevents accidental disconnection. Several manufacturers produce these devices in a range of voltages and amperages to fit everything from small electric hand tools to stationary shop machinery. They are bulkier than most straight blade plugs, but they are industrial quality. They are more expensive than household devices, but peace of mind never comes cheap.

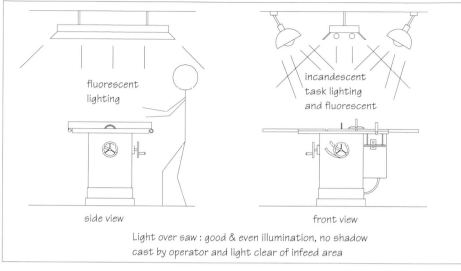

Light over saw : good & even illumination, no shadow cast by operator and light clear of infeed area

IDEAL LIGHTING PLACEMENT

POWER

Good lighting is great, but you won't get much work done unless you get power to the saw. It's a bit more involved than running an extension cord to the nearest outlet. Here are some basic rules:

- Know the voltage and current draw listed on the motor plate, and connect the saw only to a circuit of the correct size.
- Never wire the saw (or any other shop machine) directly to a shop circuit. Always use a plug and outlet so you can unplug the tool during setups and maintenance.
- Be sure the circuit and the machine are properly grounded.
- If you have to run the power cord across the floor, use cord covers to guard against abrasion and to help prevent tripping on it.

If you are not experienced in wiring and electricity, have a licensed electrician run the wiring and set up the circuits—or at least double-check your work.

Why 220V Instead of 110V?

If you're running new circuits into your shop, it's best to run 220V circuits for heavy duty motors such as those found on table saws. A motor of a given horsepower will use only half the amperage at 220V as at 110V (most motors can be modified to run on either 110V or 220V—look for a plate or label near the wiring box on the motor that shows wiring diagrams for alternate voltages). Running a motor at the higher voltage and lower amperage means less heat buildup and less voltage drop in all the wiring components, including the motor. This, in turn, means more power from less electricity and heavier work with fewer overloads.

DUST COLLECTION

Dust collection keeps sawdust from caking up inside of the saw, keeps the floor clean and safe, and keeps sawdust out of your body where it can cause potentially life-threatening lung and sinus problems. Fortunately, most modern table saws have some provision for dust collection.

You can improve the efficiency of dust collection in a contractor's saw if you can somehow enclose the back of the saw. As you might guess, this presents some difficulty because the motor and belt swing through the opening when being tilted away from 90°. Since you use the saw mostly at 90°, however, you can make a removable cover that fits closely to the protruding parts. The drawing on page 32 shows how I use a piece of ¼" plywood fit-

ted with magnetic strips to close the opening. If you are clever with sheet metal and pop rivets, you can go another step further and create a shroud around the arbor. This greatly increases the amount of suction around the blade. The trick, though, is designing the shroud to work at all angles of the arbor without interference.

The heart of your dust collection system is the blower. For the table saw, you will need a machine powerful enough to move at least 350 cfm (cubic feet per minute) of air through the line. You may find that an off-the-shelf dust collector rated as moving 350 cfm doesn't do the job if your ducting is longer than 20 feet, if it makes more than four 90° bends or if you have more than one dust-producing machine connected to it. In most cases, a single-bag dust collector of 1 horsepower or more will provide more than enough suction to meet the needs of a 10" or 12" table saw.

Unfortunately, the best location for the table saw is usually in the middle of the shop, far from any wall, and the shop space available to most of us has a concrete floor. I hate to run wires or ductwork across the shop floor. More than a constant nuisance, they can cause accidents and become damaged. My solution has been to raise my shop floor on 2x4 joists, creating a cavity for the wires and ducts. You can even use the channels created by the joists as vacuum ducts. There are two secrets to making this work:

1. Make sure all the seams and corners of the framework are well caulked to reduce air leakage.
2. Size the channels so they work efficiently as ducts.

TUNE-UP FOR MAXIMUM PERFORMANCE

You've figured out where you want the saw, you've lit up the space and run the power in, and you've set up your dust collection. The time has come to bring in the saw, set it up and put it to work—almost. First, I want to show you how you can tune the table saw to produce the most accurate, most efficient and safest work it is capable of providing. Here's what needs to be done:

- Initial setup.
- Check the arbor and blade for runout.
- Adjust the table so the miter gauge grooves are parallel to the blade.
- Adjust the extension wings so they're in the same plane as the main table.
- Adjust the throat plate (table insert) a few thousandths of an inch below the surface of the table.
- Align the motor and arbor pulleys parallel to one another. Check this by holding a straightedge against the pulleys.
- Tune up and align the blade raising and tilting mechanisms.
- Set the blade tilt angle stops.
- Fit the miter gauge bar to the miter gauge grooves.
- Set the miter gauge stops to exactly the indicated angles.
- Adjust the rip fence parallel to the miter gauge grooves (and thus the blade) and perpendicular to the table.
- Adjust the splitter, antikickback teeth, and blade guard to work smoothly and efficiently.

Each of these tasks is part of the total setup package, and all are interrelated. You'll be happy to know that most of these steps need to be done only occasionally over the life of the saw and that the time you spend here will be easily recovered. You'll work faster and make fewer mistakes with a well-tuned saw.

A single-bag dust collector powered by a 1 hp motor provides ample suction for most table saws. It is important, though, to run only one machine at a time and to keep the length of the duct work as short and straight as possible. See Sources.

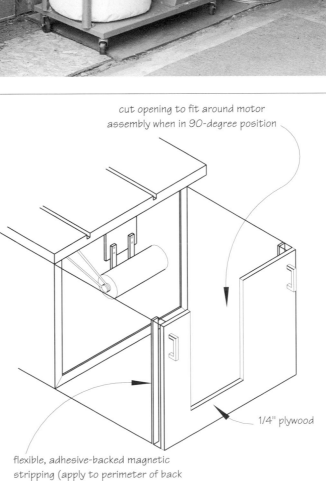

cut opening to fit around motor assembly when in 90-degree position

1/4" plywood

flexible, adhesive-backed magnetic stripping (apply to perimeter of back panel where it contacts metal case of saw)

REMOVABLE DUST ENCLOSURE
This drawing shows how to make a removable back panel for a contractor's saw.

Initial Setup

If you're setting up your table saw for the first time, follow the manufacturer's recommended assembly sequence. Winging it can result in unnecessary head-scratching and even backtracking. Most setup instructions—even those coming with foreign imports—actually make sense. The problems you may run into will most likely be missing or cross-threaded nuts and bolts, problems easily remedied by a quick trip to the hardware store. To avoid discovering these problems in the middle of assembly, lay out all the pieces and check them carefully before you begin.

If your saw came preassembled, don't take for granted that it was done right. Check for all of the parts, and be sure that all the machine's screws, nuts and bolts are in place and tight. Once you know the saw is assembled properly, you can get down to the fine points that will make your table saw a true pleasure to use

Arbor

A blade that runs true, free of wobble, is critical to everything you do with your table saw. You can't even properly tune up the other parts, such as the rip fence or miter gauge, unless the blade runs true. The two key parts that contribute to a true-running blade are the blade itself and the arbor that turns it. Our focus here is on the arbor.

With the saw unplugged and the blade removed, check the arbor shaft visually to be sure the threads are in good shape and the shaft is not obviously bent, scored or nicked. Next, rotate the shaft slowly, listening for noise and feeling for resistance or roughness. You'll be able to feel the shaft rotation much better if you remove the drive belt. Try to wiggle the arbor shaft, feeling for looseness. If you discover any looseness or roughness, you have good reason to believe that the bearings are defective (or worn out in the case of a used machine) and should be replaced. This is a job for the dealer if the saw is new or a competent mechanic if the saw is used.

Runout is a slight wobble in the blade as it rotates. The more wobble, the wider the kerf. Since it's impossible to build a saw with absolutely no blade wobble, a slight amount of runout is considered

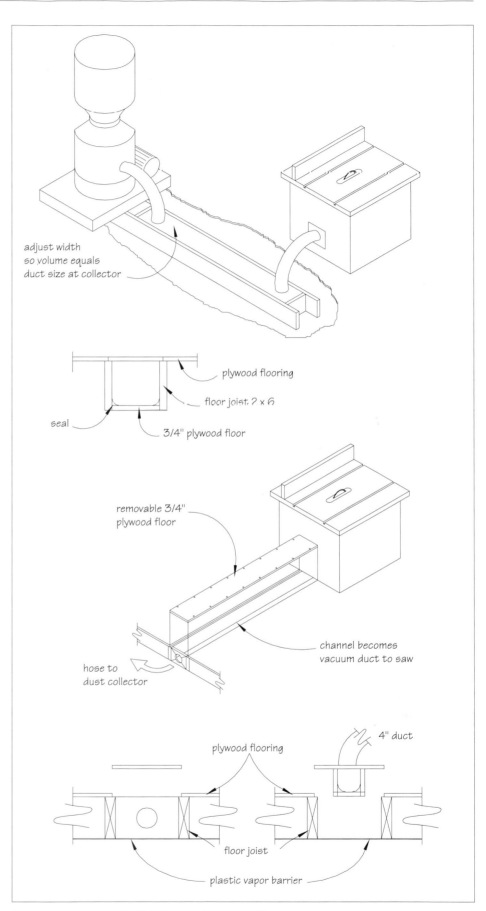

DUST COLLECTION SETUPS FOR YOUR SHOP FLOOR

normal—up to 0.012" near the edge of a 10" blade. If it's greater than this, the cut will tend to be rough and uneven, as shown, and it will be very difficult to line up the cut with your mark or layout. But before getting into the actual tests for runout, you should know some of the common causes:

- A blade that's not flat will have runout at the edge, even on a perfect saw. Since our purpose here is to check the saw, not the blade, conduct the following tests using the best blade you have—and double-check with another outstanding blade before replacing any expensive saw parts.

- A perfect blade on a perfect saw will have runout at the edge if the blade is not seated firmly against the arbor flange. To avoid misleading test results, give the entire arbor and flange a thorough vacuuming, and clean both the flange surfaces and the blade with a fine-textured abrasive pad.

- A perfect blade on a bent arbor shaft will have runout at the edge.

- A perfect blade on a perfectly straight arbor will have runout at the edge if the face of the flange is not perpendicular to the axis of the arbor.

Since it's a lot easier to tell if you have runout than to tell what's causing it, the prudent course to follow is to test for runout first. Then, if you find a problem, track down the cause.

A couple more things to keep in mind about runout: First, the question you're trying to answer is not whether you have runout but how much. Second, just like swinging a baseball bat or a golf club, a little bit of change at the holding end can make a lot of difference at the business end—in this case, a little bit of runout at the flange can produce a lot of runout at the edge of the blade.

The method shown in Low-Tech Runout Check will tell you if runout is a serious problem. All you'll need is a short dowel, your miter gauge, a feeler gauge and a good, flat blade. Most quality carbide-tipped blades are flat within .004". If you find that the wobble is worse than .012", you'll want to track down the source and take corrective action.

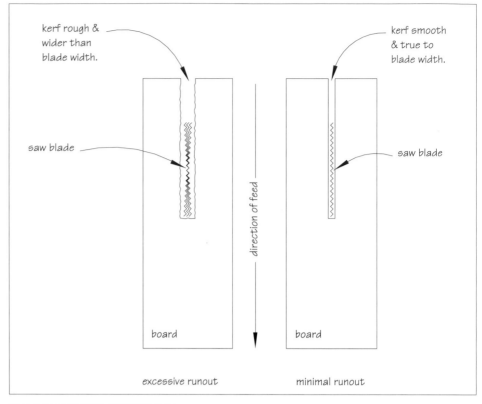

THE RESULTS OF BLADE RUNOUT

How you go about minimizing blade wobble depends on if the saw is new and on the tools and preferences you bring to the task. If you discover unacceptable blade wobble on a brand-new saw, your most sensible fix is sending it back. Correcting the problem yourself will cost a fair amount of time and/or money. If returning the saw is not an option and you don't have the experience or tools of an amateur mechanic or machinist, consider having it professionally repaired. New and used machine dealers often offer repair services, or you may be able to find an individual who reconditions woodworking equipment. You should know in advance, however, that it may not be worth the cost to repair or replace the arbor of an inexpensive machine.

If you want to deal with the wobble on your own, you can pinpoint the cause with a dial indicator. Then, disassemble the saw and either replace the offending part or have a machine shop do it for you. Saws vary widely in how they go together, so don't expect removal of the arbor to be a simple matter of unbolting it. You'll need the tools and experience of a mechanic to do the job properly.

You do have another option that may appeal to you if you don't use the saw often and are willing to live with a wobbly blade: You can experiment with the position of the blade on the arbor to find the position that gives the least amount of wobble and the cleanest cut.

Table Alignment

Accurate crosscutting with the miter gauge demands that the blade be aligned parallel to the miter gauge grooves. If it is out of alignment, the saw suffers from a potentially unsafe malady known as "heel." Mild heel causes rough cuts because the blade cuts the workpiece twice, once at the front of the blade and again at the back. More extreme heel can cause kickback if the back of the blade binds against the workpiece and lifts it.

You can check table alignment with a convenient, precise alignment jig, or, by a simple approach. Both are described on page 37.

Although the goal when setting the alignment is the same for all table saws—that is, move the table until the miter gauge grooves are parallel to the blade—the actual procedures depend on the design of the saw. For contractor's saws, where the trunnions are bolted directly to

LOW-TECH RUNOUT CHECK

Since your primary concern is to evaluate the saw, it's critical that the blade you use when taking these measurements be quite flat. If you spent more than $50 for your blade and haven't abused it, the chances are pretty good that it's acceptably flat. If you have doubts, ask your sharpening service to evaluate the blade's runout, or read the chapter on blades and then treat yourself to a new one. You can use this low-tech test to see how much your blade/saw combination wobbles at the cutting edge.

1. Unplug the saw and install the quality blade, being sure the blade is clean and there is no debris caught between the blade and the arbor flange. Raise the blade to near the top of its range and lock down the adjustment crank.

2. Clamp a ⅜" dowel to the face of your miter gauge so that one end of the dowel just touches a tooth on the infeed side of the blade. You may need to whittle flats on the dowel to keep the clamp head centered on the dowel.

3. Rotate the blade 360° at least once, mark the portion of the blade that seems to be closest to the dowel, and position this area of the blade opposite the dowel.

4. Readjust the dowel on the miter gauge so you can just slip a .010"-thick feeler gauge between the dowel and the edge of a tooth. If the teeth alternate, pick a tooth projecting toward the dowel.

5. To measure the runout, keep the miter gauge in the same position but turn the blade 180° and again slip in the .010" feeler gauge. If it's loose, add gauges in thousandths of an inch until the gauge feels snug. The amount you have to add is the amount the blade is wobbling, that is, the amount of runout.

the underside of the table, the trunnion bolts must be loosened and the position of the entire trunnion/cradle assembly adjusted. For stationary saws, the procedure is different because the trunnions and the table are both bolted to the saw cabinet rather than to each other. Here, alignment involves repositioning the table on the cabinet.

Table Flatness

The entire surface of the saw table, including its extension wings, should be perfectly flush. Most saw manufacturers provide slotted holes for the wing attachment bolts so you can adjust the wings flush with the table. To see if you need to make an adjustment, hold a straightedge across the main table and out over a wing, checking for any gaps.

The quick and easy way to adjust a wing is to loosen the attachment bolts just enough that a few sharp blows with a rubber mallet or rounded off block of wood will budge it into flush. If this doesn't work for you, the following four-step procedure should:

1. Loosen the bolts and let the wing

LIVING WITH WOBBLE

Small imperfections of the blade and the inevitable runout at the flange can cause wobble. How much wobble you wind up with depends on whether the imperfections are added to each other or tend to cancel each other out. You can improve the performance of your saw by making sure that these imperfections tend to cancel each other out. Here's how:

1. Put an indelible mark on the rim of the arbor flange.
2. Use a permanent marker to draw eight radii, 45° apart, on the side of your blade. Number them 1 to 8.
3. Mount the blade on the saw so radius #1 points directly at the mark on the rim of the arbor flange.
4. Measure the blade runout with the blade in this position using the method described in Low-Tech Runout Check or with a dial indicator. Note that this is the amount of runout with the blade in this position.
5. Repeat this procedure, measuring the runout at the remaining marked radii.
6. Put an indelible mark on the saw blade at the radius with the lowest runout.
7. Repeat the entire process for all of the saw blades that you use for critical joinery.

Now, every time you mount one of these blades, line up the mark on the blade with the mark on the flange, confident that this position will give you the least possible blade wobble. You'll find that some blades will have virtually no runout when positioned using this technique.

down to its lowest position.
2. Clamp straight sticks to the main saw table along the front and back edges so they extend out over the wing.
3. Raise the wing up to the sticks and clamp it there, but tighten the clamps only enough to hold the wing in position.
4. Tighten the attachment bolts.

Throat Plate Adjustment

The front of the throat plate should be a few thousandths of an inch below the saw table. This allows the wood to pass freely over the plate without hitting the front or binding on the table surface at the back. Throat plates often have adjustment screws for fine-tuning. If yours doesn't, you can use pieces of tape on the support ledges to raise the plate. To lower the plate, carefully file its underside.

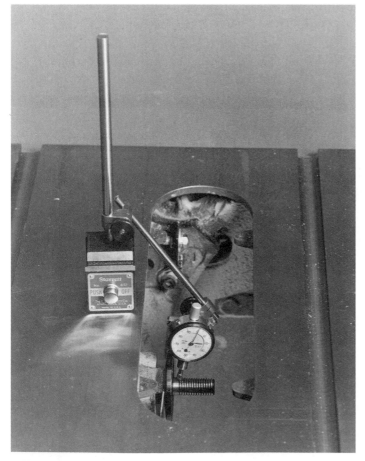

DIAL INDICATOR MEASURING RUNOUT ON SHAFT
A machinist's dial indicator gives accurate measurements in thousandths of an inch and can tell you if certain parts of the arbor are beyond acceptable tolerances. Here the plunger rests on the shaft to measure the arbor shaft runout.

DIAL INDICATOR MEASURING RUNOUT ON FLANGE
To see if blade wobble is coming from an out-of-square or defective flange, the dial indicator's plunger is set against the outer rim of the flange plate. Set up the indicator, and take your measurement from as near as possible to the outer edge of the flange. The runout here should measure less than .003". If the shaft was good but you find runout on the flange, the problem is most probably in the flange. If the flange is cast and removable, you may be able to have it trued.

Blade Angle and Height Mechanism Adjustment

Neither the blade raising and lowering crank mechanism on the front of the saw nor the blade tilt mechanism on the side of the saw is infallible. If the crank turns more than an eighth of a revolution (45°) in either direction before the blade moves, there is too much play in the mechanism. This play, called backlash, may allow the blade to shift during the stresses of cutting. A sure indication of backlash is a cut that starts square and ends at a slight angle, or changes its depth. This may only be apparent when the saw is working hard, such as when making bevel cuts in thick hardwood stock.

Another way to detect backlash without having to make test cuts is to unplug the saw and check for play in the arbor's cradle assembly by shaking it. Try it first with the blade locked at the 90° stop and then set at 20° to 30°. If you can feel any tilting or up and down movement, one or both adjustment mechanisms need to be tightened.

Adjusting the Backlash Mechanism

Fortunately, many saws have an adjustment to eliminate backlash. Begin by cleaning the cogged racks, the worm gears and the parts that mount; then adjust them. Then lubricate mating surfaces with wax, graphite, silicone, or Teflon spray. Avoid petroleum-based lubricants that attract sawdust.

Adjustment involves fine-tuning the fit between the worm gears and the cogged racks. Check your owner's manual for the procedure for your particular saw, or examine how the worm gear is mounted. Typically, it runs through a sleeve. While it may not be obvious, this may be an eccentric sleeve. By loosening a locking nut and turning the sleeve, you can adjust the worm gear to fit the cogged rack more tightly. Be sure to retighten the locking nut to fix the sleeve in place after adjusting it.

After adjusting a worm gear, change the position of the blade and recheck for backlash. It should be snug everywhere along the tilt or height range of the blade.

LOW-TECH HEEL CHECK

Checking for heel is very similar to checking for runout. The main difference is that when checking for heel you measure the distance to the same tooth at both front and back positions. Proceed as follows:

1. Unplug the saw and install a blade. Raise the blade to near the top of its range and lock down the adjustment crank.
2. Clamp a ⅜" dowel to the face of your miter gauge so that a .010" feeler gauge just fits between the dowel and a tooth on the infeed side of the blade. Mark that tooth by making a crayon mark on the blade plate just below the tooth.
3. Slide the miter gauge and dowel toward the outfeed side of the table and rotate the blade so the marked tooth is again opposite the dowel.
4. Measure the distance between the dowel and the marked tooth with feeler gauges. If it is more or less than .010", the blade is not parallel to the miter gauge groove.

HIGH-TECH HEEL CHECK

These two machine accessories—an alignment fence that clamps magnetically to the side of the blade and a dial indicator mount that slides in the table saw's miter slot—allow you to measure the amount of heel or offset between the plane of the blade plate and the miter slot with ease and a great deal of precision.

To quickly align your table to within a few thousandths of an inch, jump on the high-tech bandwagon and get yourself an alignment fence—an L-shaped length of machined aluminum. Clamping itself magnetically to the blade plate—the magnet placement is adjustable so the magnets miss the blade teeth—the fence brings the plane of the blade out onto the table surface where you can easily take measurements with a ruler or dial indicator. If you use the latter, you'll need a special mounting system that secures the base of the dial indicator to the miter groove slot. Both of these specialized tools are available through the mail—see the source appendix.

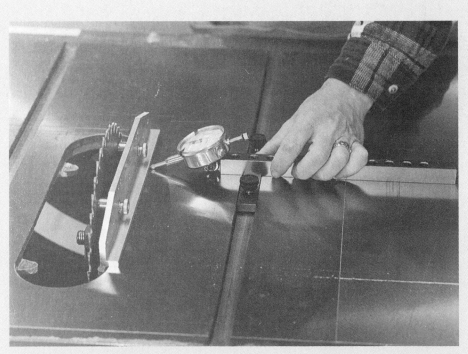

Heel check with dowel and feeler gauge.

CONTRACTOR'S SAW ALIGNMENT

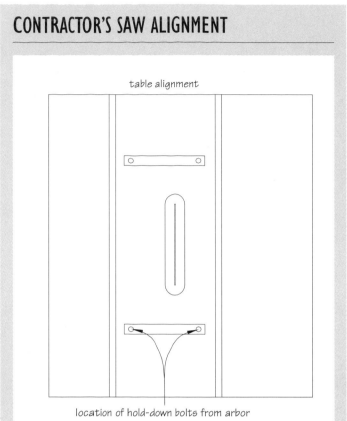

table alignment

location of hold-down bolts from arbor
assembly to other side of table

1. Loosen the bolts that hold the trunnions to the underside of
   the table, leaving them just barely snug.
2. Gently tap the trunnions left or right as necessary to bring the
   blade parallel to the miter gauge grooves. If the assembly needs
   to move but the rear trunnion won't move left, tap the front
   trunnion to the right and vice versa.
3. Recheck the alignment as described in Low-Tech Heel Check.
4. Repeat until no heel is detected.
5. Tighten the trunnion bolts and recheck the alignment.

STATIONARY SAW ALIGNMENT

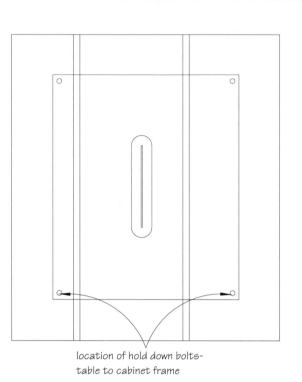

location of hold down bolts-
table to cabinet frame

1. Loosen the bolts that hold the table to the base, leaving them
   just barely snug.
2. Gently tap the table clockwise or counter-clockwise as necessary to bring the miter gauge grooves parallel to the blade.
3. Recheck the alignment as described in Low-Tech Heel Check.
4. Repeat the tapping and checking until no heel is detected.
5. Tighten the bolts that hold the table to the base and recheck
   the alignment.

Back off a bit on the fit of the worm gear if you find the mechanism doesn't move smoothly and easily. Gears that are set too tight are a pain to set up and can wear out prematurely.

Setting the Angle Stops

After you eliminate excessive backlash, adjust the angle stops. Your goal is to have accurate stops at the ends of the blade's tilt range so you won't have to check each time at these most common settings. Most—but not all—table saws have adjustable setscrews on the trunnion that stop the blade tilt angle at 90° and 45°. Check your owner's manual to see if your saw has these and how to adjust them. If you don't have a manual, you should be able to find the screws by watching which parts come close together as the tilt adjustment reaches its two extremes. Look for a screw or bolt with a locknut where parts come together.

To adjust the stops, begin by loosening the locknuts and backing the stop screws away from the ledge on the cradle. Now raise the blade as high as it will go. Hold an accurate square vertically against the blade, being sure it is touching only the body of the saw blade and not riding on a tooth. A plastic drafting triangle is ideal for this because it doesn't risk nicking a tooth on the blade. Turn the adjustment handle until there is no gap between the square and the saw blade. Adjust the 90° stop screw snug against the surface that stops tilt travel. Tighten the locknut. Next, tilt the blade to exactly 45° as measured by a 45° drafting triangle or similar tool, and adjust the 45° stop the same way you adjusted the 90° stop.

You're not finished yet! You still need to see if the saw will actually cut true at these stop settings. Make test cuts in scrap stock at both 90° and 45°. Check against a combination square, or better, perform the tests shown in the Blade Tilt Test. If the cuts are off, reset the stops until testing shows they are true.

MITER GAUGE TUNE-UP

To produce accurate crosscuts with consistent accuracy, it is important to tune up the miter gauge. Of course you'll want to

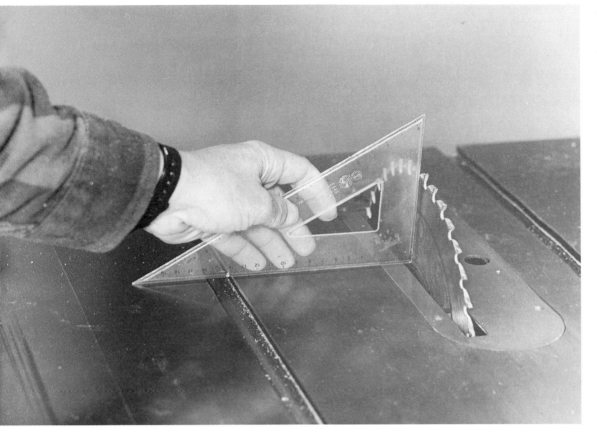

A drafting triangle is ideal for adjusting the blade square to the table—it is accurate, easy to sight, and the plastic cannot nick the saw blade's surprisingly fragile carbide teeth.

set the angle stops, but it's also critical that the gauge first run snugly but smoothly in its groove.

Begin by checking the action of the miter gauge bar in its groove. If it feels loose, you need to make it snug, yet run smoothly without binding. A quick home-made fix is to use a hammer and center punch to dimple one side of the bar as shown on page 42. The center punch creates a crater, displacing metal into a surrounding rim. The result is a bar that fits the groove more closely. Dimple only the side of the bar closest to the blade, and stagger the dimples slightly up and down on the side of the bar so they won't wear a channel in the side of the groove. Since the two table grooves probably won't be exactly the same, fit the miter gauge bar to the groove that you use most often. If dimpling makes the bar too snug, file the dimples gently with a flat mill file until the bar slides smoothly.

Setting the Miter Gauge Stops

Adjusting miter gauge stops is similar in principle to adjusting blade tilt stops, as described previously. Begin by backing off the stops. Next, square the head of the

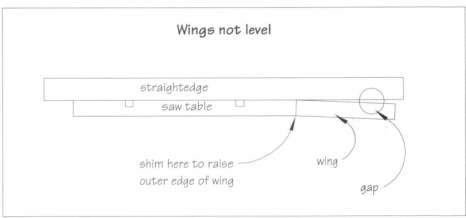

Wings not level

straightedge
saw table
shim here to raise outer edge of wing
wing
gap

ADJUSTING SAW TABLE WINGS

If the wings are flush with the main table where the two join, but the straightedge test still shows a gap, you will have to tilt the extension wing up or down to correct the problem. You can do this by inserting metal shims above or below the bolts as shown here. Brass shim stock from an auto parts store is ideal for this, but you may get away with pieces of a derelict measuring tape or aluminum can.

miter gauge to its bar by loosening the lock knob on the protractor head and then holding an accurate square against the head and bar. (Don't use the edge of the bar that has dimples in it!) Tighten the locking knob and then set the 90° stop screw adjustment. Set the 45° stop in a similar fashion, using an accurate 45° square. A top-of-the-line combination square works well for both adjustments. The commercial angle setup tool shown in the photo makes this process quick, easy and accurate. Be sure, though, to always confirm the stop positions by making test cuts in scrap.

RIP FENCE TUNE-UP

Safe and accurate ripping requires that the rip fence be parallel to the blade. If it isn't, the workpiece will either come out slightly tapered or, worse, tend to wedge between the back of the blade and the fence, creating a serious danger of kick-back. The Perils of a Skewed Fence shows these two results of an improperly aligned fence. Begin by planing a piece of hardwood to fit snugly in the miter gauge groove of the saw, leaving at least ½" above the surface of the saw table. It should be tight enough in the groove to require a light tap with a hammer to set it in. Crosscut the piece of hardwood into two short lengths, and tap them into the ends of one of the grooves 1" or 2" away from the front and back edges of the table. Now slide the rip fence over until it just touches one of the blocks. If you're lucky, it will touch both. Back the fence off just a hair and lock it securely, front and back. Now select a feeler gauge or other suitable shim that just fits snugly between the fence and the block at the infeed end of the miter gauge groove. This same gauge or shim should fit equally snugly between the fence and the block at the outfeed end. It's OK if it's slightly *less* snug at the outfeed block, but in no event should it be *more* snug at the outfeed block. (Some woodworkers actually prefer a fence that angles very slightly to the right; that is, one adjusted so the shim is very slightly loose at the outfeed edge.) If the shim is too tight at the outfeed edge,

EASY ON THE CRANK!

Once you're accustomed to a saw, you may find that in the excitement of building a project you crank rapidly on the blade-height or tilt control until the adjustment comes up hard against the stop at the end of the adjustment range—crank, crank, crank, thunk! If your saw could talk back, it would probably turn your ears red. A worm gear and rack mechanism as used on most saws for blade-height and tilt adjustment can generate tremendous force—so much that you can actually twist and distort the entire carriage and trunnion assembly at the heart of your saw. Save yourself the grief of a saw that never seems to stay well tuned: Keep your eye on the blade position, and slow down as you approach the end of the adjustment range. Bump gently against the stop at the end of the range, rather than banging into it.

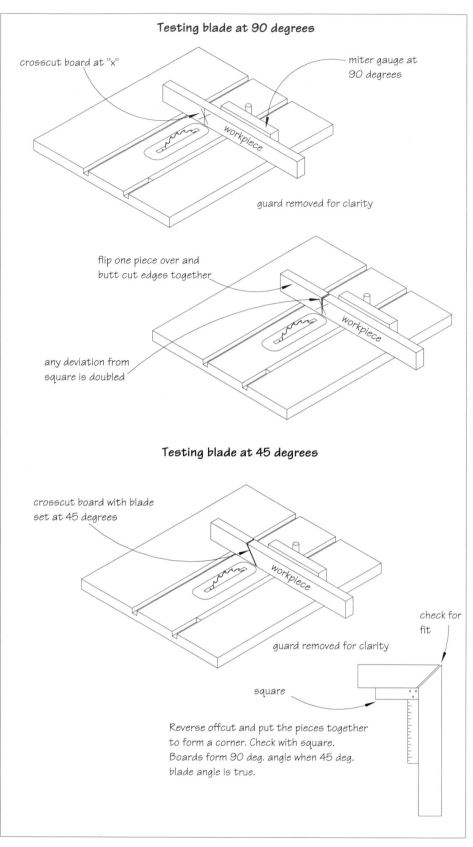

Testing blade at 90 degrees

crosscut board at "x"

miter gauge at 90 degrees

workpiece

guard removed for clarity

flip one piece over and butt cut edges together

workpiece

any deviation from square is doubled

Testing blade at 45 degrees

crosscut board with blade set at 45 degrees

workpiece

check for fit

guard removed for clarity

square

Reverse offcut and put the pieces together to form a corner. Check with square. Boards form 90 deg. angle when 45 deg. blade angle is true.

TEST BLADE TILT

When you are happy with the adjustment of the stops, check the readings you get from the blade tilt scale on the front of the saw. Most saws have an adjustable pointer for reading this scale. With the blade at 90° to the table, adjust the pointer to 90° on the scale. Now tilt the blade all the way over to the 45° stop and hope that the pointer points to 45° on the scale. If it doesn't, you'll have to either forget about using the scale for adjusting the tilt to odd angles or make an adjustment that the manufacturer probably didn't intend for you to make. See Repositioning a Tilt Scale.

REPOSITIONING A TILT SCALE

A common problem with table saw tilt scales is that when the pointer is set to read correctly at one end of the scale, it's off at the other end. This happens when the center of the arc of the scale doesn't coincide with the pivot center of the tilt mechanism. To fix this, you must move the scale. If the scale on your saw is a metal plate attached to the cabinet, repositioning it is worth considering. If the scale is just a piece of plastic tape, you'd probably destroy it trying to get it off. Repositioning the scale takes some fiddling, but the result is worth the effort if you do much sawing at tilt angles other than 45° and 90°. Here's the procedure to follow:

1. Make sure that the angle stops on your saw are correctly adjusted to stop the blade tilt at 45° and 90°. (See the previous section for the adjustment procedure.)
2. Set the pointer to read correctly with the blade at 90° to the table. (On most saws, this means having the pointer on "0" since the scales usually indicate the amount of tilt rather than the angle of the blade to the table.)
3. Crank the arbor away from zero to get the pointer out of the way. Now align a straightedge with the zero mark on the tilt scale and with a fine felt-tip pen draw extensions to the zero mark above and below the scale plate on the saw cabinet.
4. Remove the scale plate from the saw cabinet by removing the screws, drilling out the rivets, or prying it away from its adhesive, as appropriate.
5. Use a straightedge and a marker to join the two extension marks of the zero mark on the saw cabinet (where the scale plate was before you removed it).
6. Tilt the blade to 45°.
7. Hold the scale on the cabinet, positioned so the zero mark on the scale is aligned with the line you drew on the cabinet. Keeping this alignment, slide the scale along your line until the pointer is exactly on the 45° mark.
8. Tape it in place, and check that the pointer points correctly when the blade is perpendicular to the table and tilted 45°. Just to make sure, check it at one or two positions in between.
9. When you've got it right, reattach it to the cabinet with sheet metal screws or pop rivets.

Extending zero mark on cabinet face

arbor at 45 degs.

45   22 1/2

extend lines along 0 deg. mark onto face of cabinet.

plate shifts slightly to align pointer with 45 deg. mark on plate.

- maintain 0 alignment

---

adjust the fence as explained in the owner's manual. If your fence doesn't permit this adjustment, don't despair. You can align the fence by adapting the auxiliary fence approach explained next.

GUARD AND SPLITTER ADJUSTMENT

An improperly adjusted splitter and blade guard assembly can escalate from a minor annoyance to a safety hazard. In one scenario, a stiff-acting guard forces you to push on the workpiece to get the plastic guard to raise out of the way. Then, when the guard does go up, your added effort pushes the wood forcefully and unexpectedly into the blade. In another scenario, a misaligned splitter and guard mounting bracket binds the wood against the rip fence.

To reduce these hazards, keep the pivot points of the guard and splitter teeth well lubricated, and regularly check to see that the leading edge of the plastic guard is smooth and free of nicks. Use a fine file to repair any roughness or damage. Also, to decrease resistance, wax the surfaces of the guard that ride up over the wood.

The splitter and blade guard support should be centered in the saw kerf. Proper centering is easy to check. Just rip a foot or so into a piece of plywood, turn off the saw, and check that there is equal clearance between the splitter and the two sides of the kerf. The actual amount of clearance will depend on the kerf of the blade and the thickness of the splitter. The saw's manual should tell you how to adjust the position of the splitter to center it in the kerf, but if you don't have a manual, you should be able to figure it out.

If you use blades with different kerf widths, the splitter will only be centered in the kerf of the blade you used when making your adjustments. This is one argument against using blades of different kerf widths. If you need to accommodate different kerfs and don't want to readjust the position of the splitter every time you switch blades, try adjusting it for your thinnest blade and then checking that you still have some clearance with the other blades. Make certain everything is working well when ripping—the operation when a properly functioning splitter is most important.

MAINTAINING THE SAW

Now that your saw is properly set up, it pays (literally if you intend to make a living at woodworking) to keep it that way. You may want to set up a regular maintenance schedule for your saw, or you can rely more on a weather eye and frequent inspections to catch potential problems. Of course, if you use your saw regularly, inspection becomes a routine—simply note any changes that take place over time. For example, a mental red flag should go up if you have difficulty turning the cranks, if measurement indexes are slightly off or if more force than usual is

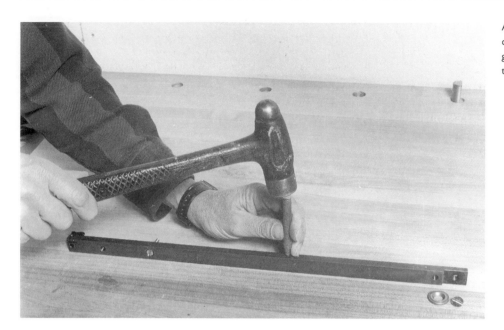

A quick hit with a hammer against a center punch creates a raised crater rim on the side of the miter gauge bar—a nice trick for snugging the fit of the bar to the groove.

A more adjustable and precise way to fit the gauge bar to the groove is available with a commercially made kit that uses phenolic plugs as slick rubbing surfaces to eliminate slop. Allenhead setscrews allow you to adjust the amount they protrude from the side of the gauge and thus the fit of the bar in the groove.

DUGINSKE'S MITERMATIC TABLE SAW SETUP SQUARE

This plastic setup tool makes it a snap to set the miter gauge head to a perfect 90°, 45°, 30° or 22½° angle. See Sources.

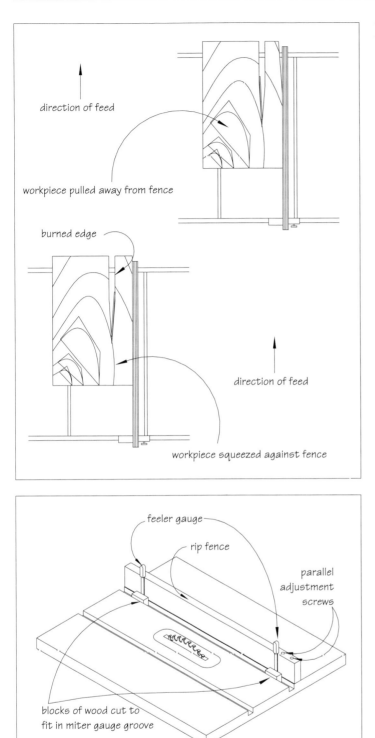

direction of feed

workpiece pulled away from fence

burned edge

direction of feed

workpiece squeezed against fence

feeler gauge

rip fence

parallel adjustment screws

blocks of wood cut to fit in miter gauge groove

Adjust fence until feeler gauge

Distance same at both blocks

RIP FENCE ALIGNMENT

An easy and accurate way to ensure that the rip fence locks up parallel to the blade is to align it parallel to one of the miter gauge grooves, which you have already aligned parallel to the blade as one of the first steps in your tune-up.

THE PERILS OF A SKEWED FENCE

Your fence likely has provision for adjusting alignment. Check the owner's manual for details on your specific fence. If you don't have a manual, look for parallel adjustment screws similar to those shown in Rip Fence Alignment.

square

auxiliary fence

saw rip fence

table

shim as required until auxiliary fence is square to the saw table

drill through fence

countersink flat machine screw

threaded insert

SHIMMING AN AUXILIARY FENCE SQUARE TO THE SAW TABLE

Since few rip fences allow any tilt adjustment, the only correction at your disposal is to shim an auxiliary fence. Some modern fences come with an auxiliary fence that you can shim. If yours does not, you'll have to make a wooden auxiliary fence and shim it (or hand plane it) so it is straight and perpendicular to the table.

required to push a sheet of plywood across the table. Set aside time to deal with each as it occurs. Every now and then, give the saw a general checkup. Tighten any loose fittings, check adjustments for accuracy, blow out the sawdust from inside the workings, and lubricate stiff parts.

Cleaning

The inside of a table saw is not a pretty place. Sawdust, especially when combined with petroleum-based lubricants or pitch, can gum up the workings in a hurry. A regular blast of compressed air as your shop vacuum or dust collector draws off the blowout is a convenient way to keep things running smoothly, but a brush also does the trick. Less frequently, you'll need to clean thoroughly with a brass wire brush and steel wool. Clean the tabletop with mineral spirits and steel wool, or 400-grit or finer wet/dry sandpaper to remove stains or rust.

Lubrication

You will most appreciate good lubrication on the table surface. A rough surface caked with rust or pitch can cause a surprising amount of drag. Well lubricated with wax or a spray lubricant, the slick table makes it almost effortless to move heavy workpieces across the saw. Regular lubrication also reduces rust and pitch buildup. While wax has been the traditional lubricant of choice (furniture or floor wax is commonly used), several modern spray dressings that do an excellent job are now available. Stay away from anything that contains silicone, which can transfer to the wood and cause problems with finishes. I like the modern sprays for their ease of application and superior moisture resistance, but whatever you choose, be sure to get the lubrication down into the miter gauge grooves.

It is also important to keep the interior moving parts well lubricated. Refer to Table Saw Lubrication for specific lubrication points and suggested lubricants. Although wax can be used, lubricants such as graphite or Teflon spray are easy to apply. Stay away from petroleum-based products; they attract sawdust and quickly lose their effectiveness.

Cleaning the Worm Gear With a Small Wire Brush
A small wire brush is the ideal tool for removing sawdust and built-up wood pitch from the cogs of the worm and rack gear mechanisms.

PREVENTATIVE SAW MAINTENANCE

The first rule of preventative maintenance is to impose as little unnecessary wear on the saw as possible. Keeping the blades sharp, the tabletop and the workings properly lubricated, and the various parts adjusted and tuned up will let your saw do its job with as little strain on the components as possible. The payback to you will be fewer repairs in the future as well as better work in the present. Keep aware of the feedback the saw gives you. Fix small problems as they occur, and you will reduce the likelihood of having to deal with major ones that result from cumulative wear and misalignment.

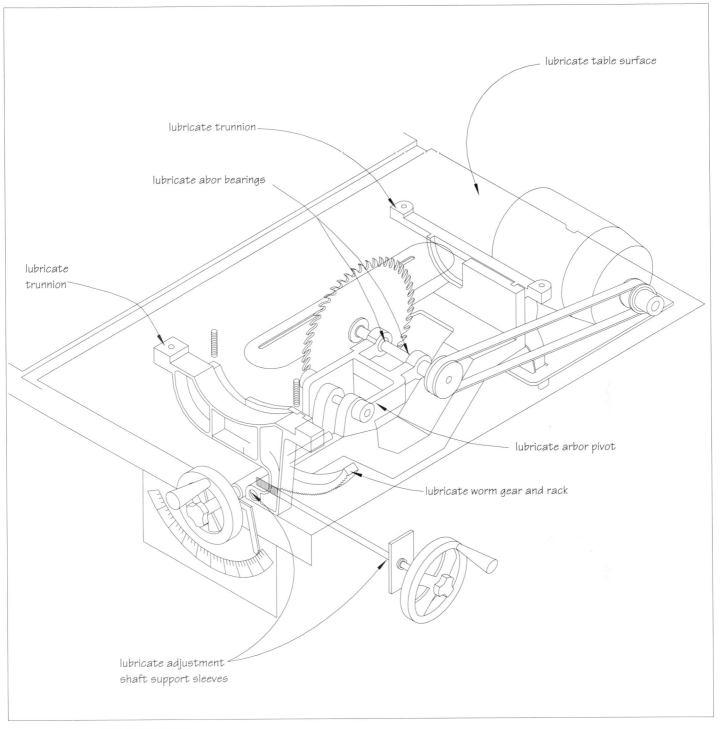

lubricate table surface

lubricate trunnion

lubricate abor bearings

lubricate trunnion

lubricate arbor pivot

lubricate worm gear and rack

lubricate adjustment shaft support sleeves

TABLE SAW LUBRICATION DIAGRAM

Table Saw Accessories

Having set up and tuned your table saw, you'd think I'd let you get right to work. There is nothing stopping you, of course; the machine is essentially all set to go. But if you are looking for the safest, most accurate and most versatile performance, you will first want to consider the merits of some shop-made and commercially available accessories for the table saw.

In this chapter I'll begin with accessories that contribute primarily to increasing the safety of this powerful and potentially dangerous tool. These include advanced blade guard and splitter systems that allow more types of cuts, are easier to use and yet significantly increase the level of protection. Also included are push sticks, hold-down systems that keep the workpieces under control and keep your hands well away from the blade, and support fixtures to ensure that large workpieces, such as full-size sheets of plywood, run flat and straight through the blade.

Next, I'll show you accessories that can vastly improve the efficiency, accuracy and overall performance of your saw. Be forewarned: I'm going to do my best to convince you to upgrade your rip fence and miter gauge if they aren't up to snuff. I'll try to goad you into buying or building some form of moving table for crosscutting, and maybe even talk you into a power feeder for the sake of both performance and safety. These accessories will admittedly cost you some money, and some time if you choose the shop-made versions, but they will enormously increase both the performance of your saw and your pleasure in using it over the coming years.

In the next chapter I'll introduce you to the broad array of cutting tools that are now available for the table saw.

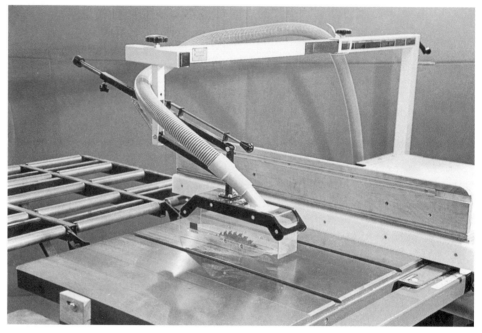

BIESEMEYER OVERARM GUARD IN USE
A square tubular steel arm supports the spring-loaded, counterweighted Plexiglas blade guard as it rides on top of the workpiece. A dust collection port is built into the top of the blade guard, and the entire assembly can be moved laterally with a crank to fine-tune its position over the blade or to move it entirely out of the way.

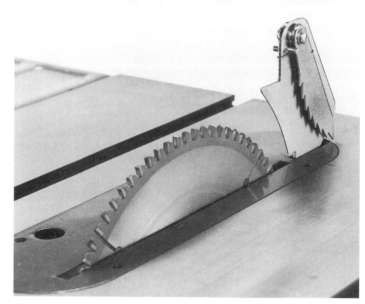

REMOVABLE SPLITTER WITH PAWLS
This splitter incorporates a pair of steel pawls to provide anti-kickback protection when using the overarm guard system shown above. A snap catch holds it in place, allowing quick, tool-less removal.

BLADE GUARDS AND SPLITTERS

The standard blade guard on table saws sold in America is supported by the splitter. This requires that the splitter pass entirely through the stock. This obviously won't work for table saw operations that don't separate the wood into two pieces. Since such operations include common cuts like rabbets and dadoes, you may be tempted to leave off the splitter rather than take the time to refit it.

To provide effective antikickback protection when ripping, overarm-type guard systems require that you install a special splitter where the splitter of the standard guard system was attached. A splitter is necessary to prevent stock from pinching on the blade as the freshly ripped wood reacts to the release of internal stresses, a condition that can cause binding and kickback. When rabbeting and dadoing you can pop out the splitter by pulling on a spring-loaded knob, retract it below the level of the table, or grab a wrench and unbolt it, depending on the design of the splitter.

But if you do neglect to refit the splitter and guard, you compromise your safety when doing the more common and more hazardous operations, such as ripping. My solution to this problem is to replace the standard guard with an aftermarket system that not only stays on the saw but offers significantly greater visibility when setting up and making cuts. Its secret: The guard is suspended from an arm overhanging the table, eliminating the need for a support rising up through the saw kerf.

One variety of overarm guard, as shown in the photo, features built-in antikickback pawls, eliminating the need to have pawls mounted on the splitter (you still need to add a splitter, however). For these spring-loaded pawls to grab well, you have to adjust the guard cage so the pawls exert sufficient pressure on the workpiece.

If you install a guard system that does not include a splitter, you'll have to make separate provision for a splitter when ripping solid wood. Instead of buying and installing one of the commercially made splitters that attach to the cradle frame,

BESSEY SYSTEM IN USE
The plastic cage of this guard system incorporates spring-loaded pawls to ensure the work doesn't kick back. A splitter, independent of the guard cage, attaches to the saw behind the blade. The crank on top of the support arm raises or lowers the cage to accommodate different stock thicknesses.

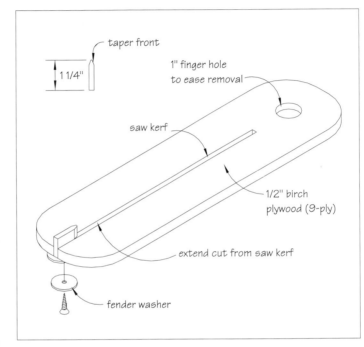

taper front

1 1/4"

1" finger hole to ease removal

saw kerf

1/2" birch plywood (9-ply)

extend cut from saw kerf

fender washer

SHOP-MADE SPLITTER/THROAT PLATE
Because this splitter is attached to the throat plate, I find that it's easier than any other arrangement I've seen to mount or dismount from the saw. Note that the fender washer at the back underside of the plate prevents the plate from rising out of the table if the blade should bind in spite of the splitter. Don't omit this part!

you can save a little money by making your own as shown in Shop-Made Splitter/Throat Plate.

PUSH STICKS

Unless you use a power feeder, you need a way to safely push stock through the blade. This is especially true when dealing with small workpieces that might bring your hands dangerously close to the blade. My rule of thumb (and I still have both) is to use push sticks if my hands would otherwise pass over the throat plate. I also use them whenever the operation prevents me from using the blade guard.

If I've installed hold-downs (explained later in this chapter), then I need only push the stock through with a straight stick bearing against its end. Otherwise,

push sticks will have to hold the stock tight to both the fence and the table as well as push it through. Because of these many requirements, I like sticks like the shoe-type shown that bear on the surface of a workpiece as well as push on its end. Another variety has a broad sole for holding wider stock flat to the table. Other types of push sticks that I'll introduce you to here include a specialized notched push stick that holds the stock against the fence from the opposite edge and tall and narrow pushers for keeping control of narrow stock between the blade and the fence.

Commercially Made Push Sticks

By holding the work secure to the table surface, shoe-type push sticks prevent the back of the workpiece from danger-ously climbing up as it comes into contact with the rising teeth at the back of the blade.

A feature I like on commercially made push sticks is a nonslip base. Some of these push sticks come with two bases: one square section designed for general pushing, and the other with a V-groove. I use the latter when I need to hold the workpiece tight against the fence as well as down to the table surface, such as when running narrow boards over the dado blade to create a rabbet. In this situation, the pusher eliminates the need to rig hold-downs on the table surface.

A third advantageous feature is the location of the handgrip—high out of the way of the blade and the top edge of the fence. I especially appreciate a high handle location when I'm ripping narrow stock—an operation that can bring the pushing hand close to both the blade and the fence.

Shop-Made Push Sticks

My shop-made push stick design incorporates three of the features I like most in the commercial product: the long, nonslip base; the adjustable stop block; and the location and orientation of the handle up high and angled to fit my hand, while directing the thrusting force down and forward. I usually make my pushers from high quality ¾" hardwood scraps from cabinetmaking projects. I may use thinner plywood if I'm making a pusher for a specific purpose, such as ripping strips less than ¾" wide. I avoid fir plywood because interior voids might weaken the push stick. A stick that could break during use could be more dangerous than none at all. Fir also tends to splinter, even after sanding. I avoid using solid wood because the push block area weakens after being riddled with saw-kerfs.

If you take your time getting the curves pretty and the handle angle just right when making your first pusher, you can use it as a pattern for making more using the techniques explained earlier for making throat plates. Not only will this give you spares, but you can take care of Christmas gifts for all your woodworking buddies!

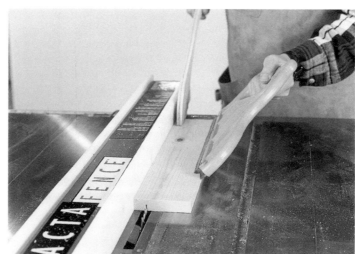

PUSH STICKS IN USE
Using push sticks ensures a board will pass safely and accurately through the blade. Here, I use a shoe-type push stick to push against the end of the board (and to hold it flat to the table), and a notched push stick to keep the board aligned to the rip fence.

Using Push Sticks

I always use push sticks when feeding stock by hand and lengthwise through the blade, such as when ripping stock to width. Before starting the table saw, I lay two push sticks—a shoe type and a side type—just to the far side of the rip fence. Placed there, I can reach them quickly and easily yet there is no chance they might vibrate into the blade and be kicked off the table or into me.

When sawing stock more than a foot long, I start the cut by guiding the wood with my hands. When the trailing end of the stock approaches within 6" of the blade, I switch to one or more push sticks. By holding the side of the stick against the fence, as shown in the photo, it's less likely to slip out of position. This is especially important when I'm cutting out a rabbet, a situation where a slip of the pusher's position could result in the wood tipping and creating a miscut.

When the stock is narrower than the push stick, the stick often goes into the blade along with the stock. Don't worry about it; just keep pushing. But remember to check the pushing block portion of the stick. You'll need to make a new stop when more than one-third of the push area has been cut away.

HOLD-DOWNS

One of the most common causes of accidents with table saws is kickback. Splitters and antikickback pawls go a long way toward preventing it. But the use of hold-downs further increases safety and helps keep your cut where you want it. Hold-downs add an additional, powerful force to keep the workpiece from drifting away from the fence or table surface and binding against the blade. In combination with a splitter, they let you keep your hands well away from the blade. Your hands are not needed to provide any holding force. Hold-downs can be shop-made, wooden, featherboards or commercial,

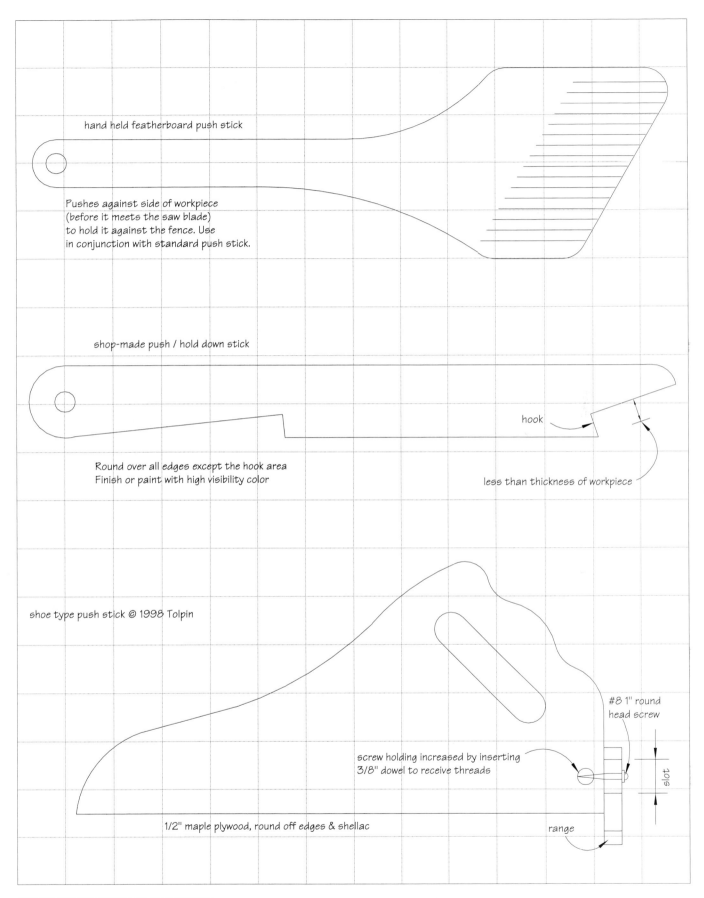

hand held featherboard push stick

Pushes against side of workpiece
(before it meets the saw blade)
to hold it against the fence. Use
in conjunction with standard push stick.

shop-made push / hold down stick

hook

Round over all edges except the hook area
Finish or paint with high visibility color

less than thickness of workpiece

shoe type push stick © 1998 Tolpin

#8 1" round
head screw

screw holding increased by inserting
3/8" dowel to receive threads

slot

1/2" maple plywood, round off edges & shellac

range

EXAMPLES OF SHOP-MADE PUSH STICKS

spring-loaded, roller-type guide wheels.

Hold-downs provide more than just safety. By keeping the stock tight against the fence and the saw table, they contribute to more consistent, precise cuts. They are especially important when dadoing, rabbeting and making moldings, since any lifting or side-to-side movement will change the shape of the cut, requiring a great deal of reshaping and cleanup. Unless I'm cutting just one small workpiece, I take the time to install holddowns. If that sounds like a time-consuming nuisance to you, look ahead to the Quick-Mount Guide Wheels that I use, or to the discussion on shop-made featherboards later in this chapter.

Guide Wheels

I have had good results using a pair of rubber wheel guides as hold-downs. The wheels hold a workpiece firmly to both the rip fence and table surface, freeing my hands to simply push the board through without worrying about alignment or getting too close to the blade. Because the wheels turn in only one direction, they give some additional insurance against kickback. I have come to use guide wheels for nearly all ripping and panel-sizing operations, and remove them only when I'm crosscutting boards or using sliding fixtures.

The guide wheels shown at right use wedge-shaped, neoprene rubber wheels mounted on a spring-loaded arm assembly. You can adapt them to different-size workpieces by sliding the wheel carriages out on their mounting plates. They can extend ⅝" and 5" from the side of the fence. The hold-down pressure is adjustable as well. By turning a thumbscrew against a spring, I can balance firm downward pressure with the right amount of push resistance. To reduce the chance of kickback, the wheels are mounted on one-way bearings that lock instantly with any back pressure.

Be aware that you may need to remove the blade guard when using guide wheels. When the fence must be close to the blade, there may not be enough room for both the blade guard and the wheels. While the guide wheels provide adequate kickback protection, I worry about working around the exposed blade.

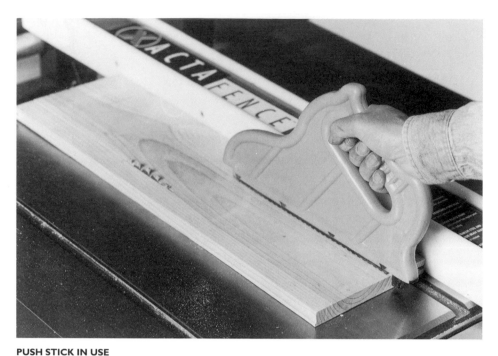

PUSH STICK IN USE
Hold a shoe-type push stick against the side of the rip fence to prevent it from rocking or shifting during the cut.

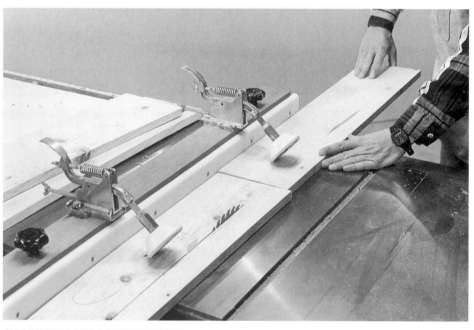

GUIDE WHEEL HOLD-DOWN SYSTEM
Attached to a quick release mounting board, these one-direction wheels hold the stock firmly to the table and fence, reduce kickback, yet offer only a moderate amount of resistance. Note that I am using a second board to push the first through the blade.

Guide wheels may also prevent you from using your push stick, at least in the way you are accustomed to using it. Often, you must push against the workpiece from directly behind. I either push with a flat-ended stick lying on the table or, if I'm making multiple cuts, I use the next board in line to push the last one through as shown.

Featherboards

Well before the woodworking industry put guide wheel systems on the market, woodworkers held stock tight against the fence and down against the table with flexible sticks called featherboards. The design of most featherboards, including those shown in Shop-Made Featherboards (see next page), also helps prevent kickback, though not as effectively as either metal anti-kick pawls on a splitter or single-direction guide wheels. Shop-Made Featherboards shows how to build several different versions. The first version is designed to mount to the rip fence to hold the stock against the table surface. (Two variations of the table-mounted featherboard are shown: one for use with a T-slot and the other for a U-slot.) The second mounts to the table, exerting pressure against the side of the stock to keep it tight to the rip fence. I generally use both the table-mounted and the fence-mounted versions in conjunction to ensure full, positive control of the workpiece. Small enough to be kept in a drawer close by the saw (perhaps a drawer hung under your saw's side extension table), you can mount and adjust these featherboards in less than twenty seconds.

Using Shop-Made Featherboards

All of the featherboards are set up in a similar fashion: Position the table-mounted boards ahead of the infeed edge of the blade. Don't go past the front edge of the blade or you might bind the wood against the blade, causing burning and risking kickback. Place a pair of vertical, fence-mounted featherboards just ahead and just behind the blade. You can clamp them to the fence or, better, bolt them to my universal auxiliary fence.

Press the featherboards against the stock until the fingers are slightly bent as they bear against the wood. Try the workpiece with the power off and the blade down. Back off the featherboards if you feel too much resistance, that is, if the board lurches past the hold-downs instead of moving slowly and steadily. When you have the featherboards situated just right, secure them tightly. Finally, store these fixtures as near as possible to the saw so you won't have an excuse not to use them.

Commercially Made Featherboards

The unusual featherboard (see photo) depends on a strong magnet to hold the wooden block in place. Lexan fingers or an optional roller pressure bar bear against both the top and the side of the workpiece. The big advantage of the magnetic clamp is its nearly instantaneous setup and removal. You slap it down in

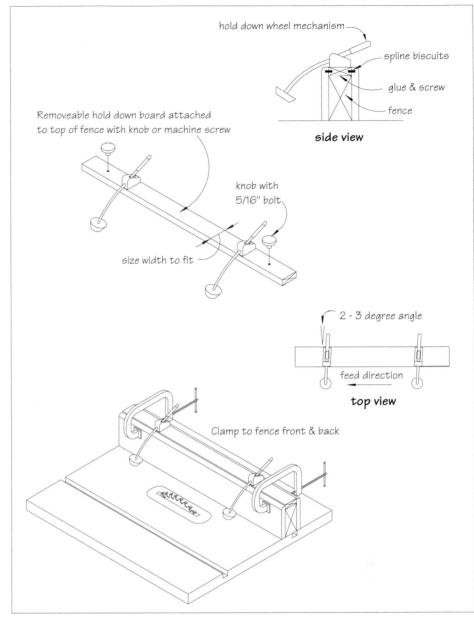

place to set it up and push the block on its side to release the magnet for removal. A disadvantage is that it won't work on aluminum tables or wood-faced rip fences. The manufacturer does offer a 4"-high steel plate to apply to a non-steel rip fence if desired.

I wouldn't, however, depend on this type of hold-down to control large workpieces or stock. If the magnet should shift, the pressure applied by the fingers will decrease making the hold-down's fingers far less effective. This system is, in my opinion, excellent for controlling small

workpieces, especially for a short run when you don't want to bother with a more complex, though reliable, setup.

STOCK SUPPORT

The typical saw table is simply not large enough to safely support pieces of wood much longer than two to three feet or panels larger than three to four square feet in area. You are going to need added support to handle large stock, even if it comes from a workshop partner. The additional support lets you maintain control so large stock doesn't shift during a

QUICK-MOUNT GUIDE WHEELS
To make the guide wheel system easy to set up (and take away my excuses for not bothering with it), I mount them on a board that attaches easily to the fence as shown here. Using threaded plastic knobs, I can install or remove the system in a matter of a few seconds.

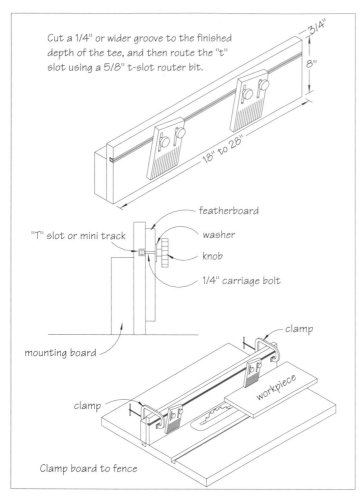

Cut a 1/4" or wider groove to the finished depth of the tee, and then route the "t" slot using a 5/8" t-slot router bit.

3/4"
8"
18" to 28"

"T" slot or mini track
featherboard
washer
knob
1/4" carriage bolt
mounting board
clamp
clamp
workpiece

Clamp board to fence

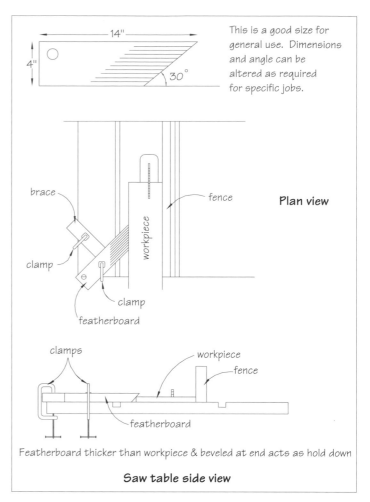

14"
4"
30°

This is a good size for general use. Dimensions and angle can be altered as required for specific jobs.

brace
fence
workpiece
Plan view
clamp
clamp
featherboard

clamps
workpiece
fence
featherboard

Featherboard thicker than workpiece & beveled at end acts as hold down

Saw table side view

CONSTRUCTION DRAWINGS OF SHOP-MADE FEATHERBOARDS

Make your featherboards from solid, straight-grained hardwood or from a sheet of void-free hardwood plywood. Because the "fingers" are thin but must be strong and flexible, I recommend using the more expensive Baltic birch plywood which has more layers of veneer than standard hardwood plywoods. When laying out the finger cuts, be sure to make them at least 5/16" thick (as measured perpendicular to the edge, not across the angled end), but not over 3/8" (or they lose flexibility). Use the index jig as shown in "Kerfing" in chapter eight to cut the fingers quickly and accurately. The only difference in setup from the kerfing jig is that you will set the blade and the index pin at a 45° angle. Round the edges and corners of the jig to ease handling and seal it with varnish or shellac.

TABLE-MOUNTED FEATHERBOARD IN USE

Shop-made featherboards from scraps of wood, mounted on both the fence and to the table surface, keep a workpiece well under control, ensuring an accurate and safe cut.

MAGNETIC BASE FEATHERBOARD

The fastest way to come up with a featherboard is to slap this magnetic-based block with lexan fingers in place. If the saw has a clean steel surface, this device will exert a surprising amount of force without slipping.

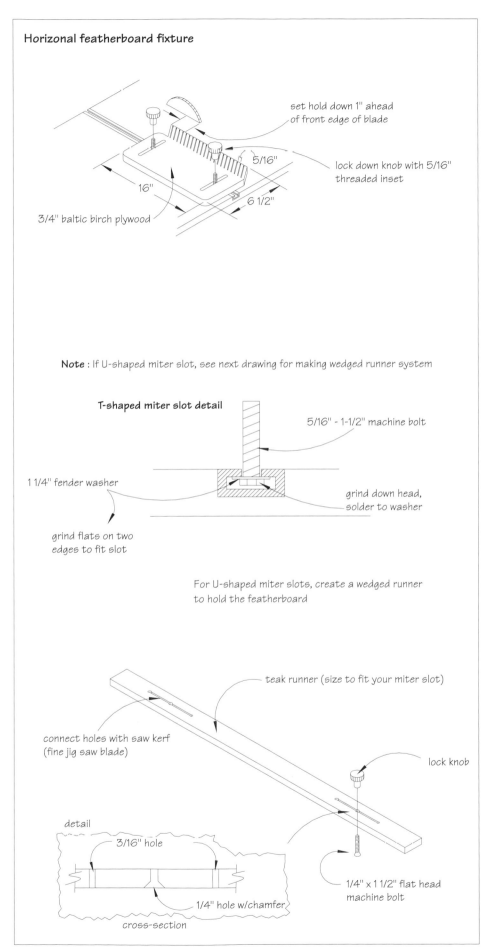

Horizontal featherboard fixture

set hold down 1" ahead of front edge of blade

lock down knob with 5/16" threaded inset

5/16"

16"

6 1/2"

3/4" baltic birch plywood

Note : If U-shaped miter slot, see next drawing for making wedged runner system

T-shaped miter slot detail

5/16" - 1-1/2" machine bolt

1 1/4" fender washer

grind down head, solder to washer

grind flats on two edges to fit slot

For U-shaped miter slots, create a wedged runner to hold the featherboard

teak runner (size to fit your miter slot)

connect holes with saw kerf (fine jig saw blade)

lock knob

detail

3/16" hole

1/4" hole w/chamfer

cross-section

1/4" x 1 1/2" flat head machine bolt

cut due to its own weight, or fall off the end of the table, damaging more than your nerves.

You have a lot of options: You can use freestanding, commercially made roller supports, shop-made versions that can be wider, more massive and therefore better performing, and you can add extension tables to the sides and the back of the saw. You can make the extension tables so they fold down out of way when not in use, making more shop space available.

Freestanding Support

For years my outfeed support partner was a simple, commercially made single roller at right. It worked well enough for long, narrow boards but only marginally for wide panel stock, which tended to tip to one side unless I centered it perfectly. I recently replaced the support with a shop-made version designed to offer significant improvements. The new version's heavy weight and dual post supports make it extraordinarily stable and nearly impossible to tip over. The large diameter of the cylinder catches the end of the work with less chance of jamming. And the wide roller offers ample support when I work with panel stock. Complete construction details are shown in Shop-Made Roller Stand.

Side Support

The single roller stand is not designed to be used at the side of the saw to support panel stock—it lacks the length of travel needed in this situation. To support wide panels, you need a series of rollers along the side of the saw working like a conveyer belt. I use two different types: a shop-made fixture utilizing a row of ball glides which I set on my jointer table as shown in the photo and illustration, and a fold-up stand that uses these same ball glides. The fold-up stand provides a wide base of support for those times when I must handle a full-sized sheet of plywood by myself. Because the legs collapse against one another, the stand stores flat out of the way on the wall. Another advantage of both of these fixtures is that, unlike cylindrical rollers, the ball rollers allow the workpieces to move freely in all directions. This prevents any tendency for the stock to work away from the rip fence.

COMMERCIALLY MADE SINGLE ROLLER STAND

The unusually wide base of this commercially made roller stand helps stabilize it when supporting heavy workpieces. Yet the base folds up to ease storage when not in use.

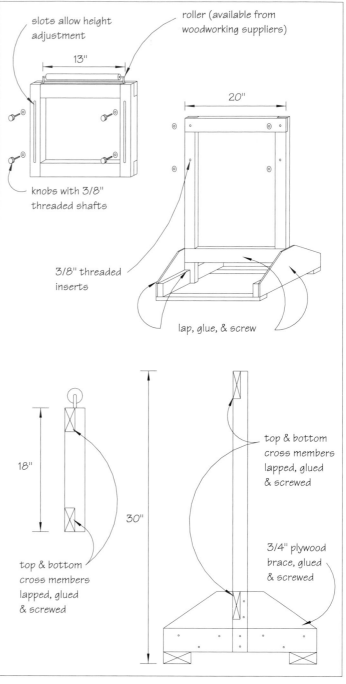

slots allow height adjustment

roller (available from woodworking suppliers)

13"

20"

knobs with 3/8" threaded shafts

3/8" threaded inserts

lap, glue, & screw

18"

30"

top & bottom cross members lapped, glued & screwed

top & bottom cross members lapped, glued & screwed

3/4" plywood brace, glued & screwed

SHOP-MADE ROLLER STAND

Positioning the outfeed support

2 deg.

roller

2' to 3'

saw

top view

Setup of roller stand - outfeed support

feed

1/8"

saw

stand

side view

To catch stock as it feeds off the end of the table saw, place the stand two to three feet behind the saw (closer if the stock is shorter than three feet). Set the roller height about 1/8" below the height of the saw table to account for sagging of the workpiece and to minimize snagging. If you are setting this up in your shop, as opposed to an unlevel job site, mark the posts at the top of their sleeves so you can reset this level quickly in the future. Unless your floor is absolutely level, it will pay to mark the position of the stand on the floor with paint or duct tape.

Fixed Outfeed Supports

When I started doing finish carpentry work on construction sites, I took along my trusty old roller stand to provide outfeed support. Sometimes it worked, and sometimes it didn't. There were times when it was nearly impossible to find a smooth and level place for both the saw and the support. To solve the problem, I designed and built an outfeed support that attached directly to the saw. See the drawings for instructions on how to build my design.

On my stationary saw, I have installed a commercially made outfeed support system that also folds down out of the way if necessary (though it's rare I need to do this in a shop situation). Before I moved my jointer to the side of my table saw and

SIDE SUPPORT FIXTURE FOR JOINTER
Set on the bed of the jointer, this simple, lightweight fixture provides a quick and reliable way to provide side support for panel stock and sliding fixtures in use on the table saw.

Jointer-mounted side support

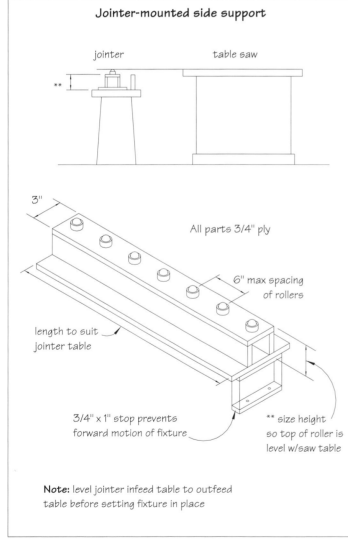

Scissors-type side support

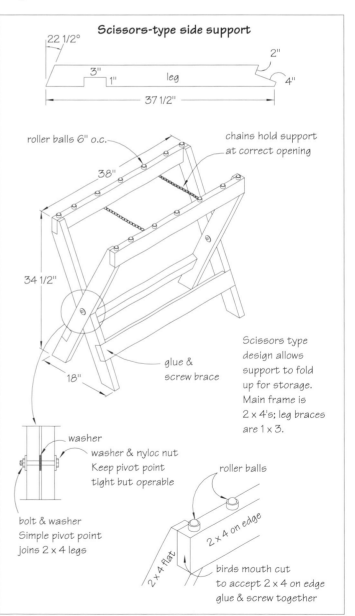

SIDE SUPPORTS
Here you see two different types of shop-made side supports. The one on the left is a jointer-mounted side support, while the second example on the right is a folding scissors type that allows the support to fold up for storage.

built the jointer-mounted support fixture, I also used a commercial ganged roller system to help support panel stock and my crosscut box to the side of the saw. The cylindrical rollers offer less friction than the table surface of my shop-made support, even when I keep my table as slick as possible. They are also wider, providing more secure support for large sheet stock.

Extension Tables

Today, the manufacturers of most contractor's and stationary saws offer an optional side extension table that extends support up to 52" to the right side of the blade. The extension table not only provides secure support for large workpieces running between the fence and blade, it also offers a convient and efficient location for mounting a router. By making the table saw extension into a router table, you can use the table saw's rip fence when routing. You can also easily connect the table saw's dust extraction system to the router location.

You can, of course, build your own extension table using wood frames and posts as I show in Shop-Made Saw Table Extension. If you go this route, be sure to use stable hardwoods for the framework to help ensure that the table stays flat. I also recommend that you cover both sides of the plywood or fiberboard table surface with plastic laminate. If only the top side is covered—and thus sealed—the bottom can absorb moisture and cause warping or bowing. I also add a pair of drawers to hold commonly used items such as push sticks, featherboards, blade wrenches, hold-down bolts and throat plate inserts.

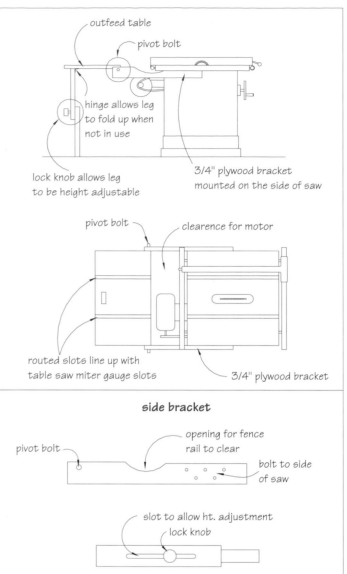

outfeed table
pivot bolt
hinge allows leg to fold up when not in use
lock knob allows leg to be height adjustable
3/4" plywood bracket mounted on the side of saw

pivot bolt
clearence for motor
routed slots line up with table saw miter gauge slots
3/4" plywood bracket

side bracket

pivot bolt
opening for fence rail to clear
bolt to side of saw

slot to allow ht. adjustment
lock knob
adjustable leg

SAFETY *tip*

ANGLE YOUR OUTFEED SUPPORT ROLLER!

Angle the outfeed roller about 2° to draw the stock toward the fence. If you don't do this, and the roller is angled away from the fence, it will tend to pull the stock away, throwing off the cut and precipitating a kickback. If you're going to be working with particularly heavy stock, throw a sandbag across the base of the stand to ensure against tipping.

CONTRACTOR'S SAW FOLD-DOWN OUTFEED SUPPORT
To make the saw and support easily transportable, I kept construction relatively light and designed the fixture to fold down against the back of the saw. The grooves in the table accomodate the miter gauge guide bars (or sled fixture guide bars) as they extend past the end of the table. I covered the surface of the outfeed table with a sheet of texture-free plastic laminate. I spray it regularly with a non-petroleum based lubricant to minimize friction. To accomodate uneven site situations, I made the single support leg adjustable in length.

COMMERCIALLY MADE FIXED OUTFEED SUPPORTS
I use heavy duty, commercially made roller systems to the outfeed and side of my stationary saw, taking advantage of their great stability. The outfeed support has three positions: folded down against the back of the saw, level to the table surface, and level to the bottom of the miter gauge grooves in order to clear the guide bar.

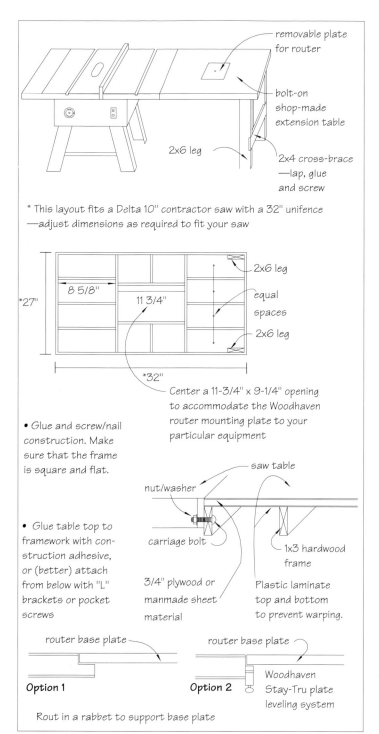

removable plate for router

bolt-on shop-made extension table

2x6 leg

2x4 cross-brace —lap, glue and screw

* This layout fits a Delta 10" contractor saw with a 32" unifence —adjust dimensions as required to fit your saw

8 5/8"

11 3/4"

*27"

2x6 leg

equal spaces

2x6 leg

*32"

Center a 11-3/4" x 9-1/4" opening to accommodate the Woodhaven router mounting plate to your particular equipment

• Glue and screw/nail construction. Make sure that the frame is square and flat.

saw table

nut/washer

• Glue table top to framework with construction adhesive, or (better) attach from below with "L" brackets or pocket screws

carriage bolt

3/4" plywood or manmade sheet material

1x3 hardwood frame

Plastic laminate top and bottom to prevent warping.

router base plate

router base plate

Option 1

Option 2

Woodhaven Stay-Tru plate leveling system

Rout in a rabbet to support base plate

A SHOP-MADE EXTENSION TABLE WITH DRAWERS

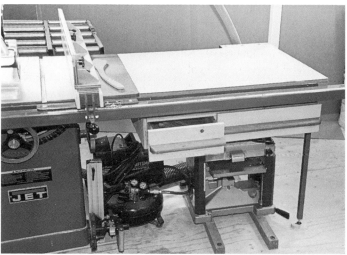

SIDE EXTENSION TABLE ON MY JET STATIONARY SAW
The extension table on my stationary saw supports stock up to 52" to the right side of the blade. I made and hung a pair of drawers under the table to keep commonly used items less than a step away.

MATERIALS FOR SHOP-MADE FIXTURES

Throughout this book, I will be showing you how to build a variety of jigs and fixtures to expand the versatility and efficiency of your table saw. To ensure that these shop-made accessories last and perform well, choose your materials carefully. For broad surfaces, I select the flattest sheets of hardwood-faced plywood (I prefer maple or birch) I can find, rejecting sheets with obvious voids or other defects. I also sometimes use laminate-faced MDF (medium density fiberboard) as it is manufactured dead flat. A drawback to MDF, however, is its high weight, fragile edges (that I strongly recommend protecting with solid wood banding), and the irritating dust it produces during milling operations.

I select solid woods for strength and stability, ideally going with kiln-dried hardwood such as maple with knot-free, straight-running grain. I carefully check for, and reject, boards that are bowed or warped. I round over all exposed edges and corners wherever possible to ease handling and to add a bit of aesthetics.

To promote stability and to help keep surfaces clean, I coat all the surfaces with two to three coats of shellac, sanding the final coat smooth. I spray wax lubricant on surfaces that must slide against the machine table or fence.

FENCE SYSTEMS

The first accessory I consider upgrading on any table saw is the rip fence. I do so because it is the most frequently used accessory on the saw and crucial to fast setups and consistently accurate cuts. Of course not all fence systems need upgrading: some standard-issue rip fences are quite good, and many manufacturers offer a premium fence as an option when you purchase the saw.

If the saw is equipped with tubular steel rails and a sheet metal fence, I am immediately suspicious. This is an obsolete design with significant drawbacks for those intending to do quality woodworking. The problem with sheet metal fences is that the sides are rarely flat and straight over their full length—a failing that means you can't depend on the fence to accurately guide workpieces in a straight line. Short workpieces suffer the most from irregular fences.

Fences that ride on tubular steel rails often stick when you attempt to adjust them, causing them to lurch along and lock down out-of-parallel to the blade. You end up fussing with a rule, measuring the distance between the fence and the miter gauge groove at both the front and the back. By the end of the work session, the heel of your hand stings from banging on the fence to knock it into alignment. All this fooling around with the fence renders the scale along the front rail essentially useless.

A third reason you might consider upgrading your fence system is to work more conveniently with 4'x8' sheet stock. It's much faster and less prone to error to always cut panels to size on the right side of the blade. But you can't cut to a width greater than 24" on the right side of the blade with most standard fences. You may be able to buy longer rails for your present rip fence but if not, look at one of the many aftermarket fences. Some of them offer maximum capacities of 122" to the right of blade.

Choices in Fence Systems

Aftermarket fence systems, all of which solve the performance problems of the older tubular-rail fences, are available from many manufacturers. Some offer an optional, superior fence at the time of purchase. Be aware that the installation process can involve drilling holes in the saw's table, building or ordering a side extension table, and generally doing a lot of fussing around before the fence operates smoothly and precisely. Installation time for most aftermarket systems can take up to four hours, though you will gain this time back through the enormously improved efficiency of your saw.

Among the many fences, you will discover some that lock only to the guide rail at the front of the saw and others that lock to both the front and back rails. In the past I have leaned toward those that lock to both the front and back, feeling that jigs that slide on the fence depend on its rigidity for accuracy and thus require a double lock. But that preference may be unfounded. My new table saw came with a single-point, front locking fence. If I apply a ten pound load to the side of the far end with the platform of a bathroom scale, it flexes less than a hundredth (.010) of an inch as measured by my dial indicator. This slight deflection will have no effect on the precision of any woodworking.

The bottom line is that all these systems enhance the performance of the table saw. Pick the version that best fits your budget (though you'll find most are within $50 of each other) and fits your needs for ripping width capacity.

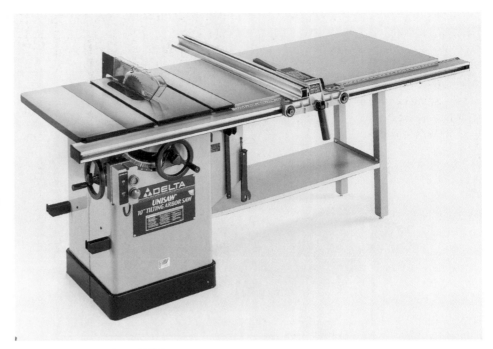

AFTERMARKET FENCE SYSTEM

An aftermarket fence system is a boon to any table saw, providing more convenience, accuracy and safety for the most common table saw operations. This advanced fence system features an aluminum extrusion that can be oriented in a variety of positions to meet different cutting situations.

UNIVERSAL RIP FENCE FIXTURE

The universal rip fence fixture is the heart of a fixture system that revolves around an auxilary fence that quick-bolts to my saw's existing rip fence. By itself, this fixture serves to guide wide stock on edge through the blade. It also incorporates a "MiniTrack" aluminum extrusion that accepts two or more shop-made, comb-type hold-downs to keep stock flat to the table surface in the location of the saw blade. But this auxilary fence's primary function is to serve as a connection-base for a galaxy of fixtures which either quick-bolt to, or slide on the fence and greatly expand the utility and ease of use of the table saw while upgrading its performance.

The most versatile of these fixtures is the Rip Fence Sled which provides a multitude of uses: short rip fence; tenon jig with integral clamps and replaceable backing strips; end bevel cutting and shaping jig; and a feather miter-joint carriage. An adjustable guide system allows sliding friction adjustment. This sled brings high precision, efficiency and control to these processes. You will see a lot of this fixture throughout this book.

In addition to the rip fence sled, these

are the fixtures I've devised for this Universal Fence System (their construction and use will be covered in later chapters). The first two fixtures slide on the auxiliary fence, the rest quick-bolt to it:

- Carriage-Type Taper Jig and Straight-Line Ripping Fixture (features adjustable clamping and guidance systems which simplify set up and ensure positive cutting action).
- Raised Panel Jig (features positive sliding action, integral hold-downs, adjustable field angle. Slides on auxiliary fence).
- Pattern Fence (allows precision replication to a template and also curved cuts to a sprung batten or template. This pattern fence doubles as a low fence for ripping narrow workpieces).
- Vacuum-Actuated Rip Fence (works with Shop Vac to control thin slices).
- Long-Extension Fence (for supporting and guiding panel stock and long boards ahead of the saw table).
- Edge Jointer (cleans up and lightly straightens edges of boards and panel stocks).
- Rabbet Fence (with integral, adjustable comb-type hold-downs).
- End Stop Fence (has adjustable stops for setting up single and double blind

slots, grooves and shaping cuts).

- Fence for Thin-Sheet Stocks (guides and controls thin, flexible panel stocks).
- Edge-Band Trimmer (allows precise flushing of edge bandings).
- Coving Jig (facilitates creation of multiple flute pattern; accepts a quick-bolt hold-down fixture; a simple spacing system ensures even flute spacing with speed and precision).

MITER GAUGES

The miter gauge that comes with most contractor's and stationary saws works fairly well—it slides freely back and forth, adjusts smoothly, and locks securely at an angle to the blade. But I often wish it would do better. I want my miter gauge to have the ruggedness and capacity to guide workpieces larger than the 8"-wide by 2'-long pieces I would feel safe sawing with a standard gauge. I would also like a miter gauge to include a stop for making a series of identical cuts, more precision in its angle stops, and better control of the stock while guiding it through the blade. As you will see later, some of these improvements and features can be added to the gauge with shop-made fixtures. Or you can get a jump on it by buying one of the many commercially made gauges that address all of these performance issues.

Commercial Miter Gauge Upgrades

The first thing you will notice about a superior miter gauge is the fence that bolts to the face of the gauge head. This fence, usually an aluminum extrusion, is straight, flat and rigid and features an integral measurement scale and sliding stop. The fence is the key to high performance: Its long, rigid support ensures that workpieces will be carried through the blade without shifting. The sliding stop, indexed to an adjustable, integral scale, speeds setup time by eliminating the need to measure and mark the workpiece. The stop is especially efficient when cutting several pieces to the same length.

Another important feature that I look for when replacing a miter gauge is an integral clamp. A gauge-mounted clamp prevents shifting of the workpiece during a cut. This is especially important when you are trying to cut dense wood at high

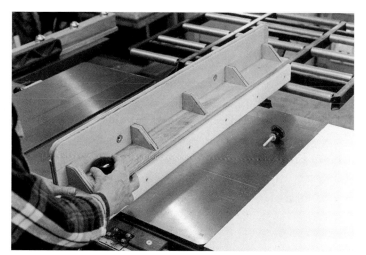

VIEW OF MY UNIVERSAL RIP FENCE FIXTURE Two handled bolts hold my "Universal Rip Fence Fixture"—the most important fixture in my shop—to the top of the rip fence. This fixture is the heart of a shop-made jig system that has vastly improved the efficiency, not to mention the pleasure, of using my table saw.

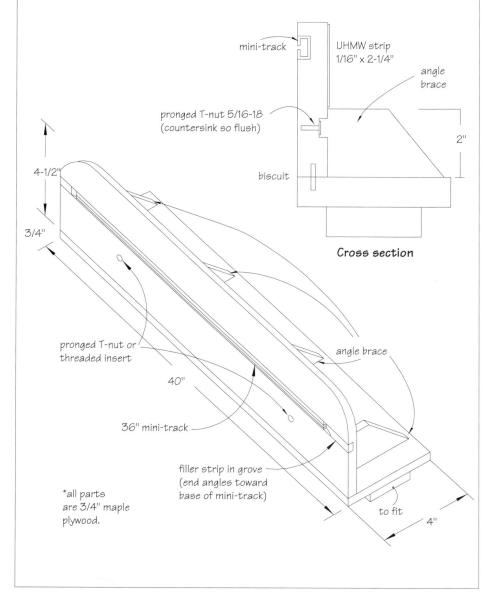

CONSTRUCTION OF A UNIVERSAL RIP FENCE FIXTURE

miter angles. In this situation the cutting forces tend to shift the stock along the fence—you can really feel this if you are trying to hold the stock with just your hands. The clamp also helps to keep your hands well away from the blade. You'll appreciate this most when sawing steep miters on wide stock, a sawing situation where finding a safe place to hold the stock with your hands is a real challenge.

I don't, however, like the type of clamp that attaches to both the gauge head and to the guide bar—it means you have to slide each piece under the bar rather than simply lay it directly down in front of the gauge. It doesn't sound like much of a difference, but if you're cutting a lot of pieces to the same length you will notice that difference very quickly. Instead, I prefer clamps that attach only to the gauge head. I particularly appreciate the clamp on the gauge I use now, shown in the photo. The clamp doubles as a beefy and comfortable push handle. Other features I look for in a miter gauge:

- A gauge head that turns to an angle greater than 45°—useful for making acute angle polygons and some unusual joint cuts. Some brands go to 90°, allowing you to rip tapers on short stock with the miter gauge.
- Easy fine adjustment of the angle. Some versions have removable pins at 15°, 22½°, 30° and 45° while others have spring-loaded pins. Spring-loaded pins are difficult to adjust close to the set stops because the spring loading tends to draw the gauge angle toward the stop. Removable pins avoid this trouble.
- Easy accurate adjustment of the sliding stop on the fence. Some versions offer a vernier scale which can make accurate adjustment quite easy.

Shop-Built Improvements

Not everyone wants to buy performance; some of us are stubborn about wanting to make our own improvements. The drawing shows you how to create a miter gauge fence system that offers a rigid, solid wood fence and a precision locking sliding stop. Though I didn't bother (because I usually measure to story sticks), you can add a stick-on rule to index the sliding stop.

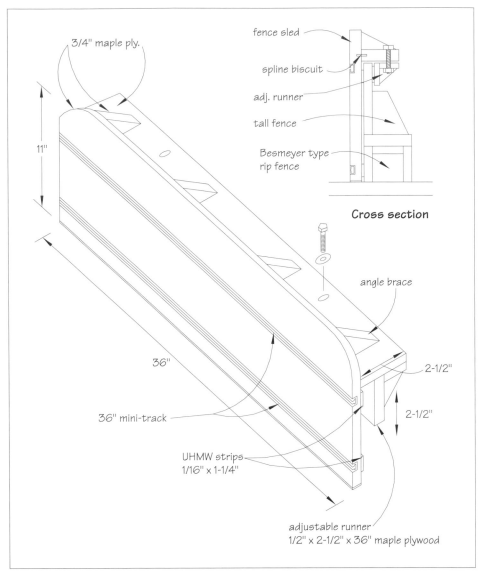

3/4" maple ply.

11"

36"

36" mini-track

UHMW strips 1/16" x 1-1/4"

fence sled

spline biscuit

adj. runner

tall fence

Besmeyer type rip fence

Cross section

angle brace

2-1/2"

2-1/2"

adjustable runner 1/2" x 2-1/2" x 36" maple plywood

CONSTRUCTION DRAWING OF MY RIP FENCE SLED

JDS MITER GAUGE IN USE

The integral clamp/push handle of this aftermarket miter gauge system not only holds the workpiece securely in place as I push it through the blade, but keeps my hands safely out of the way.

IMPROVING A STANDARD MITER GAUGE

Use hardwood for the fence; hard maple is ideal because its fine, even grain is durable and stable. To ensure that the fence is dead-straight and will stay that way, rip the fence stock in half, turn one of the two pieces end for end, and then orient the two halves so their heart sides face out. To prevent saw-dust from building up in front of the fence, chamfer the bottom edge of the fence at least ⅛". You can stick sandpaper to the face of the fence to provide a non-slip surface. (Use self-stick sandpaper or conventional sandpaper with double stick tape, and be sure to keep the sandpaper above the chamfer.)

The sliding stop straddles the fence, running over a length of self-stick measurement tape. This allows you to adjust the position of the stop without directly measuring the distance from the blade, just as you would adjust a good rip fence. Keep the stop running smoothly by occasionally waxing the inside notch of the stop.

Through-bolt the fence to the miter gauge head using handled bolts and threaded inserts (or use wing nuts and bolts) to allow for tool-less dismounting. Be sure to sink the heads of the attachment screws below the face of the fence so they won't interfere with the workpieces.

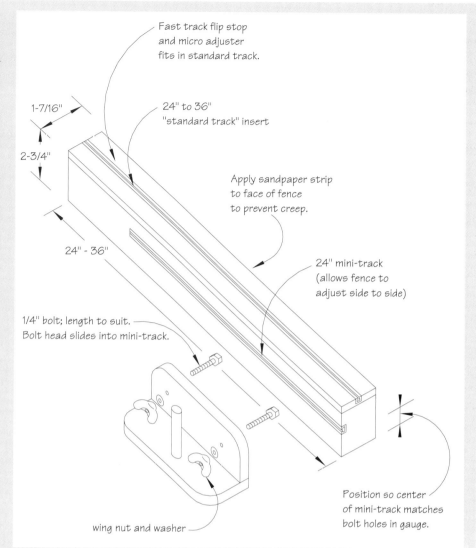

Fast track flip stop and micro adjuster fits in standard track.

1-7/16"

2-3/4"

24" to 36" "standard track" insert

Apply sandpaper strip to face of fence to prevent creep.

24" - 36"

24" mini-track (allows fence to adjust side to side)

1/4" bolt; length to suit. Bolt head slides into mini-track.

wing nut and washer

Position so center of mini-track matches bolt holes in gauge.

MOVING CROSSCUT TABLES/SLEDS

Even a tricked out miter gauge can have trouble handling larger sized workpieces. Boards longer than two to three feet and panels greater than three to four square feet are too big for most miter gauges. The resulting instability often results in inaccurate cuts and creates a potentially dangerous situation if the poorly supported workpiece twists into the blade.

The solution for dealing with larger workpieces is a moving crosscut table or sled. These saw accessories are more than just robust versions of the miter gauge, they act as carriages to support and carry the work through the blade. There is no longer any friction between the stock and the saw table to twist the stock out of alignment. Instead, friction between the stock and the moving table

or sled helps maintain alignment. Like the miter gauge, these accessories have a fence for positioning the stock and usually include clamps and a stop for making duplicate cuts.

Moving tables bolt to the side of the

SHOP-MADE MITER GAUGE FENCE
My shop-made miter gauge auxiliary fence uses an aluminum track fixture to allow side-to-side adjustment of the fence, and another extrusion to accept a commercially made sliding stop system. This fence is incredibly durable, accurate and quick to make.

saw, flush with the main table, and have their own framework and guide system. Sleds, on the other hand, slide on the table saw surface, guided by one or two rails that follow the saw's miter gauge grooves. Either fixture can help crosscut a perfectly square edge on wide boards, panel stock, drawer faces, and assemblies like cabinet doors. If the fence is adjustable, they can also help you saw precise miters in larger stock.

Commercial Sliding Tables

Sliding crosscut tables have been available as options with stationary saws for many years. Some manufacturers considered them a necessary part of the table saw system prior to the development of smaller saws and miter gauges. They had good reason. Moving tables offer an instantly available, highly accurate, and safe way to cut boards and panel stock to length. Some versions have a 52" crosscutting capacity—a full sheet of plywood.

There are, however, some disadvantages beyond the relatively high cost: You have to unbolt the fence system when using the saw for some other common uses. The table takes up lots of room on the left side of the saw, and to the front as well, in order to accommodate the guide rail. Also, the rolling table is massive—it will tire you out if you have to make numerous cuts. Finally, setting up and maintaining a sliding table is time consuming since the table travel must precisely parallel the sawblade. You know it's out of alignment when workpieces tend to bind, or have burned or rough edges. But if you have the money, the room, a stationary saw to provide a stable platform, and especially if you intend to do a lot of panel cutting, then the commercial sliding crosscut table is the way to go.

Crosscut Sleds

One of the most used and useful fixtures I made in my custom cabinet shop was a crosscut sled. I use it primarily to cut cabinet sides to length and to trim cabinet doors after assembly. I made a smaller version as well for cutting face frames and door parts to length. Compared to my powered miter box (chop saw) the sled was at least as fast and accurate, safer to use, a lot less noisy, and stirred up less dust. It also carries offcuts safely away from the blade. When you crosscut with the miter gauge on the table saw or with the chopsaw, the offcut stays next to the blade. This creates a temptation to push it out of the way with your hand, breaking

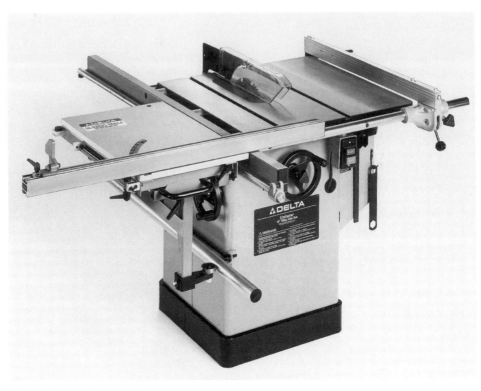

SLIDING CROSSCUT TABLE
A sliding crosscut table provides a stable and efficient platform for carrying workpieces accurately through the blade. Disadvantages, however, include having to unbolt its fence when using the saw for other purposes and the considerable room it takes up to the left of the saw.

SHOP-MADE CROSSCUT SLED IN USE
In lieu of a sliding table, I constructed this crosscut sled to perform most of my crosscutting chores. These shop-made fixtures are quick to set up for use (I keep mine hanging just a step away from the saw), and are extremely accurate if carefully built.

the rule of hands never coming within the perimeter of the throat plate. Even a blade coasting to a stop can cut through a frightening amount of flesh and bone.

Crosscut sleds are a mixed blessing. Bigger versions for crosscutting panel stock are rather heavy and require side and outfeed supports. They may also need infeed support if the workpiece is large and heavy. And unlike sliding tables which are fixed to the saw, you have to move these rather unwieldy fixtures on and off the saw as needed.

In this chapter are instructions for making two varieties of crosscut sleds—a small version for stock narrower than 16" and another for stock up to 32" wide. Because I intended to use these fixtures often, I incorporated a number of special features:

- The fence and base are made from hardwood and pattern-grade plywood.
- There is a replaceable insert in the area of the blade kerf.
- The front fence is adjustable so I can

fine-tune its alignment.
- The fence holds a sliding stop and rule.
- Integral hangers make storage easy.
- A stop prevents the blade from protruding past the front of the fixture, endangering your hands.

POWER FEEDER

A power feeder is a small motorized wheel system that holds stock firmly to the table and fence as it pushes it through the cutter. Power feeders also increase the safety of table saws by taking over the risky task of handling stock near the blade.

The motor generally has variable speeds so you can handle both dense and softer stock. Choose the horsepower to suit your most common uses. For example, you'll need at least a ⅛ hp version to rip ¾" stock at about 15 feet per minute on a 2 hp table saw. You can use this low horsepower feeder to do heavier work, but you can't ask it to run as fast or as often as a bigger feeder without risking overheating the motor.

The consistent pressure and feed speed of the power feeder significantly increases the cutting performance of the saw, and it eliminates the need to set up hold-down wheels or featherboards or to use push sticks. I even save time while the feeder is working. While it's feeding the first board, I prepare to load the next one in line. As soon as this one starts, I walk to the back of the saw and offload the first one, creating a non-stop, circular motion that results in zero downtime while the saw is running.

Power feeders do have disadvantages. You generally have to remove them when you want to use the saw for crosscutting, and they are time consuming to set up and take down. Unless you are running more than three or four boards, it can be hard to talk yourself into setting up the feeder. Also, you may have to drill and tap holes in the saw table for the feeder's support stand. Finally, power feeders don't come cheap. It is a relatively expensive accessory to buy if you will only use it occasionally.

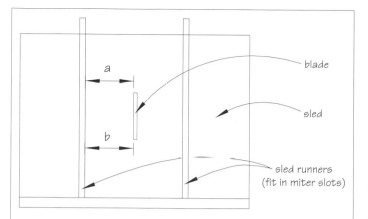
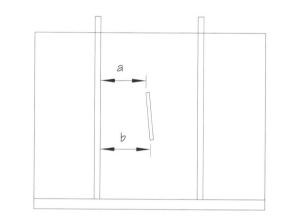

If distance a = b, sled will move parallel to blade

If distance a is not = b, sled will not move parallel to blade, because the blade is forced against the side of kerf

IMPORTANCE OF BLADE ALIGNMENT
Keep in mind that smooth, precise cuts with a sled depend on a well-tuned saw just as much as cuts with a miter gauge do. If the blade isn't parallel to the miter gauge grooves, you will see burnt edges and splintered plywood veneers. If the sled's fence isn't perpendicular to the bar that fits in the miter gauge groove you'll see out-of-square crosscuts.

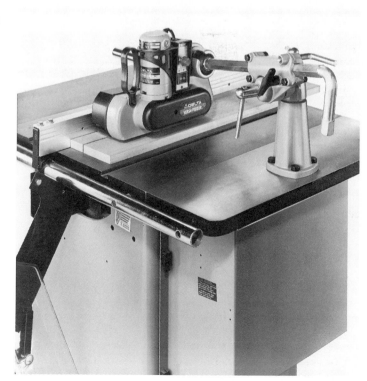

POWER FEEDER IN USE ON TABLE SAW
A power feeder is a gift you give yourself when you do production work on the table saw. It is easily the most significant way to vastly increase the safety and reduce the exertion of doing heavy-duty work on this machine.

MAKING A CROSSCUT SLED

- Make the base and fence: Make the base from ½" Baltic birch or maple—be sure to check the panel for flatness and freedom from voids. Make the fence from two strips of ¾" maple plywood, glue-laminated together against a straight edge to ensure precision. Cap with hardwood flush to the face of the fence. Cut the bottom edge of the fence face with a ⅛"x⅛" rabbet to create a sawdust clearance channel.

- Fence installation: Screw the back fence to the base with the throat plate insert in place. Install the front fence with only two screws for now: the one on the far right as a pivot, the second one through the slotted hole on far left. Be sure to install the stop system (the block on the bottom of sled and the block bolted to side of the extension wing through a slotted hole to allow adjustment). This will keep the blade from exiting past the blade guard installed on front of the sled.

- Replaceable inserts: Make the 3" wide strip from the same stock as the base—cut a number at once and predrill the four corners using an alignment jig so they all occur in the same position. Chamfer the edges so the edge of the plate won't catch on stock sliding on the sled base.

- Runners: You can use teak strips (vertical grain for stability, predrilled for attachment screw's shanks and chamfered for screw heads) or a metal slider which features adjustable cool blocks along one edge to allow for fine adjustment of sliding friction.

- Install slides to the sled: Lower the blade all the way. Laid the slides in miter slots, raised on a couple of pennies on the bottom of the slot so the top protrudes slightly above the table surface. Put a 1" length of carpet tape toward each end of the slide, then lay the sled on top with the front edge of the sled aligned parallel with the front edge of the saw table. Press the sled down on the slides and then lift it off, bringing the slides along. Screw the slides in place (screws through slides and into bottom of sled base). Now set the sled back on the saw and check the sliding action. Adjust the cool blocks with allen screws; or if wood slides, add Prussian blue machinist's ink to the sides of the miter groove's slots to see where the wood is rubbing on high spots. Scrape the high spots down—a little at time—with a cabinet scraper.

- Adjust front fence square to blade: Crank the blade all the way down. Set the sled in place on the saw table, its front edge aligned with the saw table's front edge. Hold down the sled with your hand placed on the front fence, then turn on the saw and raise the blade through the kerf plate plus about ¾". Now slide the sled forward until the kerf comes within ½" of the fence face. Turn off the saw and lower the blade. Here's the trick: Loosen the slotted screw to the left end of the fence and adjust the fence square to the saw kerf with an accurate framing square. Lock down the

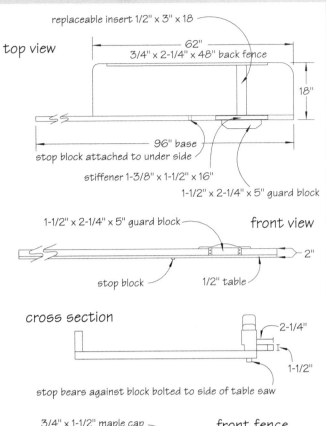

top view

replaceable insert 1/2" x 3" x 18

62"

3/4" x 2-1/4" x 48" back fence

18"

96" base

stop block attached to under side

stiffener 1-3/8" x 1-1/2" x 16"

1-1/2" x 2-1/4" x 5" guard block

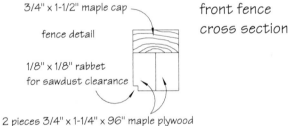

front view

1-1/2" x 2-1/4" x 5" guard block

2"

stop block

1/2" table

cross section

2-1/4"

1-1/2"

stop bears against block bolted to side of table saw

front fence cross section

3/4" x 1-1/2" maple cap

fence detail

1/8" x 1/8" rabbet for sawdust clearance

2 pieces 3/4" x 1-1/4" x 96" maple plywood

screw and make a test cut to ensure accuracy. (Test: Cut a length of 12"-wide panel stock with parallel edges in half; flip over one of the halves and see if the two cut ends align while holding the edges of the two panels against the fence. If they don't, the cut was not perpendicular to the fence.) When you are satisfied with the alignment, add more screws from the bottom of the sled base into the bottom of the front fence.

- Install indexed stop system: I use a commercially made sliding stop with a right-to-left reading tape applied to the cap of the front fence. To align the rule: Put the stop on the fence so its bearing point measures 12". Make a mark on the fence cap at the cursor line. Now align the 12" reading on the tape to this mark as you stick it in place.

Blades and Cutters

Legend has it that a Shaker woman of the mid-1800s, watching her husband tediously sawing a board in half with a handsaw, was suddenly struck with a revelation, an epiphany of tooling that would bring ease and joy to countless woodworkers to come. She reasoned that instead of placing the cutting teeth of a saw blade along a straight line where they could cut only half the time, it would make far more sense to place them along the rim of a wheel where they would cut continuously. Thus the invention of the circular blade, the heart and soul of the table saw.

Today, circular saw blades are available in a wide range of sizes and a variety of tooth shapes to meet the needs of the modern woodworking shop. All blades are a compromise: You can't, for example, combine the fastest cutting with the smoothest, most splinter-free cuts. To fully understand saw blades, you need to understand the anatomy of a blade. If you just want to be able to pick blades that work well for you, skip the next section and go directly to choosing blades. You'll also find a sections on maintaining blades, on dado cutters and on molding heads.

SAW BLADE ANATOMY

After more than a century of experimentation and development, the circular saw blade has evolved from the Shaker woman's row of points ground onto the rim of a round steel plate, to a highly engineered and complex cutting instrument. The tinkering began with the early discovery that the speed of the cut, its tendency toward splintering, and its resistance to feed pressure depended largely on the number of teeth cut along the rim. Fewer teeth cut faster with less feed pressure but produced more splintering and a coarser cut surface.

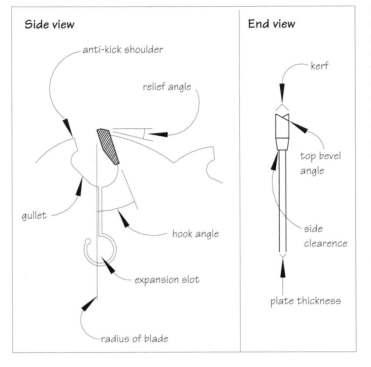

Side view
anti-kick shoulder
relief angle
gullet
hook angle
expansion slot
radius of blade

End view
kerf
top bevel angle
side clearence
plate thickness

The fast, coarse cut was acceptable for basic ripping, but woodworkers needed to crosscut with these newfangled blades as well. So blade makers increased the number of teeth to achieve a smoother cut. The price paid was a slower cut that demanded more feed pressure. Also, they found that the blade dulled sooner. Dulling is caused more by the tooth's initial impact on the wood than by the actual slicing through the wood fibers. Since these many-toothed blades needed slower feed rates, each individual tooth impacted the wood more times, and the blade dulled faster. Compounding the problem, more teeth and slower feed rates produced smaller chips that were less efficient at carrying away the edge-dulling heat.

BLADE ANATOMY
Engineers continue to tinker with the blade design to improve performance, changing the configuration and angles of the cutting tips and improving the manufacture of the plate. When carbide tips came into the picture, their durability and ability to be precisely shaped brought forth a large leap in performance. In recent years, other improvements such as thinner plates and the addition of blade stabilizers, continued to upgrade saw blades. Today we enjoy highly sophisticated, high-performance blades.

Carbide-Tipped vs. All-Steel Blades

You've heard the advertising and it's really true: Carbide-tipped blades will stay sharp more than 50 times longer than all-steel blades. This fact and the superior cutting performance of higher-quality carbide-tipped blades are the reasons why nearly every professional woodworker—and most serious amateurs—saw with carbide. Carbide is not without its shortcomings, however. It's brittle and chips easily if bumped against steel or other carbide. Good carbide-tipped blades are four to five times the price of steel blades. Finally, they are essentially impossible to sharpen yourself. Professional woodworkers have at least two of every essential blade to eliminate profit-robbing downtime. But if you're serious about woodworking, and not addicted to a lifetime habit of sharpening steel blades, consider using carbide-tipped blades.

Hook Angle

The demands of dealing with more fragile manufactured wood products, such as plywood and particleboard, and materials with a variety of plastic surfaces, forced engineers to look more carefully at the configuration of the cutting tooth. They soon discovered that the hook angle of the teeth had a marked effect on the cut. Teeth with greater hook angles (up to +20°) cut faster and more aggressively but splintered the underside of the stock more. To reduce splintering, engineers designed blades with as little as minus 7° of hook. Unfortunately, the result is much slower cutting blades that require significantly more feed pressure (read: muscle power unless you use a power feeder). Stay away from these negative hook blades; they are designed primarily for the radial arm or miter box where the cuts are short and quick. On the table saw, these blades can easily overheat and warp, ruining the cut and creating kickback. For table saw crosscutting, look for hook angles between 10° and 15°. Rip blades will have about a 20° hook.

Top Bevel Angle

Researchers also played with the top bevel angle of the teeth, learning that flat-topped teeth worked fine for ripping but contributed to the roughness of the cut when crosscutting. Taking a hint from the hand crosscut saw, they beveled the teeth so they would score the edge of the kerf before removing the stock between the edges. The result is a much smoother cut. But the angled tooth will not rip as quickly as one with a flat top, and the angled tips of the teeth will not produce a flat-bottomed kerf, which is important if the kerf will be exposed to view.

Dedicated crosscutting blades generally have top bevel angles of between 10° and 20°. Lower angles are cut into combination blades that may have to do some ripping, while dedicated plywood blades have higher angles (up to 40°).

Side Clearance

If you look closely at a blade, or at the blade anatomy illustration, you will notice that the teeth are slightly wider than the plate. This is done so that the plate will not have to rub against the side of the stock, creating blade-dulling friction and heat. Some blades, such as high-tooth-count crosscut blades, are nevertheless given minimal side clearance in order to achieve a smoother cut—this type of blade's raison d'être.

The teeth are often ground with a slight angle along their sides. This radial side clearance makes the tooth a bit wider at the cutting edge than nearer to the center of the blade, giving the tooth more clearance and less friction in the cut.

The Saw Blade Plate

Having figured out some things about the cutting teeth, the engineers turned their attention to the steel plate supporting the teeth. They soon discovered that a plate stamped out of a steel sheet could not meet the tolerances of flatness necessary to support the increasing sophistication and precision grinding of the cutting teeth. Worse, a stamped plate would often warp when heated by cutting friction, making the kerf wider and rougher than necessary.

Today, except for cheap, throwaway blades, the plates are precision cut with a laser and milled flat to within .001". The flatness of the plate is maintained by compressing a thin band of steel about one third of the way in from the blade's edge—a strategy that counters warpage from heat buildup or tension forces. Expansion slots are cut through the plate to accommodate heat expansion of the steel and to lower the noise level of the

---

THIN-KERF BLADES: PROS & CONS

Saw blades with a thinner plate and narrower teeth, cutting a kerf through the stock approximately ³⁄₃₂" wide instead of the more conventional ⅛" wide, are a relatively recent innovation. To hear some people talk, you'd think these blades were the modern equivalent of Magical Elixir Tonic, that they cure everything. While they're great in some situations, they aren't always the best choice. Here's a quick look at the pros and cons.

Pros:

- The narrower teeth remove less stock using less power, making cutting, especially ripping, easier and faster.
- An underpowered saw will often perform better with a thin-kerf blade.
- Easier cutting means less wear and tear on the saw and motor.
- The narrower kerf wastes less wood, important if you're making many closely spaced cuts in expensive stock.

Cons:

- The thinner plate is more susceptible to distortion, especially if heat builds up when cutting thick or dense wood.
- Forcing a thin-kerf blade so it slows can cause the blade to vibrate and gouge the side of the kerf.
- Using blade stiffeners to reduce distortion also reduces the maximum depth of cut. This is particularly annoying if you want to use thin-kerf blades because your saw doesn't have enough power for deep cuts.
- Switching to a thin-kerf blade requires recalibrating the saw's rip fence scale.

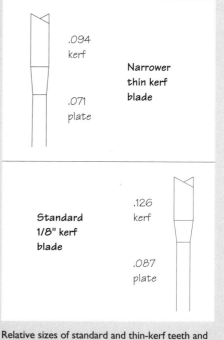

.094 kerf
.071 plate

Narrower thin kerf blade

Standard 1/8" kerf blade

.126 kerf
.087 plate

Relative sizes of standard and thin-kerf teeth and plates drawn to scale per Freud Catalog using .126/.087 vs. .094/.071.

BLADE STIFFENERS

When under cutting stresses, to produce not only a smoother cut but a quieter one as well, many blade manufacturers now recommend that we use a blade stiffener or stabilizer to dampen the vibration of the saw blade. One manufacturer claims stiffeners reduce the noise level as much as 9 dB, a 75 percent reduction. These seemingly magical devices are nothing more than flat-milled steel plates of 4", 5" or 6" diameter that you bolt to the side of the blade under the arbor nut. I use a stiffener nearly all the time, finding that it does indeed quiet the blade and produce a slightly smoother kerf.

You can put a stiffener on just one side of the blade or on both sides. Putting one on both sides may give you greater dampening, but having a stiffener between the blade and the arbor flange changes the position of the blade. This, in turn, requires recalibrating the saw's rip fence scale and any miter gauge fence scale system you may be using, and will probably require that you make a new table insert.

Stiffeners, obviously, cannot enter the kerf and therefore reduce the maximum depth of cut. The bigger and more effective the stiffener, the greater the reduction in cut depth. I put on the largest-diameter stiffener I can get away with, then replace it with a smaller one or remove it altogether when I need more depth of cut.

BLADE STIFFENER IN PLACE
Installing a blade stiffener—a circular piece of machined-flat steel—to the face of a saw blade dampens vibration to help produce a smoother cut.

spinning disk. To combat friction, especially with crosscut blades with minimal side clearance, manufacturers often coat the plate with Teflon. Even the arbor hole gets their attention: They precision mill it to close tolerances to ensure that it fits snugly on the saw's arbor, eliminating play that might induce wobble.

CHOOSING BLADES

A quick glance through a catalog of saw blades tells you there are many types of blades to choose from, depending mostly on the kind of work you intend to do. Most of the differences revolve around the grind of the teeth. There are four common grinds on carbide-tipped saw blades. The flat top (FT) grind blade has square teeth with no top bevel angle and is designed primarily for ripping. The alternate top bevel (ATB) blade features teeth with an angled top bevel, each alternating to either side. It is the blade of choice for clean, precise crosscutting. The alternate top bevel and raker (ATB&R) is a variation of the ATB, adding a square-tipped raker tooth to each set of five teeth around the blade. The raker tooth's function is to clear the kerf of chips, allowing the blade to be used for both crosscutting and light-duty ripping tasks. Finally, the triple chip (TC) grind—a two-tooth pat-

tern consisting of a beveled tooth followed by a flat-topped tooth—is engineered for cutting man-made panel stock.

The Building a Set of Blades chart lays out my recommendation for a single blade for the rank beginner, a basic set of three saw blades for serious woodworking, and an optional set that adds several more specialized blades. How, though, do you pick the correct number of teeth for any particular style of blade? The general rule suggests that the more teeth you allow to

advanced woodworking set of 5	basic set of 3 blades	one blade	no. of teeth	shape of teeth	applications
			40	ATB	general purpose
			24	FT	general ripping
			60-80	TC	man-made materials general plywood
			80	ATB	high quality 2 sided veneers
			40	FT	glue line ripping

FT=flat top
ATB= alternate top bevel
TC=triple chips

* for a 10" blade

Building a set of blades to match your needs.

SAFETY *tip*

Never use a stiffener in place of the flange washer; always insert the washer between the nut and the stiffener. Also, be sure there is no debris caught between the stiffener and the saw plate. Not only does the presence of debris render the stabilizer ineffective, but it could cause the arbor nut, and therefore the blade, to loosen.

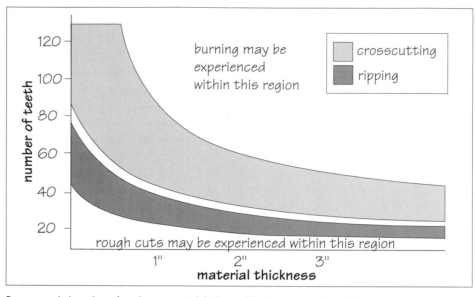

Recommended number of teeth per material thickness. [Graph courtesy of Freud]

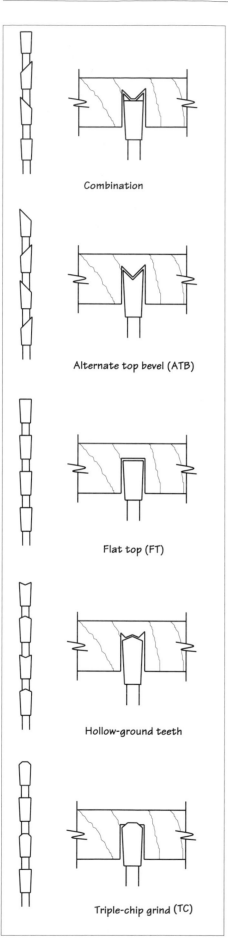

Carbide-Tipped Tooth Patterns

WHAT TO LOOK FOR IN CARBIDE

Price is one of the first indicators of whether a blade will offer high-quality carbide tips. I expect to pay at least $50 or more for a 10" combination blade that will give me clean, crisp cuts and thick enough tips to last through more than a dozen sharpenings. I don't expect much from a $35 blade—it may be advertised to cut through nails without chipping, but what that really says is that the teeth are made of carbide particles that are too soft and/or coarse to take a fine edge.

If you can, find out the grade of the carbide: The hardest, finest-grain carbide generally used in saw blades is designated C4. Though it is more brittle than C3 and lower grades, the fine grain allows it to take an incredibly sharp edge, and its hardness keeps that edge for much longer than lower-grade carbide. Note, though, that you don't always want C4 in a blade; those designed to cut nonferrous metals will have softer carbide in order to increase the impact strength.

cut into the wood at one time, up to a maximum of four, the smoother the resulting cut. But you have to compromise this with the fact that the more teeth in the cut, the more the feed resistance increases since the small teeth can't clear chips very fast. You have to slow the feed rate, especially when cutting thick stock. If you compromise by going for fewer teeth in the cut, you may sacrifice smoothness, which can be detrimental if you are cutting joints.

The best compromise is to select the number of teeth that will provide you with a reasonable feed speed while producing an acceptable smoothness of cut. The graph shows the recommended number of teeth per material thickness. For a 10" blade set ⅛" above the surface of the stock.

Recognizing a Quality Blade

Choosing a saw blade can be confusing. The cost of a 10" blade can be as low as $5 or as high as $200. How can you know what you're getting for your money? First, know what overall quality grade you're looking at. Manufacturers offer three grades targeted for distinct market groups: consumer or economy grade, contractor grade and industrial grade.

Consumer blades, also called disposables, are made from low-grade materials to loose tolerances and often are packaged in blister packs. The rule is, if you can't examine the blade through the packaging, don't buy it. These blades are suitable only for rough carpentry. Cost: $5 to $20.

Contractor blades are reasonably well made from good materials. They offer

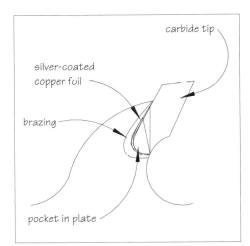

BLADE TIP DETAIL

(labels: carbide tip / silver-coated copper foil / brazing / pocket in plate)

good value for the money and should serve you well through several sharpenings. Their midrange price, however, is partly the result of fully automated production, so examine the blade carefully for roughness or defects that might have slipped through quality control. Cost: $25 to $50.

Industrial blades are made from the finest materials to tight tolerances. They produce precision cuts, last the longest between sharpenings and usually can be sharpened more often than lower grades. Cost: $55 to $200.

Next, check that the plate is flat. Place a straightedge across the full diameter of the blade, avoiding the teeth, and hold it up to a light source. If more than a sliver of light shows under the straightedge, don't buy the blade. Check with the straightedge in several positions.

The plate should also be smooth. Good blades are flattened by grinding, and the more care taken during this process, the better the blade will look.

While examining the plate, you may notice a faint, contrasting ring about an inch in from the teeth. This is the result of tensioning, a process that compresses a thin band of steel on the plate to counter stresses during cutting. Roll tensioning is the most common and leaves the faintly visible band. Hand tensioning with a hammer leaves marks but manufacturers then grind off the marks during finishing. Good tensioning is important to blade performance, but there is no way to check it. You just have to trust the reputation of the manufacturer for making blades that perform well.

Also check the arbor hole for fit and finish. Arbor holes on cheap blades are stamped out and the resulting edges may be rough or bent in or show fracture lines. The arbor holes on better blades are first punched and then reamed or ground to the correct diameter. If the arbor hole is too big, the blade will never run true. Return any blade that is the least bit loose on your arbor.

Finally, check the teeth. They should be seated in a small pocket cut into the plate, not simply parked on the face of the gullet. The brazing that holds them in the pocket should be smooth and uniform. Reject any blade with rough brazing, pitting or gaps. The grinding of the facets of the teeth is one of the most important indicators of quality. A dull, granular appearance indicates that they haven't been ground at all or only ground on the tops. The teeth on good blades are carefully ground on all surfaces with progressively finer abrasives up to 600 grit. Use a hand magnifier to look at the surfaces of the teeth; the quality of the grinding will be obvious.

MAINTAINING BLADES

Having a high-quality blade of the correct grind installed on your table saw is, of course, of primary importance for getting the best performance from your machine. But even the best blade won't perform up to snuff if it is dull or even dirty. It is also important, then, to regularly inspect your blades for damage, dullness and dirt buildup and to do something about it if you don't like what you see or feel. With a bit of experience, you'll quickly become aware if something is amiss and can step in to nip problems in the bud. In this way, you can enjoy the fruits of peak performance whenever you need to use your saw.

Inspection

Before you begin using a blade, and after a particularly rough job where the blade encountered knots or foreign metal objects, inspect the teeth with your magnifying glass. You are looking to see if any tips are chipped or fractured or missing. If you discover damage, send the blade out for resharpening or retoothing. Also look for pitch buildup as discussed previously.

Heat is the saw blade's worst enemy, but you can help avoid it by keeping the blade sharp and clean.

Cleaning

Dirty blades can act dull without really being dull. That's because sharp edges that are coated with residue can't cut properly. Furthermore, a dirty carbide-tipped blade may soon become an actually dull blade. The heat generated by the increased friction of the residue stimulates the acids in many woods to break down the binder that holds the carbide crystals together—and that causes premature dulling of the tips. Frequent removal of this residue can eliminate unnecessary sharpenings and increase the amount of cutting you can do before actually requiring sharpening.

When I first notice a heavy buildup of pitch, I spray the blade with oven cleaner. I leave it on the blade for a half hour or so, then brush it off with a stiff-bristled tire brush from the auto supply store. Never use a wire brush: It could dull the tooth edges and leave scratches that provide toeholds for rust and residue buildup. But I don't wait for routine sawing to create a heavy buildup. Daily, I spray my working blades with an ammonia-based window cleaning solution, let it sit a bit

RECOGNIZING A HIGH QUALITY SHARPENING SERVICE

Probably the easiest way to find a high-quality sharpening service is to ask those who depend on finding the best: your local professional woodworking shops. These businesses rely on both a fast turnaround and a quality of sharpening that brings the blades to razor sharpness without excessive grinding (industrial-quality blades are pricey and need to last through as many sharpenings as possible).

Another way to find the best shops is to ask a lot of questions. Here are the answers you hope to hear:

- They use ultrasound to clean the blades of dirt and pitch buildup, avoiding the need for scrubbing (an overnight soak in solution is an OK alternative).
- They inspect the teeth for chips under magnification and test the plate for flatness with a straightedge before sending the blade for sharpening.
- If the plate is not flat, they will straighten it, preferably with a kick press. Hand hammering can make bumps on the surface.
- They use expensive ($50,000 plus) liquid-cooled, computer-controlled grinders to grind the face and top of the teeth with diamond abrasive of up to 600 grit, providing the most precise and sharpest edge you can get on carbide.
- They will ship the blades back to you with some kind of protection placed around the teeth, usually a dipped plastic film.

When you get a blade back from a high-quality shop, the teeth will look highly polished and have edges sharp enough to curl cuticle on the back of your thumbnail. Your first test cuts should be smooth, creating a kerf of even depth and width and with no rough edges or splintering, even under magnification.

If your sharpening shop is out of town, I strongly suggest that you make a sturdy, reusable wood box specifically for shipping your blades. As you can see above, I make mine with ¼"-plywood sides fastened with screws to a joined hardwood frame. I write my address on one side of the removable panel and the sharpening service's

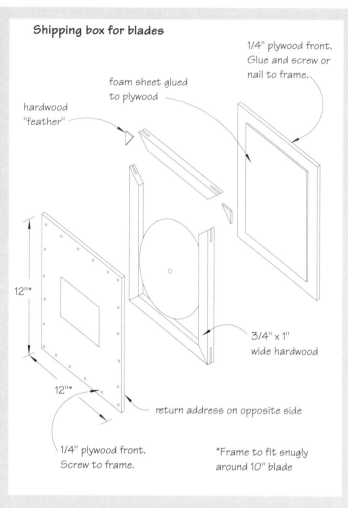

Shipping box for blades

hardwood "feather"

foam sheet glued to plywood

¼" plywood front. Glue and screw or nail to frame.

12"*

12"*

3/4" x 1" wide hardwood

return address on opposite side

¼" plywood front. Screw to frame.

*Frame to fit snugly around 10" blade

address on the other side. I screw the panel on with the shop's address showing and the shopkeeper screws it on with my address showing. He loves it because it saves him time, and I love it because I don't have to cobble together a shipping container every time I want to send out my blades.

and then wipe it off with a cotton rag. Finally, I spray the teeth and plate with nonpetroleum antirust film to nip problems in the bud.

If the pitch buildup gets ahead of you, you can remove the blade and give it a thorough cleaning using the magic of baking soda: Place the blade in a large nonstick skillet, supporting the blade on a small ceramic saucer so the edges are raised off the bottom of the skillet and do not touch the sides. Add water to cover the blade by at least ¼" and add one to two tablespoons of baking soda. Now bring the water to a boil, then turn it down and let it simmer for several minutes. Turn off the burner, let the water cool and then remove the blade from the pan. A quick rinse and light scrubbing with a nylon-

bristle brush will remove all traces of buildup, making the blade look like new. Spray the blade with a nonpetroleum lubricant (WD-40 works better than most) or wipe it with alcohol to remove any trace of moisture.

Sharpening

I do not recommend that you try to resharpen a carbide blade. The chance of getting a sharp, lasting edge with the kind of tools most of us have access to makes any attempt to do so a waste of time. Instead, when these blades get dull, send them to a well-equipped professional saw shop or to the manufacturer.

Unfortunately, not all sharpening shops are created equal. It is crucial that yours has the right equipment and experience

because unskilled hands working on crude equipment can cause the demise of your blade in as little as 3 or 4 sharpenings, as opposed to a potential of 15 sharpenings. To find a good shop, see Recognizing a High-Quality Sharpening Service.

Handling and Storage

You can extend the life of your saw blades, increase the time between sharpenings and prevent outright damage by simply handling your blades properly. Read the rules that follow, and think about them a moment. They are telling you to not do some things that may seem perfectly natural.

- Don't ever lay a saw blade on the saw table. Every time carbide touches steel, you risk chipping a tooth

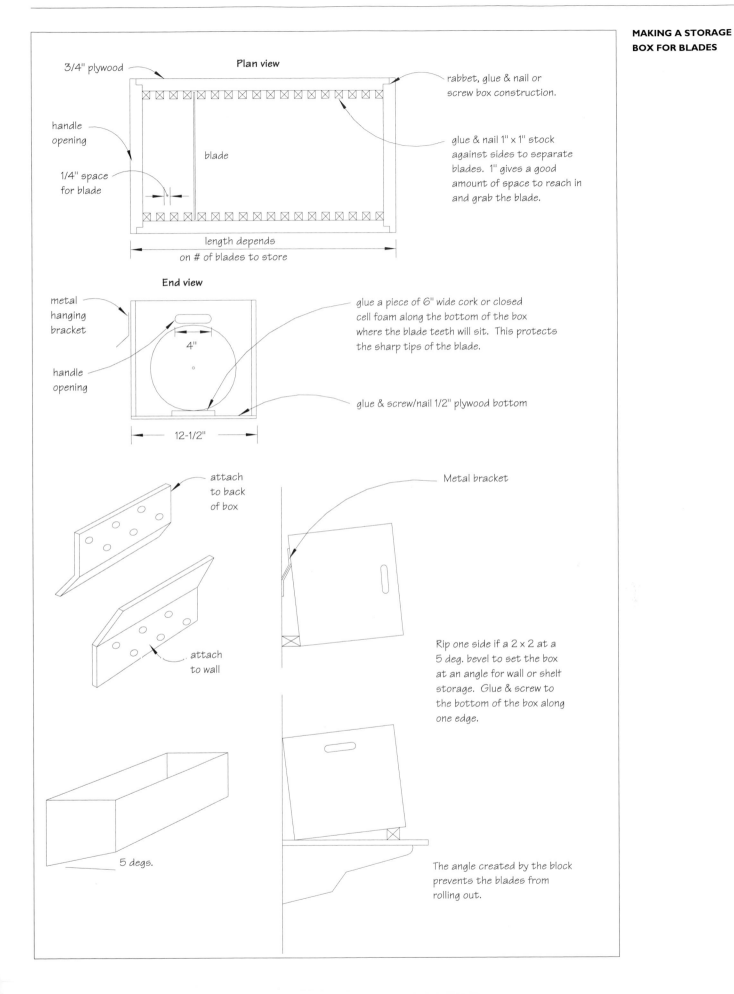

Plan view

3/4" plywood

rabbet, glue & nail or
screw box construction.

handle
opening

glue & nail 1" x 1" stock
against sides to separate
blades. 1" gives a good
amount of space to reach in
and grab the blade.

1/4" space
for blade

blade

length depends
on # of blades to store

End view

metal
hanging
bracket

glue a piece of 6" wide cork or closed
cell foam along the bottom of the box
where the blade teeth will sit. This protects
the sharp tips of the blade.

handle
opening

4"

glue & screw/nail 1/2" plywood bottom

12-1/2"

attach
to back
of box

Metal bracket

attach
to wall

Rip one side if a 2 x 2 at a
5 deg. bevel to set the box
at an angle for wall or shelt
storage. Glue & screw to
the bottom of the box along
one edge.

5 degs.

The angle created by the block
prevents the blades from
rolling out.

and the risk increases if you accidentally slide the blade across the miter gauge groove.

- Only temporarily lay a blade on a wood panel or workbench. It is always best to slide the blade vertically into a wood storage box or a vertical cubby. The drawing Making a Storage Box for Blades shows how I made mine.
- Never hang the blades one against the other on a peg or nail. If you must hang them on nails, use a separate nail for each blade, or separate the blades with wood or cardboard disks at least as large as the blades, or place thick washers between the blades, so thick that the blades' tips won't touch one another when placing or removing the top blade.
- Don't touch the carbide tips with your fingers. The acid in your perspiration can etch the carbide, prematurely dulling the edge.
- Store the blades out of the direct sun: Excessive sun heat on one side of a blade can cause the plate to warp slightly, causing runout.

DADO CUTTERS

Before the development of the specialized dado cutter, woodworkers figured out they could quickly cut grooves or rabbets by stacking two or more blades on the arbor, creating a sort of gang saw without any gaps. Not surprisingly, when engineers developed the dado cutter, they drew on that same basic concept—except they went a step further: They figured out how to make a stack of cutters adjustable in width.

The most basic adjustable dado cutter is a stacking type that requires selecting a combination of shims and chippers to place between two outer bladelike cutters to achieve the desired width. While the stacking dado creates a clean, flat-bottomed groove, it has an annoying drawback: It is time-consuming and clumsy to remove the outer cutter to get at the chippers or shims every time you need to change the width or make fine adjustments. To address this problem, the engineers came up with a wobble-blade dado, which required only a twist of a rotating collar to reset the width. But this conve-

nience introduced its own annoying drawback: much rougher cuts compared to its stacking predecessor.

The most recent development in the dado cutter is the adjustable stack dado. To eliminate the need to change chippers and insert shims, the stack expands and contracts along an eccentric hub. Guess what? It too has an annoying drawback: While you can buy a basic stack dado set for under $50, the adjustable stack dado runs to several hundred.

All dado cutters have similar specifications: They cut grooves from ¼" wide to ¹³⁄₁₆" wide, or even up to just under 1" wide in the case of some basic stack types. They vary in diameter from 6" to 12". The larger diameters will cut deeper grooves of course, but because you are asking them to remove so much material, they require more powerful motors (sometimes more than 5 hp for the 12").

When selecting a dado set, be aware that most makers recommend a dado cutter 2" smaller in diameter than the maxi-

mum blade size for the saw. For example, they recommend an 8"-diameter dado cutter for a 10" saw. While you can run a 10"-diameter dado cutter on many 10" saws, make sure the one you buy has a ⅝"-diameter arbor hole, not the 1" arbor hole of a cutter intended for a 12" saw. Also, carefully check the arbor length of your saw and the specifications of the dado set before ordering.

Finally, be aware that you will need a special throat plate to accommodate the dado cutter; most table saw makers offer one as an option or supply one with the machine. You can also make your own throat plate as described earlier. I recommend making your own if you are looking for the cleanest possible cut since you can custom fit the plate to an exact depth and width of dado, supporting the stock right to the edge of the cutting surface.

Stack-Type Dado Cutter

The stack-type dado set is basically a sandwich of cutting blades: two outside

HANGING STORAGE BOX
My shop-made blade storage box, hung on a wall near the table saw, keeps blades organized, safe from rubbing against one another and instantly available.

STACK-TYPE DADO
The classic dado set consists of two outer combination-type blades with a selection of chippers placed between them to form a kerf between ¼" and ¹³⁄₁₆" wide. Though time-consuming to set up, the stack-type dado can produce a crisp, flat-bottomed dado cut.

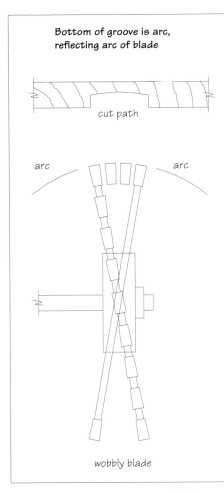

Bottom of groove is arc, reflecting arc of blade

cut path

arc   arc

wobbly blade

CROSS SECTION OF GROOVE MADE BY WOBBLY DADO

WOBBLY DADO CUTTER
You can quickly adjust a wobble-type dado set to the desired kerf width by turning its center hub. No shimming is necessary for fine-tuning—but the wobble action produces a slightly curved kerf bottom and relatively rough shoulders.

EXPANDING-STACK DADO BLADE SYSTEM
The expanding stack is the premier dado blade set: You can quickly set it to any kerf width by turning its center hub, yet it produces a crisp, flat-bottomed dado. The only drawback is that its cost is nearly twice what you might pay for other types of dado sets.

blades with a choice of 18 to 48 teeth ground for both ripping and crosscutting, and a set of chippers of varying thicknesses on the inside having 2 to 6 flat-topped teeth each. While more teeth may produce a smoother cut, the quality and type of grind on the teeth are also factors. The teeth on the outside cutters should be a single bevel angled toward inside of the stack and not flat-ground, which are usually found only on cheap sets and won't cut clean shoulders. To minimize splintering when cutting across the grain, especially on hardwood plywood, some sets have a negative hook angle on the outside cutters. These sets don't self-feed and thus cut slower and require considerably more feed pressure. I wouldn't go with a negative hook angle option unless I planned to regularly dado across plywood panels.

The dado set's chippers usually include one ¼" wide, two ⅛" and one ¹⁄₁₆". Since the outer blades are most often ⅛" wide, this selection of chippers allows you to adjust the width of the cut between ¼" and ¹³⁄₁₆" in ¹⁄₁₆" increments. If the set includes a ³⁄₃₂" chipper, you can adjust in ¹⁄₃₂" increments —a big advantage when cutting dadoes to accept hardwood plywood, which is typically ¹⁄₃₂" shy of the plywood's nominal dimension (¾" plywood is often ²³⁄₃₂").

To allow for fine-tuning the width of cut, most basic stacking dado sets include a set of washerlike paper shims as thin as .010". Unfortunately, I find these paper shims tear easily, and they're worthless if they get crinkled or damp from sitting around the shop—a condition I call shop rash. I often found myself having to make sandpaper shims—rather convenient because the higher the grit, the thinner the shim, but they're tough on my scissors. Better alternative shims are available from tool suppliers in plastic, brass and even magnetized steel. The latter is a useful innovation: The shims stay in place and sit perfectly flat to the sides of blades as you build the stack, allowing you to put

on the shims before you install the blades on the arbor. No more fumbling in the sawdust inside the table saw for that dropped shim washer.

Chippers with four or more flat-topped teeth produce a flatter and smoother groove bottom than chippers with two such teeth. This is an important consideration if you intend to expose the end of the dado in furniture construction. But it may not be important to you if you use the cutter primarily to make grooves for drawer bottoms or to create stop-dado shelf grooves.

Wobbly Dado Cutter
The single blade of a "wobbly" dado cutter is mounted between two disks that vary the blade's angle to the arbor, a sort of controlled, intentional runout, as shown in the drawing. The amount of wobble determines the width of cut. To increase the width, you simply dial in more angle. It's a quick and inexpensive way (you are only

paying for one blade) to get an adjustable dado width. But you have to pay for this convenience and efficiency somewhere: in this case, poor cutting performance compared to the stacked dado cutter.

One blade has to do all the work—and that is considerable, especially when cutting wide grooves. In use, the tilted blade generates considerable vibration, sometimes enough to loosen clamps on fixtures, and produces a rough-edged cut. Also, the tilted blade necessarily produces a groove with a rounded bottom. It is not possible for a wobbly dado cutter to cut a flat-bottomed dado or groove. That may be a problem if you intend to expose the ends of the groove. But for occasional use, the economy and convenience of the wobbly cutter may be the best way to go.

Expanding-Stack Dado Cutter

If you want it both ways—exceptional performance and the convenience of adjustable width without changing chippers or shims—you can have it. It just takes a willingness to spend more money. Several blade manufacturers offer stacking dado sets whose blades and chippers mount to a camlike hub. By turning a plate on the hub, you can dial in the desired width. I find the dial more accurate and easier to fine-tune than the wobbly cutter. Best of all, the groove produced by the adjustable stacking dado—no matter what the width—is perfectly flat bottomed. And the high quality of the outside cutters ensures splinter-free shoulders.

The use of these dado cutter systems will be covered later in the book as I apply them to specific techniques. I will tell you in advance, though, that you should read the manual for specific instructions about using and adjusting your particular cutter set; not all operate in exactly the same way. Also read the reminders about the safety issues involved with using dado cutters, not the least of which is to retighten the arbor nut after each width adjustment.

MOLDING HEADS

A molding head is an accessory that will change the kind of work you can do with your table saw. It consists of a cutterhead that fits on your saw's arbor and holds

MOLDING CUTTER HEAD
The molding cutter—a solid-steel hub that grasps three cutters along its rim—can produce a wide variety of shapes, turning your table saw into a shaper.

several, usually three, shaped cutters as shown. With the molding head installed, you can shape a wide variety of profiles into the edge or face of a workpiece.

Of course you can cut all of these shapes with a router or stationary shaper, but a molding head on a table saw offers several advantages. The first of these is power. Compared to the universal motor of even the biggest router, a table saw with a 2 hp induction motor can make bigger cuts faster and without bogging down.

An easily overlooked difference between the molding head and a router or shaper is the orientation of the shaft driving the cutter. The shaft on the saw, the saw arbor, is parallel to the saw table, while the shaft of the router or shaper is perpendicular to the table, or base of the handheld router. This makes a difference in the direction from which the cutter approaches the stock.

Because of this difference, only the molding head can cut shapes such as multiple beads or flutes in the middle of a board's face. Shapes such as an edge bead in the face of a board can be cut with a table-mounted router but only by feeding the stock on edge, guided by a tall fence. With a molding head, you simply feed the stock flat on the saw table. The table saw also offers the unique advantage of its tilting arbor. This allows you to produce unusual profiles or cut profiles in unusual places, such as across the corner of a box. To duplicate these cuts with a router or shaper, you would need to build some rather complicated, custom-made jigs.

Adjusting and securing the angle, depth and location of the molded cut is easy on the table saw; you simply crank on the arbor wheels or adjust the rip fence and lock them down. Some of these adjustments can be cumbersome on a table-mounted router or stationary shaper.

Finally, don't overlook the advantages of the larger cutting diameter of the molding head. This larger diameter produces much shallower mill marks, minimizing the time and effort you must put into final sanding before finishing.

Before you jump into using a molding head on your table saw, however, consider its requirements: Your saw must have ample mass to dampen vibration if your molding head is not well balanced, and ample power if you intend to make large cuts in a single pass. A stationary saw with a 3 hp motor will let you make the most of the efficiency and range of a molding head's capabilities. When choosing a molding head, be sure that your saw's arbor is long enough to accept the head, that the cutters will not strike other parts of the saw below the table, and that you have (or will make) a special throat plate to accommodate the cutters. Some cutterheads may require special spacers when used on some saws.

Most modern molding heads have three cutters, the number necessary to produce smooth cuts with a high degree of durability and safety. (The less work required of each cutter, the less strain each has to endure.) Avoid the older, one- or two-cutter heads; their cutters have

---

SAFETY *tip*

MOLDING HEAD SAFETY

Working with a molding head on the table saw is a potentially hazardous operation. To minimize the danger, follow these essential rules:

- Always double-check the installation of the knives in the cutterhead to make sure they are facing the correct way, that they are fully seated, and that the Allenhead screws are tightened all the way.
- Unplug the saw before installing the cutterhead.
- Never install the cutterhead in the saw unless all the cutters are installed.
- Be sure you are using any bushings and/or spacer washers required by your combination of molding head and saw.
- Always use the outside flange if your arbor is long enough, and be sure the arbor nut is tight. But do not tighten it by holding a stick against one of the knives; you may distort it, creating a potentially hazardous condition.
- With the saw still unplugged, turn the cutterhead through several full revolutions to make sure it isn't hitting any part of the table saw.

- Never run warped stock or stock that has knots. These conditions can chip or break the knives and can cause forceful kickback.
- Never mold stock less than 1' long. Short stock has a much greater tendency to kick back, so mold longer stock and cut it to length.
- Stand to the side when starting the saw, and stand to the side throughout the cut. Always use hold-downs—a power feeder is best—to secure the stock to both the table surface and to the rip or guide fence.
- Do not attempt heavy cuts in a single pass unless your table saw is adequately powered. Feed the stock just fast enough to avoid burning. This will minimize mill marks as well as any tendency to kick back.

USING A POWER FEEDER WITH A MOLDING HEAD

A power feeder contributes significantly to both safety and quality when cutting with a molding head. The feeder's consistent feed rate minimizes burn and mill marks and reduces any tendency to kick back.

Keep in mind that each individual cutter is much larger than a saw tooth and that there are only three of them. So each one takes a pretty big bite. The forces generated demand that the stock be held securely to both the table and the fence. Unless you're making very shallow cuts, the strength of your hands will not be enough. Hold-downs are necessary to prevent the stock from shifting, and an antikickback device is essential to prevent kickback should the cutters encounter a knot. In my estimation, a power feeder does this best because it nearly eliminates kickback through its firm control of the stock and its high resistance to back forces. And if kickback should occur, you need not be anywhere near the cutters or infeed path.

---

likely been subjected to huge stresses and may be fatigued or fractured.

Manufacturers have several methods of holding the cutters in place in the cutterhead. Some use a cutterhead that is significantly thinner than the width of the cutters. Their cutters have a groove in the back that slides around the cutterhead. This keeps the cutters parallel to one another and ensures that they project out the same amount. A hardened Allenhead screw secures the cutter in place. Another style uses a much thicker cutterhead and a specially shaped screw to center and secure the cutters. If you are buying a used molding head, be sure that the screw threads are not stripped.

Maintaining and Sharpening Molding Head Cutters

Always remove the knives from the cutterhead when you are finished working; leaving them installed exposes them to handling damage. Here's the routine: After use, remove all three cutters, inspect each for nicks, clean pitch buildup on the cutter faces and in the mounting

groove, spray with a protective film, and then store the knives in their case face to back.

To sharpen the cutters, hone the flat face on a series of sharpening stones. I start on an 800-grit waterstone, move to a 1200-grit and then polish on a 6000-grit. I try hard to stroke each knife the same number of times on each of the stones. This is important because the knives must remain the same length or the longer ones end up doing all the work—a condition that would degrade the cut and pose a potentially dangerous situation. Be aware that deep nicks will require a professional resharpening of all three cutters or replacement.

Ripping

Most of us understand ripping to mean sawing a board parallel to its grain, and we assume, usually correctly, that this means sawing down the board's length to create two narrower pieces. Sometimes, however, the assumption is not correct, and we find ourselves dealing with pieces of wood that have the grain running across the width. As you read this chapter and the next, keep in mind that matters such as blade choice, wood movement and the need for splitters are related to grain direction while matters such as stock guidance and whether you use the rip fence or a crosscut device are determined by the direction of the cut in relation to the shape of the stock. In general then, you'll use a rip blade to saw parallel to the grain, regardless of how you guide the stock, and you'll guide the stock with a rip fence when sawing down the length of a board, regardless of which direction the grain runs.

Sawing down a board's length to create two narrower pieces, that is, most ripping, is what the table saw does best—and is its primary function as intended by its original designers. Though you can rip boards on the band saw, and of course with hand tools, the table saw excels in offering an easily adjusted and accurate guide system (the rip fence) and a fast-cutting blade (the circular saw blade). You would have to spend a great deal more money on an industrial-size band saw to come up with the same width capacity, speed and precision afforded by a garden-variety table saw, and you still wouldn't get as smooth a cut.

BASIC RIPPING

To safely and accurately rip a board on the table saw, the board must have a straight edge to follow the fence and at least one flat face to slide along the saw table. If it doesn't, you will have to flatten and straighten it.

Begin your stock preparation by checking the wood for foreign matter, which could dull your blade or knock a chip from a carbide tooth. If you imagine a chunk of carbide coming at you at the speed of the teeth on a saw blade, you'll have a new understanding of the expression "bite the bullet." So remove any suspicious substance, or reject the stock.

To flatten your stock, first saw your workpieces to rough length. The shorter the board, the easier it is to handle and control. Plane a face flat, and check it with a straightedge and a pair of winding sticks to make sure there is no cup, bow or wind. You can continue surfacing the opposite face to bring the stock to the desired thickness, but you need only one

flat face for ripping. (I often wait and surface the second side after the board has been cut to width.) Holding the flat face against the jointer fence, plane one edge straight and square to the flat face. If the edge of the stock is so irregular that jointing it straight would be tedious, treat it as a waney board. You now have the two necessary reference surfaces for ripping the board.

Setting Up the Saw

Proper saw setup is important, both for your safety and for peak saw performance. The Pre-Ripping Checklist may seem long, but many of the items on it require no more than a quick glance. Make a habit of going through the list, eventually from memory, before each ripping operation.

Choose the best rip blade for the type

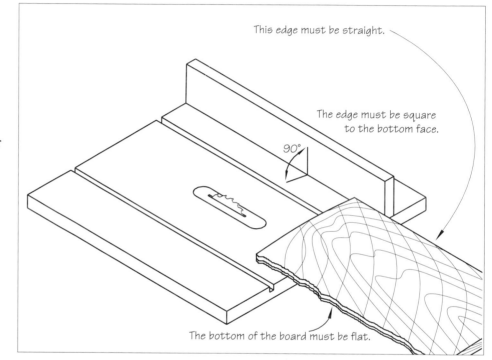

This edge must be straight.

The edge must be square to the bottom face.

90°

The bottom of the board must be flat.

and quality of stock you are working with and for the results you desire. If, for example, the wood is green or extraordinarily dense and you want a fast cut with minimum potential for kickback due to binding, choose a blade with fewer teeth, deep gullets and more set or kerf width than the average blade. An 18-tooth blade with a .153" kerf is a good choice. If you are working with stable wood and are looking for a finely cut edge so you can join the boards edge to edge without additional machine work, select a blade with more teeth and a thin kerf, such as a 24-tooth with a .126" kerf width. For light-duty ripping involving little blade stress, I go with a thin-kerf blade to conserve the wood lost to the kerf. (For a complete discussion of blades, see chapter four).

Setting the Width of the Cut

To cut the board to a certain width, set the rip fence to that distance from the inside edge of the blade. You can do this in one of three ways: by measurement, to a layout mark on the stock or a story stick, or to a sample you wish to match in width.

Measure the space between the fence and the blade with a tape measure or ruler or use the rip fence scale on the saw. While direct measurement is the most reassuring, few modern fences give an accurate measurement until locked down; then you have to unlock them to make a minor adjustment. On the other hand, the rip fence scale on the saw is only correct for blades identical to the one used when setting the pointer. In either case, make doubly certain that the measurement you're setting the fence to is correct. To quote the title of a previous book I wrote, "Measure twice, cut once."

You can set the fence to a layout mark by using either a story stick or a mark on the stock. A story stick is a piece of wood with carefully placed marks at the exact dimension required, taken directly from the opening where the part must fit or from the full-scale rendering of the object. It's particularly useful when the opening you need to measure cannot be brought into the shop. In other cases, you can mark the part itself by holding it up to the opening. Both of these methods eliminate potential inaccuracies from reading a scale incorrectly.

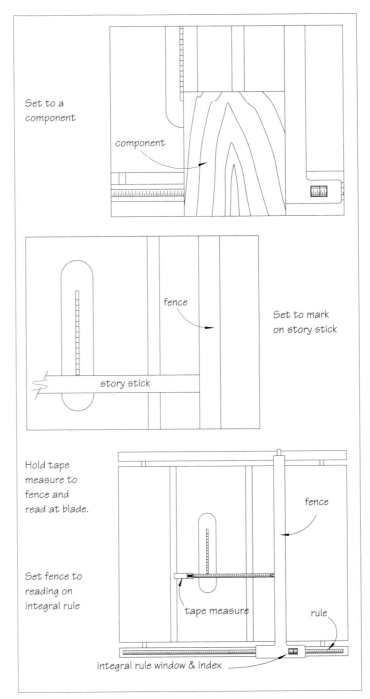

Set to a component

component

Set to mark on story stick

fence

story stick

Hold tape measure to fence and read at blade.

Set fence to reading on integral rule

fence

tape measure

rule

integral rule window & index

SETTING RIP FENCE CUTTING WIDTH
The most reliable method of all is to set the fence using a sample of the required width. (A) This is most often a previously cut part of the project that you know is exactly correct, but it can also be a left-over part from a previous project that you're copying or an accurately cut piece that you keep around the shop for just this purpose. To double-check the setting, make a short cut in the end of a piece of scrap and measure the result. Then compare it to the story stick (B) or sample or fit it to the project. You can always use a tape measure or the integral rule on your saw (C), but keep in mind this is the least accurate method.

Setting the Height of the Blade

A circular blade runs cooler and with less feed pressure when set high because the teeth are at a smaller angle of attack relative to the wood, but the increased tooth exposure is more hazardous. My rule of thumb (and I still have both) is to set carbide teeth just high enough to clear the top of the wood. (I place a sample piece of stock against the blade to visualize the height.) At the most, to reduce splintering on the underside of the stock, I'll raise the blade until the gullets between the teeth are fully exposed.

Assuring Stock Support and Room

Many woodworkers, both beginners and experienced, turn on the saw and start sawing when they're satisfied that the cut will be in the correct place. All too often they regret their haste. Halfway through a cut is no time to discover that the stock is going to push your favorite hand plane off the outfeed table where you left it, or that it takes extraordinary effort to keep the stock from tipping.

Assess the situation. Make sure nothing is on the saw table or any built-in outfeed support. Consider the length of the

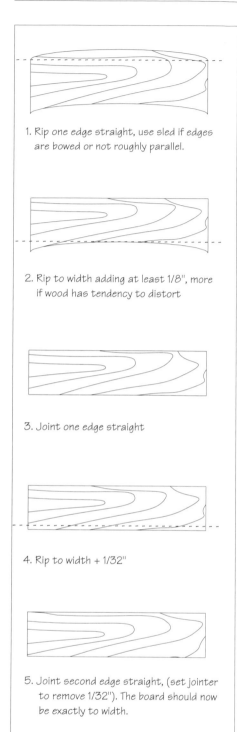

1. Rip one edge straight, use sled if edges are bowed or not roughly parallel.

2. Rip to width adding at least 1/8", more if wood has tendency to distort

3. Joint one edge straight

4. Rip to width + 1/32"

5. Joint second edge straight, (set jointer to remove 1/32"). The board should now be exactly to width.

RIPPING TO A CRITICAL WIDTH
Because wood seldom stays perfectly straight after ripping, I often add at least ⅛" (even more if the first pieces indicate the wood has a tendency to move a lot) to allow for rejointing, especially if the finished width dimension is critical. If width isn't critical, I still add about ½" to allow for planing the edges smooth. The drawing above shows my process for ripping stock to a critical width.

STANCE FOR RIPPING—INITIAL
Begin the rip cut by supporting the board level to the saw and tight to the rip fence. Unless the board is under 3' long, you may have to begin a step or two back from the front of the saw.

STANCE FOR RIPPING—FOLLOW THROUGH
Feed the stock through the blade using a push stick and blade guard for safety. Brace your hip against the front of the saw for the follow-through.

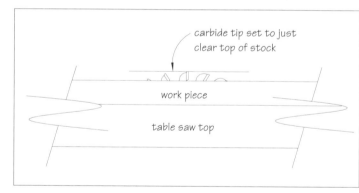

carbide tip set to just clear top of stock

work piece

table saw top

SETTING BLADE HEIGHT AGAINST STOCK

stock. Ask yourself if you will be able to let go of the stock when the cut is complete without having the stock fall to the floor. If there is any doubt, test by lowering the blade below the table and running the stock through. If your test shows a need, set up additional outfeed support and weight the base. Sand bags are convenient for this. (You'll find a more complete discussion of outfeed supports in chapter three.)

Making the Cut
Now you are ready to turn on the saw and make the cut. Place the board on the front edge of the table surface, well back from the blade. Orient the board so the planed face is on the table and the straight edge is against the fence. Turn on the motor, let the blade come up to speed and then move the stock into the blade.

Be aware of your stance: You should be standing to the left of the blade so you're out of line of possible kickback, as shown in the photos. Set the front of the board on the saw table, and feed it slowly into the blade, keeping your eye on the edge of the board against the rip fence. Walk toward the saw in a straight line (no waddling!) as the board feeds into the blade.

Push with your right hand while your left hand applies light pressure toward the fence in front (your side) of the blade. If you are using a table-mounted featherboard, you can rely on it to exert this pressure; in this case, place your left hand on your hip to keep it out of the way. Never place your hand in your pocket; you may need it instantly to control the workpiece or to switch off the machine. Continue feeding the stock into the blade at a steady rate, being sure the edge of the board stays tight to the rip fence. When you reach the saw, brace yourself by placing your left foot against the base of the machine and your hip against the front edge of the table. Switch to a push stick when your hand is within 1' of the blade. If you are using another person rather than outfeed supports to catch the board, instruct your helper to only support, never pull or otherwise control, the board.

As you make the cut, listen to the motor: If it is bogging down, you are pushing too fast. Avoid going too slow, however; this increases friction and thus heat

buildup at the blade, which can cause the edges of the wood to scorch.

When the cut is complete and the board clears the back of the blade, continue pushing the stock onto the outfeed supports. Place the ripped workpiece in a holding area if you are ripping more pieces and clearly mark it if it is to become a specific component.

Dealing With Problem Wood

A small percentage of boards come from the lumberyard cupped or warped. If the board is thick enough, you may be able to plane out the warp or cup and proceed

PRE-RIPPING CHECKLIST

- Sharp rip blade in good condition and stabilizer (if appropriate) installed.
- Throat plate flush with table.
- Blade 90° to table surface.
- Splitter in line with blade.
- Blade turns without interference.
- Kickback pawls hang loosely and prevent backward movement of stock.
- Blade guard swings up easily.
- Fence set to desired distance.
- Blade parallel to rip fence.
- Blade no higher than necessary.
- Stock has sufficient room to move past the blade unhindered.
- Outfeed support in place and weighted, if necessary, to prevent tipping.
- Dust collection system is connected and working properly.

AUXILIARY FENCE FOR RIPPING

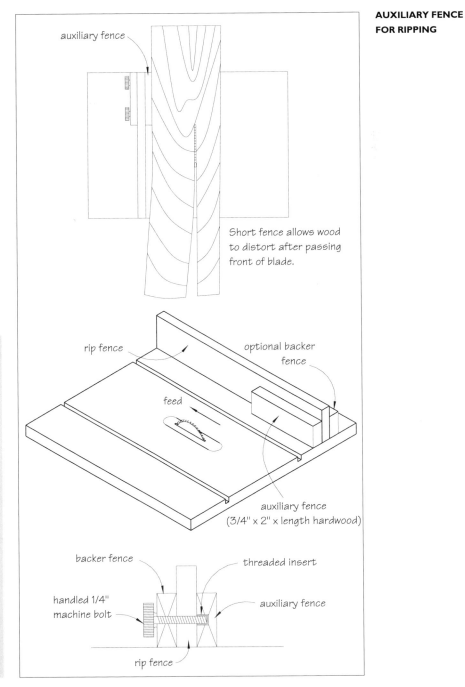

auxiliary fence

Short fence allows wood to distort after passing front of blade.

rip fence

optional backer fence

feed

auxiliary fence (3/4" x 2" x length hardwood)

backer fence

threaded insert

handled 1/4" machine bolt

auxiliary fence

rip fence

normally with your millwork. However, there is no guarantee the board will stay flat after being ripped. Some boards contain areas that tend to bend in opposite directions and balance each other; ripping may sever the link between them, allowing them to go their opposite ways.

Sometimes it is better to first rip a deformed board and then plane out the warp or cup. In this way, you will not have to remove as much material and stress may be relieved by having ripped the board. The problem, though, is that ripping deformed stock can be hazardous. If you rip it with the cup up, it tends to rock on the table as you progress through the cut. But if you rip it with the cup down, it can suddenly collapse flat at the end of the cut, pinching against the blade. In either case, the blade will tend to toss the board right back at you.

The safest way to rip problematic wood is with either a handsaw or a band saw. Both may bind up in the cut, but neither will cause a dangerous kickback. If I do use the table saw, I follow these precautions: First, install my splitter and anti-kickback pawls or hold-downs with integral antikickback qualities (shop-made comb-type featherboards or the one-way rollers shown in chapter three). Next, I install a shop-made, short auxiliary fence on the universal rip fence fixture that runs to 1" behind the front of the blade (see the drawing). Alternatively, I secure my rip fence sled (see chapter three) at this position (see photo). This allows the board the freedom to spread after passing through the blade, without hitting the fence and pushing the side of the blade. If

the board is cupped, I run it through the blade cupside down. Though the board will collapse to the table when the cut nears completion, the splitter prevents it from binding on the blade. I never run it cupside up because the rocking motion invites binding and kickback.

If the board is warped, which is easily determined by setting it on the table and seeing if it rocks on its corners, I usually avoid using the board altogether.

RIPPING WITH A POWER FEEDER

A power feeder saves your back and arms, significantly reducing fatigue during a stint in the shop, and the feeder makes the ripping quick and accurate. Follow these safety guidelines when you use a power feeder:

- Know the machine—especially how to stop it quickly.
- Avoid loose clothing; never wear your shirt cuffs loose.
- Support long stock on the infeed and on the outfeed.
- Be sure the edge of the stock bearing against the rip fence is straight. The faces of the board should be relatively flat and parallel to one another.
- Never leave the feeder running unattended.
- Shut off the feeder before shutting off the saw.
- Unplug the machine before touching and handling its wheels for cleaning or adjustment.

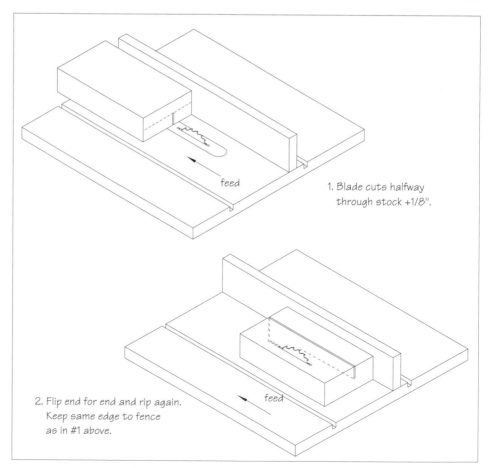

1. Blade cuts halfway through stock +1/8".

2. Flip end for end and rip again. Keep same edge to fence as in #1 above.

RIPPING SEQUENCE FOR THICK STOCK

feed

feed

POWER FOR RIPPING

Ripping puts more demand on your table saw than crosscutting. One reason is that a ripsaw chisels through the wood rather than slicing. Another reason is that ripping typically involves a longer cut. The best way to keep the saw up to speed while still ensuring the longevity of your machine is to increase its power and efficiency when asking it to cut lengthwise through boards. Here's how:

- Be sure your saw is getting adequate power. If it's on an extension cord, make sure the cord is of adequate gauge. To keep power loss to a minimum, stay well within the amperage rating that came with the cord.
- Use a dedicated rip blade. For the cleanest and most efficient cut, choose a blade with teeth ground for chisel cutting. The teeth will be flat-topped and have a hook angle of about 20°. If your stock is green or reactive and the kerf tends to close up after it exits the blade, install a blade with fewer teeth per inch and greater side clearance. Thin-kerf rip blades do well with dry, stable wood: They remove less wood, thus require less power to move the blade through the wood.
- Make sure the blade is clean and free of pitch buildup. Of course, the sharper it is, the easier it can remove material and get through the wood, placing less demand on the motor.
- To prevent binding, use a splitter to keep the kerf open behind the blade. Be sure the splitter is aligned with the blade. If it's not, it may rub against one side of the kerf, thus increasing resistance.
- Switch to a smaller-diameter blade to increase the power of your saw when cutting denser wood. Because of the smaller radius, the wood has less leverage on the blade. The smaller diameter sacrifices some cutting depth but is faster during the cut.
- Maintain a steady, moderately fast feed rate. If you go too fast, you won't give the blade enough time to make the cut and the motor will bog down. If you're too slow, the wood and the blade will heat up, risking blade warp and binding in the kerf.

SETUP FOR RIPPING LONG STOCK
When ripping long stock, be sure to use an infeed support to help you keep the board level with the saw table.

I find that warped boards often continue to warp, even when cut down to relatively narrow pieces. When I do rip a warped board, I clamp it onto the sled I use for waney stock. To keep the board from rocking, I insert a shim under the high corner.

Power Feeder Setup

Before ripping, with or without a power feeder, always wax the table and fence surfaces to reduce sliding friction. Be sure the saw blade is sharp so the feeder won't have to work any harder than necessary. Also ensure that the feeder's wheels are free of pitch buildup; clean them with a solvent if necessary.

Begin the setup by installing the feeder support mast securely to the table, being sure that the bolts are tight. With the saw blade below the table, set a scrap of the stock to be ripped on the table. Swing the feeder into position over the scrap, locating the wheels in front of the blade and as close as possible to the rip fence. (A large power feeder may span the blade if there is enough room between its wheels.)

Adjust the position of the feeder so that all the wheels bear evenly on the wood. Angle the machine slightly (⅛" to ¼" offset) so that its outfeed side cants toward the rip fence. Next, remove the scrap and lower the feeder about ⅛". Be sure all the machine's locking levers are secured, including the lever at the swivel base of the mast. Set up a vacuum hose for dust pickup if the feeder is set up to receive one.

Without ripping, run a test piece across the table. The feeder should grab firmly enough to pull the board out of your hands and should keep the board's edge tight to the rip fence. Readjust the feeder position if necessary. Double-check the locking levers to ensure they have stayed tight.

Running the Power Feeder

Now you are ready to let 'er rip (so to speak). Turn on the saw and allow the blade to come up to speed. With the feeder set on a slow feed rate, hold a board flat on the table and tight against the rip fence. Slide the board forward until the feeder grabs it and takes over the task of pulling the board into the blade. Because things will now begin to happen quickly,

SAFETY *tip*

NEVER FREEHAND ON A TABLE SAW!

You can cut a taper by simply drawing a line on the stock and cutting freehand along the waste side of the line with a hand circular saw or band saw. Do not do this on the table saw. I've watched some old-timers do this and get away with it—at least while I was watching. But I've also noticed that many of them can't count to ten on their fingers, and not because they are mathematically challenged. To taper on the table saw, use a taper jig to hold and guide the board through the blade.

it's a good idea to have a helper to off-load the ripped stock as you feed in fresh material. Increase the feed speed until you hear the motor bogging down a bit. Then back off the speed slightly. Over the course of a big production run, you may have to slow the feed rate to accommodate a duller blade.

RIPPING THICK STOCK

What do you do when the stock is too thick to rip all the way through? Rip it twice: first with the blade set to cut a little more than halfway through; then again with the board flipped over. Ripping Sequence for Thick Stock shows how. I mark the side running against the rip fence so I'm sure to hold it against the fence for the second cut; otherwise the kerfs may not meet. Accuracy also depends on the two faces of the board being surfaced flat and parallel to one another and perpendicular to both edges.

Ripping thick stock often presents difficulties, including insufficient power, wood movement and inability to use the blade guard and/or splitter. If your saw lacks power, see the discussion on motors in chapter one. Wood movement is a common problem with thick stock because of the length of time it takes for thick stock to adjust to a change in humidity. If the stock is quite dry on the interior but more moist near the surface because of a recent rise in humidity, the kerf may tend to close during a cut. If it does so and grips the splitter, you'll have to saw in a series

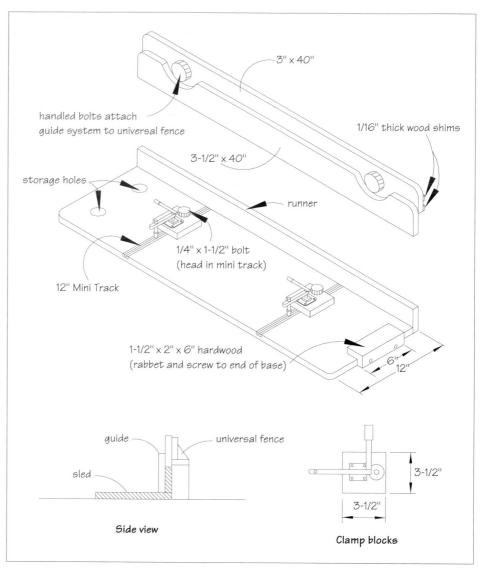

STRAIGHT-LINE RIPPING SLED

of passes of increasing depth. This widens the kerf of the previous pass while increasing the depth of the kerf. The situation is much more dangerous if your saw design doesn't allow you to use the splitter when sawing less than all the way through the stock.

Many saws use a splitter that extends higher than the top of the blade in order to attach the blade guard to the splitter. If your saw is of this type you will, unfortunately, have to remove the guard and splitter to make all but the final cut. But unless you are absolutely certain your stock is rock stable, safety demands you to use a splitter. In this situation, I use a shop-made throat plate with a built-in splitter as described in chapter three.

Also, be sure to use hold-downs that provide at least some kickback protection.

Reinstall the blade guard before making the final, separating cut.

RIPPING LONG STOCK

Ripping stock longer than about 6' can get tricky because the balance point of the stock is several feet away from the saw at the beginning of the cut, thus you can't stand close to the saw to ensure the wood is flat on the table and tight against the rip fence. If you have a helper, you can stand by the saw and let the other person support the weight of the board behind you as you feed it into the saw. When the balance point of the board approaches your hands, the helper is free to walk to the outfeed side of the saw to catch the offcuts.

Without a helper, you need support and hold-down aids to keep the board under control. Besides the outfeed support, which you should leave on the saw full time, add a single-roller infeed support positioned beyond the board's balance point and level with the saw table. When the board is in position to start the cut you should be able to let go of it and not have it fall to the floor. Set up hold-downs—either featherboards, guide rollers or a combination of both—to guide the board. Be sure the splitter, antikick-back pawls or hold-downs, and blade guard are in place and working properly. The longer and heavier the board, the more you will have to rely on these accessories to ensure a safe and accurate cut.

Now you are ready to proceed. Support the leading end of the board on the front of the saw table, turn on the saw and begin feeding the board into the blade, standing a step or two away from the saw. When the back of the board leaves the infeed support, walk in a straight line with the board until you come against the front of the saw, where you can brace yourself as you feed the rest of the board through the blade.

RIPPING OFF WANEY EDGES

If your stock does not have a straight edge because the board is bowed or has a waney edge (it was not straight-edged after being sawn from the log), you have two options: You can cut the edge straight with a portable saw guided by a straight-edged board, or, if you think you will run into the problem often, you can use one of several shop-made fixtures to guide the stock through the saw. The first fixture supports the stock as it is carried through the blade (see photo). The edge of the fixture is captured against the rip fence to guide the board in a straight line. Another effective fixture, especially for stock longer than about 3', is the pattern fence (see chapter eight). To use the pattern fence for ripping off a waney or bowed edge, you simply attach a straight-edged stick (at least 1' longer than the stock) to the board to act as the guide template.

RIPPING A TAPER

There are times when you don't want a rip cut to run parallel to the edge of the

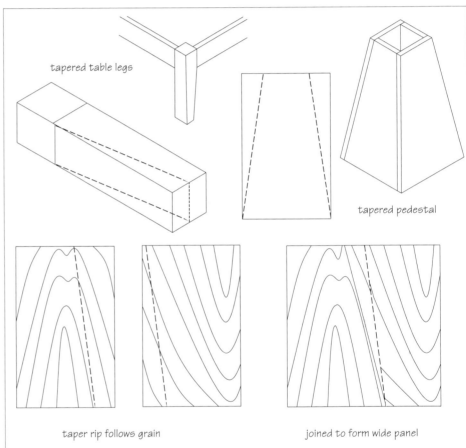

tapered table legs

tapered pedestal

taper rip follows grain

joined to form wide panel

TAPER RIP APPLICATIONS

board. When making table legs, for example, you may want the bottoms of the legs to be thinner than the tops so the legs will appear delicate. Or if you're preparing stock for edge-gluing, you may want the rip cut to follow along a grain line so the edge joints will be less conspicuous. You can also make tapered cuts at a bevel to create polygon assemblies, such as tapered boxes for pedestals.

Commercial jigs work well enough for a single-tapered rip (or tapers on two adjacent faces), but to cut a taper on the opposite face of the stock, you have to readjust the jig. These jigs have another disadvantage: Especially long workpieces extend past the end of the jig and hit against the rip fence. Also, it can be difficult to hold the workpiece securely to the jig. To get around these problems, I make my own jig.

Because the jig is a sled—it is, in fact,

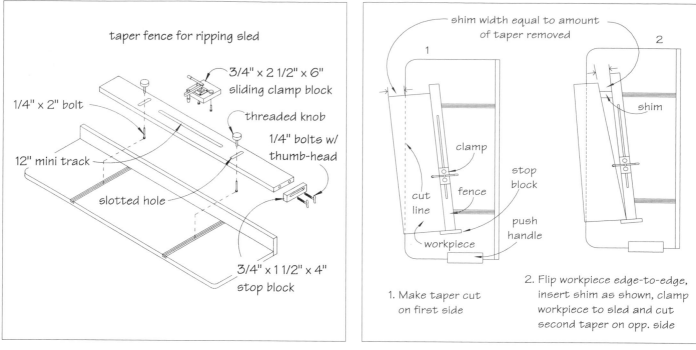

SHOP-MADE TAPER JIG

SETTING UP TO CUT A DOUBLE TAPER

the straight-line rip sled with a specialized fence—you can clamp the stock to the jig's base, increasing safety and accuracy. Its unique design accommodates stock to any length without hitting the rip fence.

Cutting the Taper

Because you can orient the layout marks of a taper cut directly to my unique shop-made taper jig, there is no need to calculate or guess at angle settings.

An advantage of my shop-made taper jig is that I needn't know the angle or inch per foot of the taper in order to set up the cut. Instead, I simply mark the location of the taper cut on the workpiece and then orient the marks to the edge of the jig, which indicates the cut line of the saw, as I slide the fence against the inside edge of the workpiece. To make the cut, tighten the fence to the sled with the knobs, clamp the workpiece to the jig with the toggle clamps on the fence, turn on the saw and run the jig against the rip fence. The jig's runner system ensures the jig stays tight to the fence and allows you to use only your right hand to push the assembly through the blade.

To cut a double taper (an equal angle on opposite edges of the workpiece), you simply insert a shim cut to the maximum thickness of the taper cutoff, as shown in the drawing. First cut the taper on one

side of the workpiece, then release it from the jig. Next, insert the shim as shown, clamp the workpiece back into the jig and again make the taper rip cut.

RESAWING

The purpose of resawing is to rip through a board edgewise producing two or more thinner pieces. I often resaw to create veneer, which I apply to plywood for a stable panel. I also resaw boards in half, then edge-join the halves, creating panels with a unique grain pattern called a bookmatch.

I usually resaw on my band saw because it can cut a wide board in one pass (up to 8" wide on my machine) because its narrow kerf wastes less wood and because the band saw is safer if the wood distorts. However, the band saw can be time-consuming to set up for just one or two cuts. With proper precautions, the table saw offers a fast and effective way to resaw boards up to 6" in width (on a 10" saw). Wider boards end up with an uncut area that must be ripped with a handsaw or on the band saw.

To ensure an accurate cut, surface flat and straight the face of the stock that will bear against the rip fence. Both edges of the board should be straight and square to this face.

For resaw work, I use a smooth-cutting rip blade with 24 teeth and a ⅛" kerf, pro-

ducing a surface that doesn't require much sanding and thus loss of thickness. I avoid combination blades because they are slower-cutting and thin-kerf blades, which can overheat and warp in deep cuts. Lock down your arbor with the blade at 90° to the table and double-check that the face of the rip fence is square to the table.

Because you will probably have to remove your standard guard and splitter bracket, use a throat plate with an integral splitter. Do not resaw without a splitter; a thin offcut distorts easily and can bind against the blade.

Set the rip fence to the desired width and the height of the blade to cut a little more than halfway through the workpiece. If you have a blade-stabilizer plate, you may have to remove it in order to

---

SAFETY *tip*

BEWARE OF TAPER RIP OFFCUTS

Taper rip offcuts typically have a sharp, wedge-shaped end with the potential to become trapped between the blade and the opening in the throat plate, especially if the taper is short. Your best defense is to use a zero-clearance throat plate and pay attention to the progress of the cut.

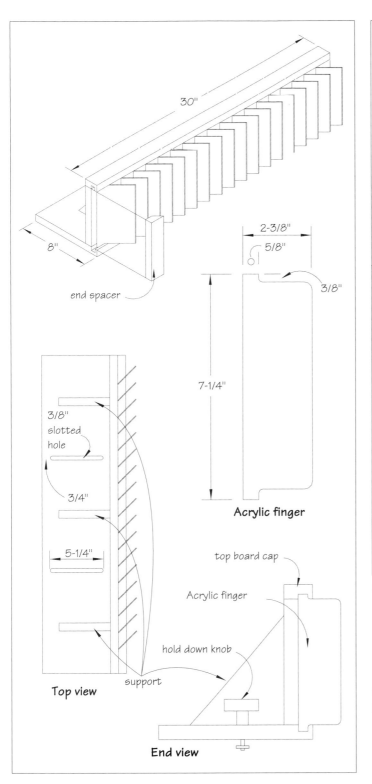

30"

8"

end spacer

2-3/8"

5/8"

7-1/4"

3/8"

Acrylic finger

3/8"
slotted
hole

3/4"

5-1/4"

top board cap

Acrylic finger

hold down knob

support

Top view

End view

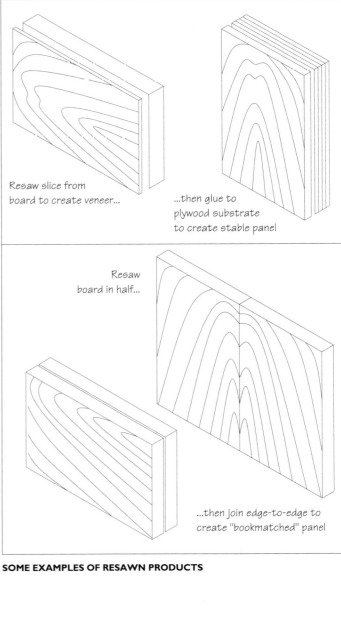

Resaw slice from
board to create veneer...

...then glue to
plywood substrate
to create stable panel

Resaw
board in half...

...then join edge-to-edge to
create "bookmatched" panel

SOME EXAMPLES OF RESAWN PRODUCTS

**VERTICAL FEATHERBOARD
FIXTURE**

maximize the depth of cut. If the stock is dense, such as hard maple, you may find you can only cut at a 1" depth for the first cut, with subsequent passes at 1" increments.

The way I obtain an accurate and safe cut is to use a vertical featherboard fixture. This unique fixture ensures that tall workpieces are held tightly to the fence when being ripsawn, eliminating the need

to use hand pressure against the side of the boards. The result is a safer, more controlled cut. Unlike featherboards that clamp flat to the saw table, this fixture holds the feathers—in this case Plexiglas fingers—vertical. The notches of these ⅟₁₆"-thick Plexiglas pieces insert into grooves and are held at a 45° angle by spacers screwed to the face of the jig. A board fastened along the top of the face

captures the notches in a groove and allows the fingers to be easily removed and replaced if necessary.

To build the fixture, cut the groove in the base and then fasten the vertical face and buttress supports. Screw the end spacer in place flush to the end of the vertical face, and insert the first Plexiglas finger. Screw in the next spacer, and insert the next finger. Continue until you reach the last finger, and then attach the last end spacer. Now lower the top board in place, capturing the protruding notches of the fingers in its groove. Screw it in place.

To use the resaw featherboard, install the saw's throat plate with integral splitter. Set the rip fence to the desired width of cut, lower the blade and set the stock against the rip fence. Now set the fixture over the lockdown bolts and slide the fixture over until its Plexiglas fingers bear snugly against the side of the stock. Lock the fixture to the saw table by turning the hold-down knobs. Lift the stock out of the way, raise the blade and commence resawing. You'll notice that the multiple, highly flexible Plexiglas fingers allow the board to slide smoothly forward with little resistance, yet they resist any backward movement. All you do to control the board

is to push it through the blade with a push stick held against the end of the top edge of the board.

The Resaw Process

After making the first cut(s) to halfway through the stock, reverse the board end for end, place the same reference face against the fence and saw the other half. If the width of the board won't allow a clean separation, finish with a freehand cut on the band saw or use a hand ripsaw. A fellow woodworker I know intentionally leaves ⅟₁₆" or so connecting the two parts of the workpiece. He's more comfortable having the parts attached to each other, however tenuously. Ripping the two halves apart with a handsaw is quick and easy for him since he only leaves a tiny bridge. If you intend to continue resawing

the board to create more slices, surface the reference face and repeat the sawing procedure.

If you are resawing to cut the board into two pieces equal in thickness, surface both faces flat and parallel to one another. Set the rip fence to a width just shy of one half the thickness of the stock after accounting for the kerf. Cut one edge of the stock to maximum depth, then flip the stock end for end and run it through again, producing the first slice. Now reverse the board edge for edge and cut in the same fashion to produce a second slice equal in thickness to the first.

GANG RIPPING

If you need to make a lot of same-sized narrow strips, and you want to avoid the tedium of producing one strip at a time,

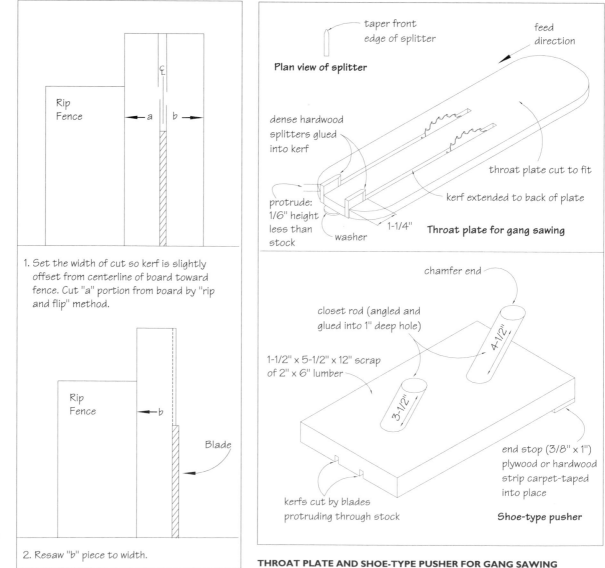

1. Set the width of cut so kerf is slightly offset from centerline of board toward fence. Cut "a" portion from board by "rip and flip" method.

2. Resaw "b" piece to width.

RESAWING A BOARD INTO TWO EQUAL PIECES

taper front edge of splitter

Plan view of splitter

feed direction

dense hardwood splitters glued into kerf

throat plate cut to fit

kerf extended to back of plate

protrude: 1/6" height less than stock

washer

1-1/4"

Throat plate for gang sawing

chamfer end

closet rod (angled and glued into 1" deep hole)

1-1/2" x 5-1/2" x 12" scrap of 2" x 6" lumber

4-1/2"

3-1/2"

end stop (3/8" x 1") plywood or hardwood strip carpet-taped into place

kerfs cut by blades protruding through stock

Shoe-type pusher

THROAT PLATE AND SHOE-TYPE PUSHER FOR GANG SAWING

try gang ripping. You'll need to install two or more blades on the table saw with spacers in between. You'll also make and use a zero-clearance throat plate with integral splitters and a shoe-type pusher, as shown.

To do this, first make a standard throat plate. Install the plate, clamp a board over the plate (or slide the rip fence over a portion of the plate away from where the blades will be) and raise the spinning pair of blades into the plate. Turn off the saw, remove the plate and extend lines back from the kerfs to locate the positions of the splitters. Cut slots with a jigsaw and insert the splitters. The splitters should be hardwood with grain oriented vertical and height less than the thickness of the stock so they will not interfere with shoe-type pushers. Test the location of the splitters by cutting into a piece of scrap, stopping as the end of the scrap approaches the splitters. I taper the thickness of the splitters narrow to the front of the saw so they won't catch on the edges of the kerf.

I make my shoe-type pushers from a dry length of 2'x6' construction lumber, cutting the length slightly less than the distance of the front of the saw table to the front of the blade (if it's longer, the shoe tends to tip the workpiece). I use closet poles for handles, canting the back handle away from the rip fence slightly to ensure plenty of hand clearance. I carpet-tape the push ledge—a ⅜"-thick strip of hardwood cut to the full width of the shoe—to the rear of the shoe. Never use screws or nails; they could ruin your blade tips—or worse.

I use two identical combination blades for gang ripping; the two outer blades of a standard dado set would work well also. It is important that the blades be identical in type and size so they will cut with the same efficiency. Also, do not exceed the capacity of your arbor; the nut should be fully threaded on the arbor shaft. Don't cheat by eliminating the flange washer.

To make blade spacers of the correct thickness, first measure the side clearance of the blades you intend to use. Since the side clearance on one side of each of two identical blades is the same as the total side clearance of both sides of one blade, the easy way to find the dimension is to subtract the plate thickness of a blade

FEATHERBOARD FIXTURE FOR RESAW WORK IN USE
My shop-made vertical featherboard holds tall workpieces securely and accurately against the universal rip fence fixture to ensure the board is accurately resawn.

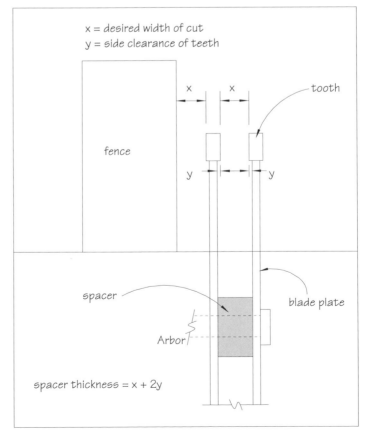

x = desired width of cut
y = side clearance of teeth

fence
tooth
x   x
y   y
spacer
blade plate
Arbor
spacer thickness = x + 2y

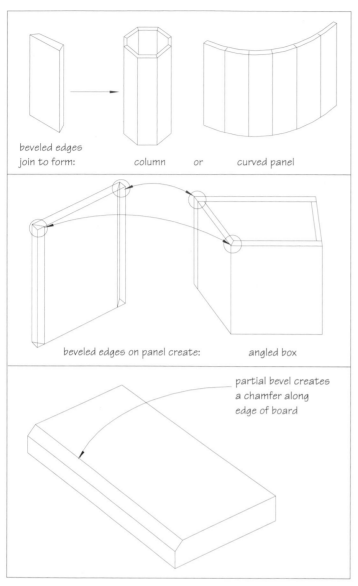

beveled edges
join to form: column   or   curved panel

beveled edges on panel create: angled box

partial bevel creates
a chamfer along
edge of board

BEVELED RIP PRODUCTS

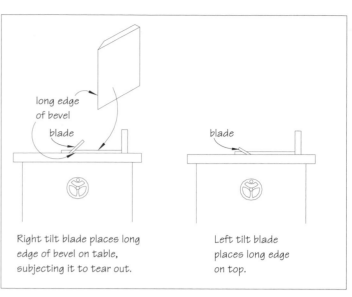

long edge
of bevel
blade

blade

Right tilt blade places long
edge of bevel on table,
subjecting it to tear out.

Left tilt blade
places long edge
on top.

LEFT VS. RIGHT TILT CONFIGURATIONS

from its kerf width. Add this to the thickness of the strips you want to rip to get the thickness of the spacers you need. Set the rip fence to the thickness of the strips you want by test cutting strips of scrap. Lay these test strips next to each other, edges down on the saw table, to see if they lie flush to one another. Adjust the rip fence as necessary until the strip produced between the blades is equal to the strip produced between the rip fence and the first blade. Gang ripping is best done with the help of a partner who can catch the strips and help pull them past the splitters. I always use a push shoe to hold the strips down on the table as I feed the stock.

RIPPING BEVELS

The modern table saw makes ripping a bevel easy: Just tilt the blade by turning a crank, adjust the fence, and saw. Some older saws designed midcentury tilt the table instead of the blade. This arrangement is less convenient but still easy. Either setup produces beveled edges that you can join into columns with three or more sides. With appropriately low bevel angles on enough narrow boards, you can even produce columns or panels that are easily cleaned up into curved surfaces. Beveled edges on casework panels produce boxes with angled corners. If you make the bevel cut through only a portion of the edge, you create a chamfer—a decorative detail.

Setting Up the Saw

Though it's easy enough to make the beveled rip, there are some special considerations. On most table saws, the blade tilts to the right, which is where the rip fence is normally located. If you are ripping narrow stock at a bevel, the rip fence may interfere with the blade, or the clearance between the blade and the fence may become uncomfortably narrow, even with a push stick. Another problem you may encounter is the standard blade guard assembly hitting the fence, restricting the degree of tilt or the width of the cut. Two easy solutions to these problems are to add a low auxiliary fence (see chapter eight) or to switch the fence to the left side of the blade. The low auxiliary fence solves the interference problem, but with very narrow stock, it doesn't solve the problem of pushing the stock through. Switching the fence to the left side of the blade solves both problems but offers a limited width capacity, which means wide

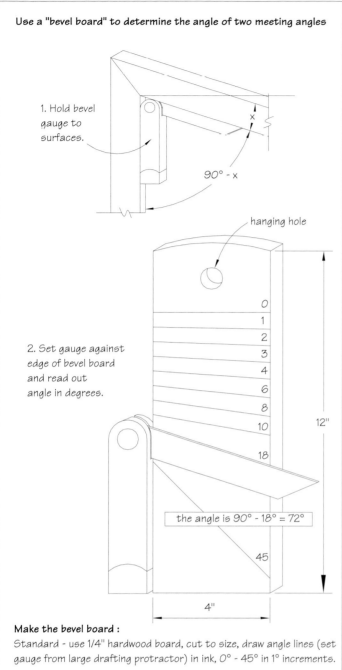

Use a "bevel board" to determine the angle of two meeting angles

1. Hold bevel gauge to surfaces.

90° - x

hanging hole

2. Set gauge against edge of bevel board and read out angle in degrees.

0
1
2
3
4
6
8
10

12"

18

the angle is 90° - 18° = 72°

45

4"

Make the bevel board :

Standard - use 1/4" hardwood board, cut to size, draw angle lines (set gauge from large drafting protractor) in ink, 0° - 45° in 1° increments.

Deluxe - make board from 3/16" to 1/4" Plexiglas. Etch angle lines with a sharp awl. Rub permanent ink into lines.

BOATBUILDER'S BEVEL BOARD

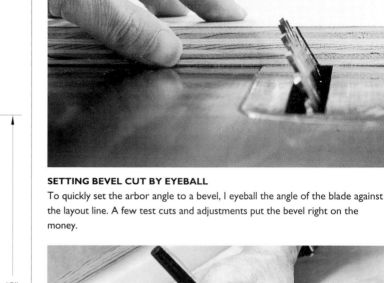

SETTING BEVEL CUT BY EYEBALL
To quickly set the arbor angle to a bevel, I eyeball the angle of the blade against the layout line. A few test cuts and adjustments put the bevel right on the money.

MARKING KERF POSITION ON THROAT PLATE
I can quickly set the rip fence to any desired width by marking the location of a beveled kerf cut into a piece of scrap on a strip of tape applied to the table ahead of the blade.

stock will have to be bevel-ripped with the fence on the right side of the blade.

This brings up another fundamental problem with bevel ripping with a right-tilting saw: Because the long edge of the bevel usually occurs on the exposed side of the workpiece, especially when making columns or boxes, you want this edge to be smooth and splinter free.

Unfortunately, when bevel-ripping on a right-tilt saw with the fence on the customary right side of the blade, this edge winds up on the bottom of the cut—the exit side of the stock, where most splintering occurs. Since I often make cabinets from sheet stock, I chose a left-tilting table saw for my stationary saw. The drawing shows the difference. Except for

these fence considerations, setting up for bevel ripping is essentially the same as that for basic ripping.

Basic Procedure
Begin by setting the angle of the blade. If I know the size of the angle in degrees, I place an angle gauge against the side of the blade and then crank the arbor to get

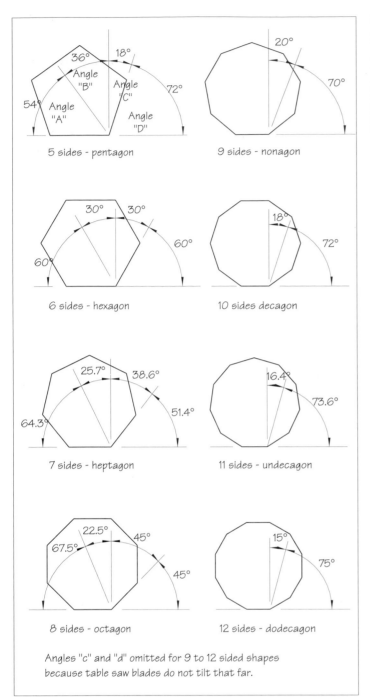

ANGLES FOR MANY-SIDED WORK PIECES

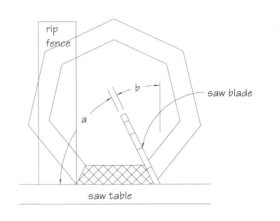

Angle "a" : Use when measuring from the saw table surface to bevel the edges of staves for gluing up.

Angle "b" : Use when measuring blade tilt with the saw's tilt scale to bevel the edges of staves for gluing up.

ANGLES FOR BEVELING STAVES

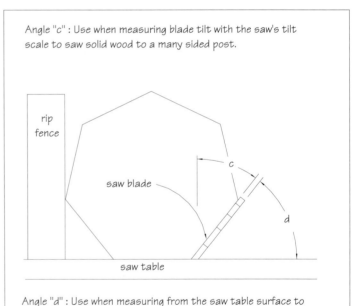

Angle "c" : Use when measuring blade tilt with the saw's tilt scale to saw solid wood to a many sided post.

Angle "d" : Use when measuring from the saw table surface to saw solid wood to a many sided post.

ANGLES FOR SAWING SOLID POSTS

the correct reading. (I only use the saw's angle indicator on the front face of the machine to give me a coarse reading of the blade's position.) I then lock down the crank and make a test cut, checking the angle with the shop-made gauge shown in Boatbuilder's Bevel Board.

If I'm cutting the bevel to match an existing angle on a full-scale drawing or actual structure, I don't bother to find out the number of degrees. Instead, I mark the angle on the end of the workpiece by

transferring it with the bevel gauge. I then set the workpiece on the table saw so I can eyeball the angle of the blade against the layout mark. I test cut to double-check the angle, adjusting the arbor angle as necessary.

To set the width of cut, I use the same test scrap (assuming it's the same thickness as the workpiece) and hold it against the fence and in front of the blade. I can easily sight across the layout marks to set the fence (see photo). Again, I make test

cuts to ensure accuracy.

Another way to set the rip fence to width is to mark the location of the kerf on the throat plate. To do this, set the fence at any convenient distance, run a scrap of wood into the blade a ½" or so and then back it out. Shut off the saw. When the blade stops, hold the scrap against the fence and mark on the throat plate where the kerf exits the bottom of the scrap (see photo). Note that the kerf position varies for each angle. I avoid a confusion of lines

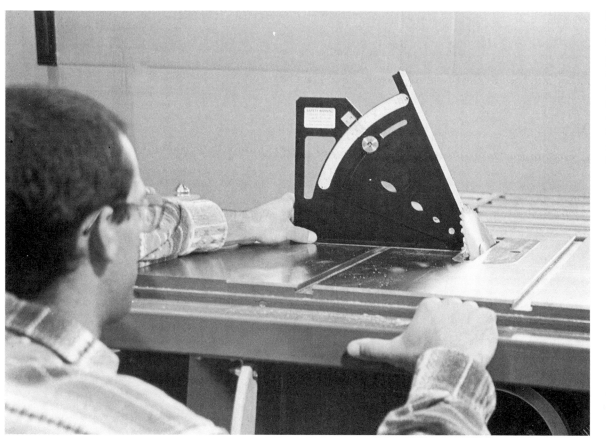

**SETTING HEPTAGON
TILT ANGLE 25.7°**
Using an AngleWright
precision protractor
designed specifically for
the table saw (see
source in Appendix), I
can set the arbor to a
specific angle. Here I'm
reading 25.7° to set up a
heptagon cut.

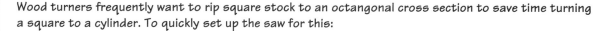

Wood turners frequently want to rip square stock to an octangonal cross section to save time turning
a square to a cylinder. To quickly set up the saw for this:

1. Tilt the blade to 45 degrees.
2. Lay the square against the blade.

3. Bring the fence up to touch the side
   of the stock and lock it.

4. Bevel-rip all four corners.

45°

fence

fence

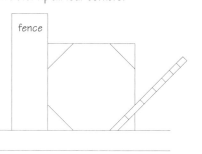

QUICK OCTAGON SETUP

by putting the mark on a piece of masking
tape and removing it after these particular
bevel cuts are made.

If the cut is going to be narrow (either
to the left or right of the rip fence), you
can make more room for the blade guard
and your push sticks by installing the low
auxiliary fence shown in chapter eight. In
making the bevel rip cut itself, follow the
same procedures outlined for the basic
rip cut.

CUTTING POLYGONAL SHAPES AND ASSEMBLIES

By cutting bevels around the circumference of a squared length of wood, you can
create many different polygonal posts.
The angle of the bevel determines the
number of facets and thus the type of
polygon. If you want to create a polygon
by edge-joining a series of boards or
staves, set the blade at a different angle:

the tilt angle [B] as shown in the drawing.
For any other type of polygon, apply this
formula: tilt angle = 180/N where N = the
number of sides. 180/7 = 25.7.

To taper the column in size from one
end to the other, cut the beveled rip at a
lengthwise angle. Using the same fixture
introduced earlier for making a straight-
sided taper cut, set the blade at the
desired angle and then carry the board
through the cut on the fixture.

Crosscutting

Crosscutting is a fairly general term. Among other things, it can refer to cutting across the grain, across a narrow strip of material that doesn't really have grain direction (such as most manufactured panel stock) or cutting more or less across the grain but at a bit of an angle. In this book, I will use the word "crosscut" to mean a cut that is 90°, plus or minus just a few, to the direction of the grain, and pretty close to 90° to the length of the board. I will use the term "miter" to mean a cut that is between 90° and 45° to the direction of the grain and the length of the board. If the cut is less than 45° to the grain direction, it is more like a rip than a crosscut, and, as I did in the last chapter, I'll call that cut a taper or a taper rip. As I also explained, you really need to pay attention to both the direction of the grain and the shape of the stock. Use a crosscut blade when the cut will be between 90° and 45° to the direction of the grain. Guide the stock with crosscutting devices such as the miter gauge, sled or sliding table when the cut will be 45° or more to the length of the stock.

In addition to the angle between the line of the cut and the edge of the board, we often find ourselves making bevel cuts. Bevel cuts are made at some angle other than 90° to the face of the board. When the cut is at an angle to both the edge and the face of the stock, as in bevel miters or bevel tapers, most woodworkers call it a compound angle cut.

In this chapter, I will discuss crosscuts, bevel crosscuts, miters and bevel miters, and present tables and formulas for the bevel and miter angles for a wide range of compound angle cuts.

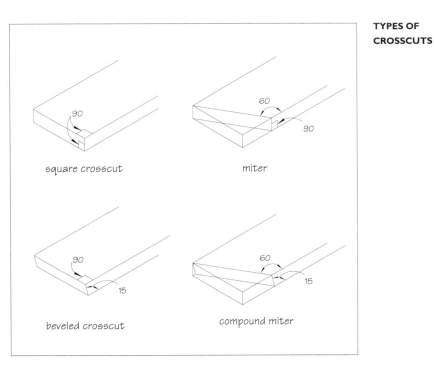

TYPES OF CROSSCUTS

square crosscut

miter

beveled crosscut

compound miter

BASIC CROSSCUTTING

The small-shop woodworker can choose from the two basic types of crosscutting guides: the miter gauge and the crosscut sled. Each have their place, usually determined by the size of the stock. Just as you wouldn't take a Mack truck to fetch a quart of milk from your local convenience store, it doesn't make much sense to use a massive, cast iron sliding table to trim a jewelry box drawer front to size. It amazes me, though, to see how many neophyte woodworkers try to do the opposite—trim a large cabinet door with a miter gauge, the equivalent of fetching a few cubic yards of gravel with the family sedan.

Crosscutting With a Miter Gauge

The miter gauge is appropriate if both the width and the length of the stock are within easily eyeballed limits. In width, the stock should fit comfortably between the miter gauge head and the blade with a

> **S A F E T Y *tip***
>
> ### NEVER CROSSCUT FREE-HAND ON A TABLE SAW!
> If you inadvertently twist the stock even a tiny bit, the blade will jam in the kerf and throw the piece off the table with tremendous force.

couple inches to spare and with the miter gauge head at least partially on the saw table. Don't try to use the miter gauge if the width of the stock causes the head of the gauge to extend off the table top—the head is liable to catch or the edge of the table partway through the cut.

A workpiece is too long for the miter gauge if the middle of the board—the balance point—will be off the edge of the saw table both after and before the cut. To crosscut larger stock, use a crosscut sled or sliding table.

But even these size limits are too gen-

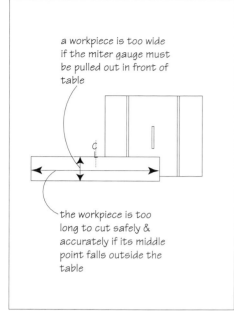

a workpiece is too wide if the miter gauge must be pulled out in front of table

the workpiece is too long to cut safely & accurately if its middle point falls outside the table

BOARD SIZE LIMITATION WHEN USING MITER GAUGE

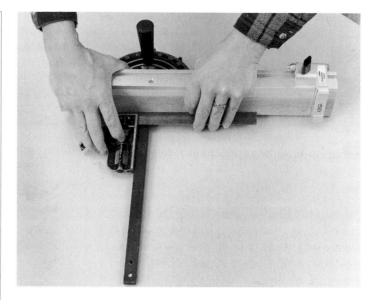

SETTING MITER GAUGE TO COMBINATION SQUARE
It's quick and accurate to set the miter gauge to 0° by holding a try square between the head and the bar.

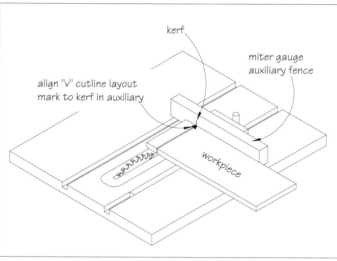

kerf

miter gauge auxiliary fence

align "V" cutline layout mark to kerf in auxiliary

workpiece

SETUP OF BOARD ON MITER GAUGE AUXILIARY FENCE

erous for the miter gauge as it comes from the manufacturer. Furnish your miter gauge with an auxiliary fence, as described in chapter three. Through side-to-side adjustment, it should be able to extend beyond the blade on the right and to the edge of the table on the left. Without the fence, crosscutting is dangerous and less accurate because of the small bearing surface afforded by the miter gauge head. The lack of adequate support can allow the board to shift during the cut, jam against the blade and kick back.

To prevent shifting of the workpiece, always hold it against a stop block clamped to the fence, even if you're only cutting one piece to that length. Also apply a strip of sandpaper to the face of the fence with double stick tape or spray adhesive to further prevent shifting.

The Cutting Procedure

Set up the miter gauge for making a square crosscut by squaring the gauge head, and thus the attached fence, to the bar. Use a commercial setup fixture as described in chapter two, or simply hold a combination square against the gauge. With the blade raised about ⅜", make a test cut across an 8"-wide strip of ¼" plywood to confirm the setting. Readjust the head and angle stop as necessary. When satisfied, raise the blade about ¼" above the thickness of the stock

and push the gauge forward until the blade cuts to this height into the fence. Then align a mark on your stock with this kerf when crosscutting.

To crosscut a board to length, first mark the length on the face of the stock that will be up during the cut. Make this *V* mark at the edge of the board that will be against the miter gauge fence. Place an *X* on the waste area of the board so you won't confuse which side of the *V* mark the kerf must fall on. Now, assuming the waste is to the right, place the stock against the miter gauge fence and align the mark with the left edge of the kerf you cut into the fence. To ensure the board won't shift during the cut, slide a stop (either a commercial fixture or a square block of wood) against the left end of the board and clamp it firmly to the auxiliary fence. You can fine-tune the position of the board by loosening and gently hand-

tapping the stop to either side, or by turning the microadjustment screw on certain commercial miter gauge systems.

Now make the cut by pushing the miter gauge across the table with your right hand as your left hand holds the board against the fence (on my commercial miter gauge, the integral clamp also serves as a push handle). Push the assembly of board and fence past the blade. For the smoothest and most accurate cut, don't pull the board backward past the blade after cutting it off. Instead, shut off the saw, wait for the blade to stop, and then remove the board and its offcut.

Crosscutting With a Double Miter Gauge System

A clever way to increase the accuracy when cutting with a miter gauge is to add a second gauge, joining them together with a fence. This system is easier to build

TRIMMING AN END SQUARE

To trim one end of a board square prior to cutting the other end to length, you can use the Flip-Up Stop System, the Spacer System or the Double Miter Gauge System.

FLIP-UP STOP SYSTEM

Use either a ruler or a layout stick to set a commercial or shop-made flip-up stop as the stop block for the crosscut. To make the preliminary square cut, flip the stop up out of the way and then hold the stock firmly against the fence. Cut one end square, making sure you remove any end splits. Now flip the stop down, turn the board end for end, place it against the stop and make the cut to length.

SPACER SYSTEM

This method may be low tech, but it works just fine. Start by posi-

tioning a stop block as necessary for the final length cut and clamping it to the fence. Now set a second block of wood, exactly the same thickness as the stop block, just to the left of the kerf in the fence. Hold the board against both blocks and trim one end of the stock square. Then remove the second block, hold the end of the board against the first block and cut to length.

DOUBLE MITER GAUGE SYSTEM

If you have two miter gauges for your saw, you can trim one end square with the second miter gauge in the right-hand miter gauge groove. Then shift to the left-hand gauge, holding the square cut against a stop block set for the desired length. Use an auxiliary fence on the right-hand miter gauge for the same reasons you use one on the left-hand gauge.

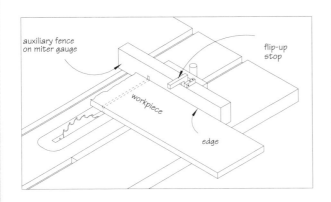

first cut: set stop to length of cut, then flip out of the way.
Cut about 1" in from rough end of board.

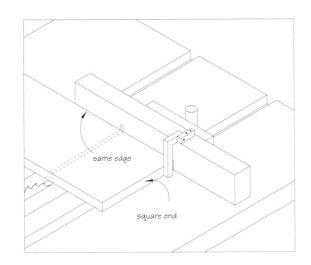

second cut: flip board end for end, place squared end against flipped-down stop and cut to length

FLIP-UP STOP SEQUENCE FOR END SQUARING

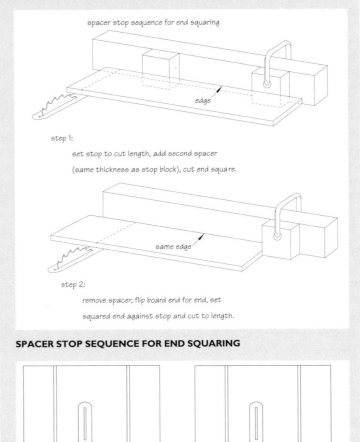

spacer stop sequence for end squaring

step 1:

set stop to cut length, add second spacer

(same thickness as stop block), cut end square.

step 2:

remove spacer, flip board end for end, set

squared end against stop and cut to length.

SPACER STOP SEQUENCE FOR END SQUARING

1. make first cut to square end of board with work in right-hand miter gauge

2. cut work to length with miter gauge in left-hand groove, and auxiliary fence set up with stop set to finished lenath

DOUBLE MITER GAUGE SEQUENCE FOR END SQUARING

and lighter than a crosscut sled, while offering nearly as much accuracy and versatility. But like the sled, the double miter gauge carries the offcuts away from the blade where they cannot vibrate into the blade and kick back. Because I designed the fence fixture with a sliding bolt attachment, I can adjust the miter gauges to angles other than 90° to the blade.

Make the fence from two strips of ¾" maple plywood, glued together against a straightedge (such as a 48" level). Cap the fence in the area where the fence encounters the blade; use a 12"-long piece of hard maple as a stiffener (the fence becomes weakened with the saw kerf). Inlay two lengths of MiniTrack on the side of the fence facing the miter gauge heads, and attach the heads with bolts and knobs, as shown in the drawing in chapter five. The track allows the heads to slide from side to side as they change their relationship to each other at angles other than 90° to the blade. If you wish, you can add a sliding stop to index the cut, speeding multiple cuts and increasing accuracy by providing a positive stop against the end of the workpiece.

Cutting Multiple Short Lengths

While you can cut multiple pieces from the end of long stock by repeatedly using the stop on the miter gauge's auxiliary fence, the procedure is awkward and dangerous when cutting short lengths. There is a better way.

Keep the long, uncut end of the stock against the miter gauge fence, and cut the desired pieces from the other end—so the offcut is the desired piece. To position the stock for the cut, butt it against a stop to the right of the blade, then hold the stock firmly to the miter gauge fence as you push the piece forward to make the cut.

Most woodworkers using this procedure clamp the stop block to the rip fence so the block is easy to adjust by moving the rip fence. This works fine as long as

> **SAFETY** *tip*
>
> Never hold onto the workpiece on both sides of the blade. This could cause the offcut to bind just before it releases from the workpiece.

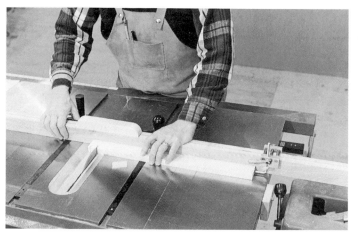

DOUBLE MITER GAUGE SYSTEM
Joining two miter gauges with a fence increases the accuracy and safety of the crosscut.

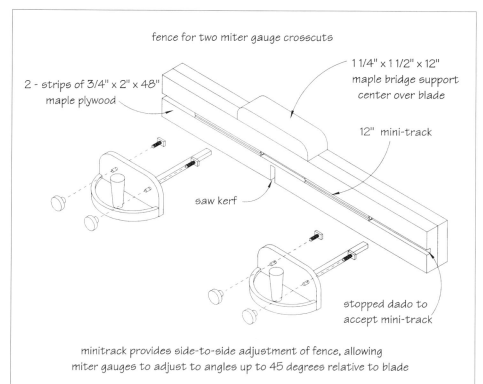

fence for two miter gauge crosscuts

2 - strips of 3/4" x 2" x 48" maple plywood

1 1/4" x 1 1/2" x 12" maple bridge support center over blade

12" mini-track

saw kerf

stopped dado to accept mini-track

minitrack provides side-to-side adjustment of fence, allowing miter gauges to adjust to angles up to 45 degrees relative to blade

CONSTRUCTION DRAWING OF FENCE FIXTURE

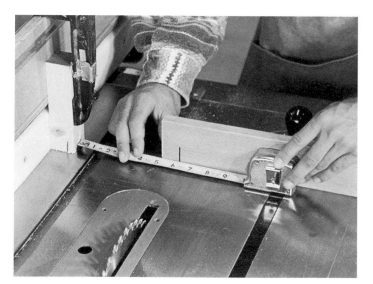

SETTING UP A STOP ON A RIP FENCE
This photograph shows measuring from the stop block (clamped to the fence) to the kerf in the miter gauge fence.

you make certain the stop block is well forward (toward you) of the blade. If the stop block overlaps the front of the blade even a little bit, there is a serious danger that the offcut will twist and jam between the blade and the stop block. This is a common error for inexperienced woodworkers who simply put the stop block where it's most convenient to measure the distance to the blade. To do it right, mark the desired length on the stock, measuring from the right end of the stock. With the miter gauge well forward of the blade, line up the mark with the right side of the kerf in the miter gauge fence. Now slide the rip fence over until the stop block on the rip fence just touches the end of the stock, and lock down the fence. You can now cut multiples by butting the stock against the stop block, holding the stock firmly to the miter gauge fence, making the cut and repeating as necessary. When offcuts start to accumulate between the blade and fence, turn off the saw, let the blade come to a stop and then remove them.

Crosscutting With a Sled

The standard miter gauge, despite being quite versatile and convenient, has several shortcomings: The head is likely to catch on the edge of the saw table if you try to crosscut wide stock, friction between the stock and the saw table can make it difficult to keep the stock in position against the fence, the area of contact between the stock and the gauge is usually limited to the edge of the stock, and the small dimensions of the gauge make it difficult to securely lock the protractor head to the bar, to name a few.

The crosscut sled overcomes these shortcomings by introducing a thin, flat "subtable" between the bar that follows the miter gauge groove and the head, or fence. This subtable eliminates direct friction between the stock and the saw table, and increases the area of contact with the stock, allowing you to cut much wider and heavier workpieces with precise control.

Crosscut sleds are often custom-made to meet individual needs and preferences, though commercial ones are available. Many woodworkers have a collection of these sleds, each designed to meet specific needs. I use larger-size sleds to cut

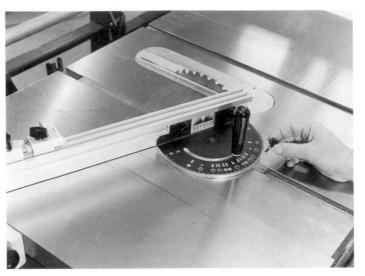

AFTERMARKET MITER GAUGE
Note the pin that locks head to certain common angle settings.

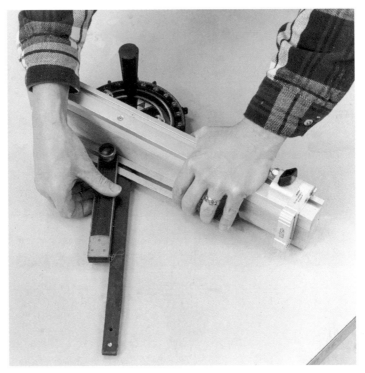

SETTING THE ANGLE OF THE MITER GAUGE
I set the miter gauge to index a nonstopped angle setting by holding a bevel gauge set to the desired angle between the gauge head (with its fence system) and the bar.

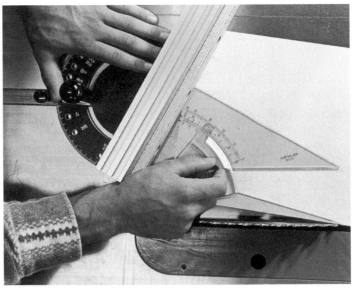

SETTING THE MITER GAUGE TO AN ADJUSTABLE TRIANGLE
The scale is on the triangle, white paper is underneath. They are positioned relative to the miter gauge head and bar.

STOP BLOCK FOR SHORT OFFCUTS

This unique shop-made end stop features a quick-acting end stop and an integral table clamp, bringing speed and safety to the process of cutting multiple small pieces from the end of a board. It offers a safer option (relative to using a block clamped to the rip fence) for indexing short cut lengths from the end of a workpiece. By eliminating the rip fence, you rule out the hazard of having an offcut jam between the spinning blade and the face of the rip fence and fire back at you. As a bonus, setting up the cut with this fixture is fast.

As shown in the drawing to the right, build the fixture from scraps of ¾" and ½" maple plywood. Hardware includes a 24"-long piece of MiniTrack (which you will inlay into a groove), a flat-based T-nut and some knobs. The guide runner, a strip of ¼" plywood, holds the base square to the miter gauge groove, and thus the blade. To properly orient the base to the guide runner strip, set the strip into the miter groove on some pennies or washers placed in the bottom of the groove (to lift the strip slightly above the saw table). Apply double stick tape to the strip, and then lay down the base as you orient it perpendicular to the groove with the help of a framing square. Be sure the end of the base projects about ¼" past the left side of the blade. Lift the base and the stuck strips, and screw them permanently in place. Cut away a section of the strip to allow room for the T-nut. Now place the fixture back on the table, turn on the saw and run it into the blade, cutting off the projecting ¼" of the base. This end of the base plate can now serve as an index for setting the stop.

To set up the fixture for use, move the rip fence out of the way (at least 24" away from the blade) and lay the fixture along the front edge of the saw table with the runner set into the miter gauge groove. Turn the base plate lockdown knob to secure the fixture in place. Set the stop to the desired length by measuring (or indexing to a story stick) from the blade end of the base plate to the end of the sliding stop. Lock down the stop. Note: If a different blade is used, or the end of the base becomes worn, slide the fixture forward so you can measure from the stop directly to the blade; then slide the fixture back to the front edge of the saw table and lock it down. To make the cut in the workpiece, hold its edge against the miter gauge, which is set in the left-hand groove, and slide it over until its end bears against the stop. Now move the miter gauge forward, carrying the work through the blade. Repeat the process until the board becomes too short to hold against the miter gauge head. The photo to the right shows the fixture in use.

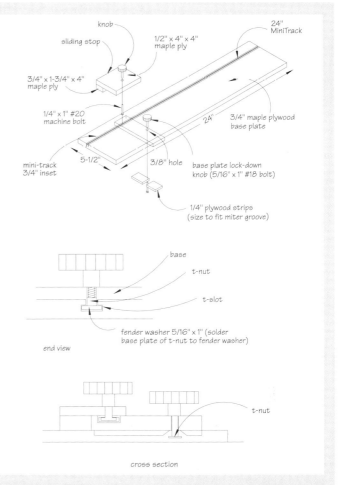

---

plywood case components and cabinet doors to length, and smaller sleds to cut frame parts and moldings (see chapter three for information on how to build these sleds, and chapter eight for a specialized sled for cutting small and odd-shaped workpieces).

When using a sled, especially a larger variety, make sure it is supported level to the side and back of the saw (if cutting large panels it may need support to the front as well). I always use my jointer-sup-port fixture and the outfeed rollers mounted to the back of my saw when using sleds. Adequate support is much more than just convenience. By freeing your mind and muscle to concentrate on guiding the sled and stock, your work will be much safer and more accurate because the danger of losing control is all but eliminated.

Cutting with a sled is delightfully straightforward. After ensuring adequate support, sweep out the miter gauge slot(s) and lay the sled on the table. Set the stop block if necessary to index the width of cut. Now pull the sled far enough back from the blade to allow the workpiece to lie against the fence without touching the blade. Keeping your hands shoulder-width apart to either side of the blade, slide the work against the block, turn on the saw and push the sled across the table until it hits the integral stop. Turn off the saw, allow the blade to stop and then pull the sled back to remove the workpiece and offcut.

Crosscutting End Bevels

If a workpiece is less than 8" wide, you can lay it horizontal and cut the end bevel using the miter gauge with an auxiliary fence as a guide. But if you need to cut a bevel or chamfer on the end of a wide board or panel, you need some way to guide the workpiece upright through the blade. If the workpiece is perfectly flat and easy to handle (less than a square foot), you can use the universal fence fixture as a support guide. If, however, the workpiece is bowed—or you want assurance of accuracy—use the rip fence sled fixture to take advantage of its integral clamping system, which holds the board flat for you as the fixture carries it through the blade.

MITERS

As I mentioned at the beginning of this chapter, a miter is a cut across a board or strip of panel stock at an angle of 45° to nearly 90°. I consider less than 45° a taper. Though compound miter saws get all the press for miter work—they are, admittedly, easy to set up and are portable for jobsite work—the table saw is still my tool of choice for mitering. I find I can saw miters with more precision and safety on the table saw than on the powered miter box. The secret is in the rigidity of the table saw's arbor and support structure and the use of a good, stock-supporting fixture like the miter gauge or sled.

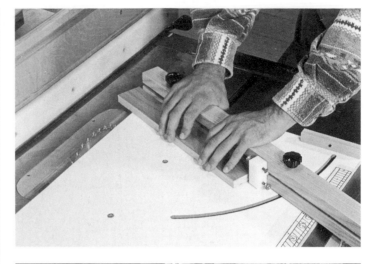

DUBBY SLED IN USE SHOWING ITS ANGLED FENCE SYSTEM, OFFCUT ON TABLE

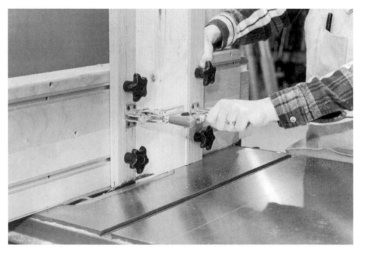

SHOP-MADE CROSS-CUT SLED IN USE
I'm pushing a sled with the workpiece indexed to stop; side and back roller supports in view.

CUTTING AN END BEVEL
I can crosscut an end bevel with a high level of accuracy and safety—even if the board is slightly bowed—by using my rip fence sled fixture. The secret is the two vertical stops that prevent shifting and the toggle clamps that secure the board flat to the fixture.

Using a Miter Gauge

The miter gauge is essentially a protractor, and cutting the end of a workpiece at a specific angle is a simple matter of fixing the head of the miter gauge at that angle. Most standard miter gauges have stops for cutting miters at 45° and 60° from the edge of the workpiece. Aftermarket varieties have additional stops for miters of 80°, 75° and 67.5°.

Gauges vary, however, in how their scales are labeled. Some gauges label the position for a square crosscut as 90 and miter settings by the angle between the cut and the edge of the workpiece. Others label the position for a square crosscut as 0 and miter settings by the number of degrees that they deviate from a square crosscut. Some mark the angles both ways.

When adjusting a miter gauge to an

angle for which there is no stop, you have to decide between adjusting by the angular measurement in degrees and adjusting to the actual application. I usually prefer to avoid the potential errors of measurement by setting a bevel gauge from the project itself and then setting the miter gauge to the bevel gauge.

To adjust the miter gauge to a setting for which there is no stop, first set your bevel gauge according to the project plans, or directly from the actual surfaces that you need to match. Now hold the stock of the bevel gauge against the bar of the miter gauge and swing the head of the miter gauge until the fence aligns with the tongue of the bevel gauge. Lock down the miter gauge. Test cut scrap to ensure you have set the correct angle.

If you choose to set the miter gauge by the measurement of the angle (sometimes you have no choice), you can use the scale that's built into the miter gauge if it's sufficiently accurate and readable. Otherwise, use an adjustable drafting triangle as shown. Note that a piece of white paper slipped under the triangle makes it easier to read. Or you can use an adjustable triangle made specifically for woodworking.

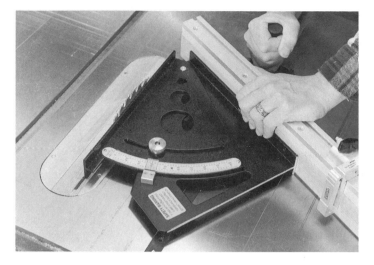

ANGLEWRIGHT GAUGE
This adjustable triangle, featuring large index surfaces and a precision angle scale, is made specifically for woodworkers. Source in appendix.

PREVENTING CREEP

A sure way to stop creep is to use the open position whenever possible. In this position, the cutting strain pushes the workpiece against the stop, eliminating creep entirely. If the workpiece is long, however, you may have no choice but to go with the closed position to gain the support of the tabletop surface (unless you take the time to set up infeed supports). In this case, set up the miter gauge to minimize creep in one or more of these ways: (1) Increase the bearing surface of the end stop by cutting it to complement the angle of the miter cut; (2) use double stick tape to attach a strip of sandpaper to the face of the auxiliary fence; (3) install retractable pins (the tips of screws) to the fence; (4) use the integral clamp of an aftermarket miter gauge to hold the workpiece against the miter gauge bar, or use a throat clamp to hold the workpiece against the face of the fence.

OPEN AND CLOSED MITER POSITIONS

Closed Position

ADVANTAGE
- The natural, comfortable position of the body is safely out of the line of fire of the blade.

DISADVANTAGES
- The cutting forces tend to pull the stock away from the stop block.
- At the end of the cut, the miter gauge tends to run out of groove and the stock needs outfeed support.

Open Position

ADVANTAGES
- The cutting forces tend to push the stock against the stop block.
- The miter gauge bar and the stock remain well supported at the end of the cut.

DISADVANTAGE
- A safe body position, out of the line of fire, feels awkward to many.

closed miter position:
cutting action shear force pulls workpiece away from stop

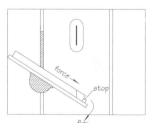

note: you could extend the fence to the right of the blade and set the stop on the right, but the disadvantage is that the gauge or fence can flex and throw off the cut

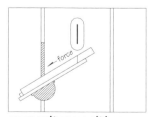

open miter position:
cutting action shear force pushes workpiece against stop

MAKING A MITER SLED

Refer to my notes for building a crosscut sled in chapter three before constructing this fixture, as the same principles of construction and setup apply. There are, however, certain things to watch for with this sled.

When selecting a piece of plywood for the base of the sled, be sure it is perfectly flat; a bow or warp across the long diagonal will throw off the miter cut. Also, carefully orient both fences to 45° before locking them down with additional screws (see the detail in the drawing for testing a cut for a perfect 45°). Finally, because an angled crosscut tries to move a workpiece sideways during the cut, don't neglect to add a strip of sandpaper to the face of both fences to increase friction.

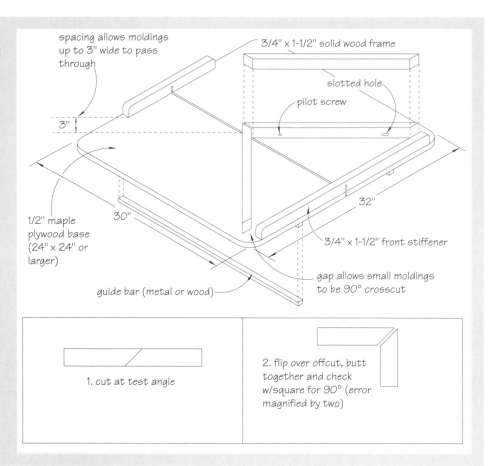

spacing allows moldings up to 3" wide to pass through

3/4" x 1-1/2" solid wood frame

slotted hole

pilot screw

3"

1/2" maple plywood base (24" x 24" or larger)

30"

32"

3/4" x 1-1/2" front stiffener

guide bar (metal or wood)

gap allows small moldings to be 90° crosscut

1. cut at test angle

2. flip over offcut, butt together and check w/square for 90° (error magnified by two)

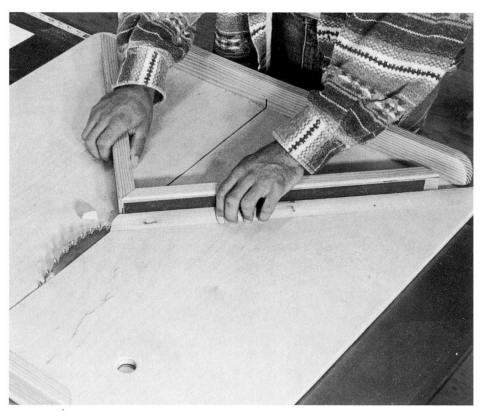

SHOP-MADE MITER SLED IN USE
Small molding in the process of being cut; small trim offcuts are in view.

When setting the angle, you have a choice of which way to swing the head. With the miter gauge in the left-hand slot, swinging the head clockwise creates a "closed" cutting situation while swinging it counterclockwise creates an "open" cut. Refer to the sidebar summarizing the pros and cons of these two positions. It is worthwhile to consider these pros and cons and then, regardless of the position you choose, keep in mind the potential dangers of that position.

Though there may be more advantages for the open position, I almost always take the closed position. That way, I can minimize the dangers of the closed position but can't do anything about the awkwardness of the open position. To make the closed position work safely, I provide outfeed support and I clamp the stock to the auxiliary fence. The clamp keeps the stock from creeping along the fence (referred to simply as creep) and keeps my hands safely away from the blade. I also stick sandpaper to the miter gauge fence to increase friction.

Mitering With a Sled

When you want to cut 45° miters with great efficiency, safety and accuracy, use a shop-made dedicated miter sled similar to the crosscut sled discussed earlier. The sled's fences are permanently attached at a specific angle, speeding setup time and ensuring accuracy. By using a pair of fences, one on the right and one on the left, you can cut both sides of the miter joint with the same fixture. Unlike the miter gauge, the miter sled is guided by two runners, helping to eliminate shifting of the sled during the cut. Finally, the base of the sled carries offcuts, even tiny trim cuts of small moldings, safely away from the blade. A drawback is that the sled's base eats up a little cutting-height capacity. Refer to the complete plans for the miter sled.

Quick Setup Miter Jig With Stop

When I want to cut a square or rectangular frame, I use the quick setup miter jig for quick cuts. The design (adapted from woodworker and magazine editor Tim Snyder) allows me to make both end cuts on each frame piece. Without having to reset a stop, the first cut creates one mitered end, the second cut the finished length. As you can see in the drawing above, the trick is using both sides of the fence with the front side of the fence outfitted with a sliding and locking stop system.

Make the base of the fixture from a flat sheet of ¾" maple plywood and the fence from a 2¼" strip of the same material. Attach the runner to the base as described earlier, and groove the top of the fence to receive a length of MiniTrack (alternative: make a T-slot for a toilet bolt).

To attach the fence to the base at a precise 45° angle to the blade, use your combination square to draw a line at 45°, beginning 4" back from the far end of the base. Screw the fence along the line with just two screws initially: a screw at the top to act as a pivot and a screw through a slotted hole near the bottom to allow for fine adjustment. Allow the end of the fence to project slightly past the edge of the base so the blade can trim it precisely to length. Make a test cut by cutting a miter in one end of two scrap strips of wood. If the angle is 45°, when you hold

the miters against one another the joined strips will form a perfect right angle. When satisfied, add screws to secure the fence to the base.

To use the jig, make the first cut by holding the workpiece against the back edge of the fence, projecting its end an inch or so past the blade. A strip of sandpaper applied to the fence edge with carpet tape or spray adhesive prevents any tendency for slippage (which can throw off the angle). Mark the desired length of this frame component on the long side by measuring from the tip of the miter. Insert

the mitered end into the stop and slide the stop until the layout mark aligns with the mitered end of the fence. Lock down the stop. Proceed to cut this component to length and then its mate. If you are creating a square, all four sides are cut at this setting.

Angle Fixtures for Mitering

A simple angle fixture for cutting miters gives you some of the advantages of the dedicated miter sled without building (and having to store) a complete sled. Moreover, you can use the angle fixture

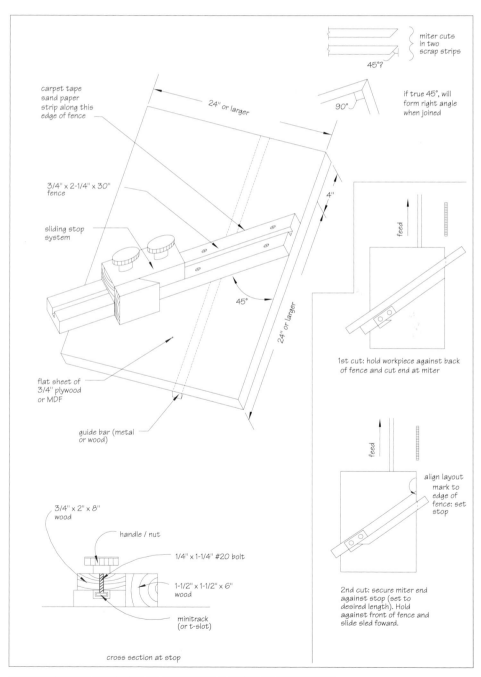

CONSTRUCTION DRAWING OF QUICK SETUP MITER JIG WITH STOP

with either a miter gauge or a crosscut sled. With the miter gauge or sled fence still at the position for a square crosscut, clamp the angle fixture to the fence and hold the stock against the front edge of the fixture. You don't have to tediously set and reset the miter gauge every time you need to cut a miter; by making angle fixtures for the miter angles that you cut often, you'll never have to worry about whether an angle stop is correctly set and you can set up nonstopped angles as quickly and easily as the more common angles.

CUTTING POLYGONS

In the chapter on ripping, I discussed beveling staves for gluing into curved surfaces and bevel-ripping solid stock to create solid, many-sided posts. The flat-stock equivalents of these shapes are the many-sided frame and the solid polygon. Since they are created by mitering instead of by beveling, you can use the bevel angles from the list of table saw miter and bevel angles at the end of this chapter to adjust

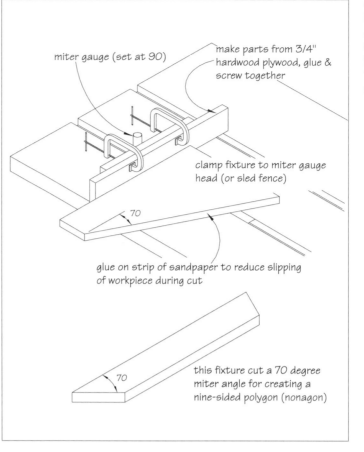

miter gauge (set at 90)

make parts from 3/4" hardwood plywood, glue & screw together

clamp fixture to miter gauge head (or sled fence)

70

glue on strip of sandpaper to reduce slipping of workpiece during cut

70

this fixture cut a 70 degree miter angle for creating a nine-sided polygon (nonagon)

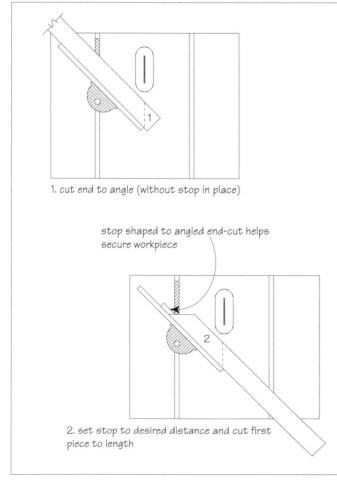

1. cut end to angle (without stop in place)

stop shaped to angled end-cut helps secure workpiece

2

2. set stop to desired distance and cut first piece to length

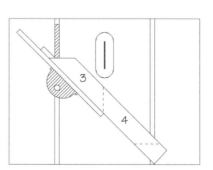

3

4

3. flip board over, set to stop and cut second piece

4. flip board and cut last segment

ACCURACY IS ESSENTIAL

A frame with as few as 6 sides involves 12 miter cuts, one on each end of all 6 frame members. If your miter gauge or sled is off by as little as a 0.5°, the error of closure will be a whopping 6°—and the need for precision goes up with the number of sides. If miscut parts are brought together tightly, the cumulative error will show as either a frame that doesn't come together or one that overlaps at the last joint.

A fail-safe way to check the angle setting is to cut all of the parts from scrap stock, tape the miters tightly together and see how the last piece fits. If it won't go in, readjust the angle closer toward being a square crosscut. If there's too much room for the last piece, readjust the angle to deviate farther from a square crosscut. Then use the new angle to trim both ends of all of the parts and try again. Note that for this test to work the parts must be cut to the same length, so use a stop fixture.

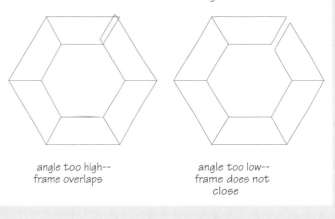

Results of miscut angles

angle too high--
frame overlaps

angle too low--
frame does not
close

your miter gauge. (In practice, you can probably calculate the angle faster than you can look it up in a table: Dividing 180° by the number of sides gives you the miter gauge setting for the frame members, assuming your miter gauge reads 0 for a square crosscut.)

If you are at all frugal with your time and your wood, you will quickly realize that you can save both by flipping a board over for each subsequent cut of frame members, as shown. Select your stock carefully if you intend to cut it this way, however. If grain and coloration aren't similar on both sides of the stock, the segments making up the frame will look poorly matched. Since frame members of this sort are usually fairly small, and since flamboyant grain doesn't usually look good in small parts, I commonly choose quartersawn stock for frames. Most often, this avoids the mismatch problem, allowing me to cut with the greatest economy. Otherwise, when circumstances dictate that the same face of the stock show on all parts, I abandon economy and either set up two miter gauges, cutting one miter on the left-hand gauge and the opposite miter on the gauge to the right, or, if I'm making a square or rectangle, use my shop-made miter sled, cutting the first miter with the stock against one fence and the second miter with the stock against the other.

Cutting Compound Angles

You can, with care, combine miters and bevels to create shapes with tapered, or tilted, sides. There are two ways to go about it: the direct, or preindustrial, method and the bevel-miter method. Your best choice will depend on the size of the stock, the capacity of your saw

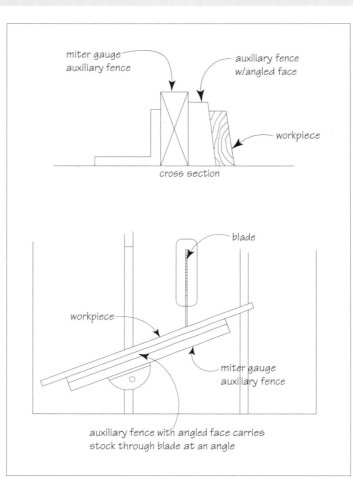

DIRECT METHOD FOR CUTTING COMPOUND MITERS

miter gauge auxiliary fence

auxiliary fence w/angled face

workpiece

cross section

blade

workpiece

miter gauge auxiliary fence

auxiliary fence with angled face carries stock through blade at an angle

and your ability to create a mental image of what you're doing and keep it in mind as you work.

The Direct Method

The direct method works best with relatively narrow stock, such as for shallow boxes, picture frames with tilted sides or

TABLE SAW MITER AND BEVEL ANGLES

Pitch		Number of Sides									
		3	4	5	6	7	8	9	10	11	12
0°	Miter angle	60.0°	45.0°	36.0°	30.0°	25.7°	22.5°	20.0°	18.0°	16.4°	15.0°
5°	Miter angle	59.9°	44.9°	35.9°	29.9°	25.6°	22.4°	19.9°	17.9°	16.3°	14.9°
	Bevel angle	85.7°	86.5°	87.1°	87.5°	87.8°	88.1°	88.3°	88.5°	88.6°	88.7°
10°	Miter angle	59.6°	44.6°	35.6°	29.6°	25.4°	22.2°	19.7°	17.7°	16.1°	14.8°
	Bevel angle	81.4°	82.9°	84.1°	85.0°	85.7°	86.2°	86.6°	86.9°	87.2°	87.4°
15°	Miter angle	59.1°	44.0°	35.1°	29.1°	24.9°	21.8°	19.4°	17.4°	15.8°	14.5°
	Bevel angle	77.0°	79.5°	81.2°	82.6°	83.6°	84.3°	84.9°	85.4°	85.8°	86.2°
20°	Miter angle	58.4°	43.2°	34.3°	28.5°	24.3°	21.3°	18.9°	17.0°	15.4°	14.1°
	Bevel angle	72.8°	76.0°	78.4°	80.2°	81.5°	82.5°	83.3°	83.9°	84.5°	84.9°
25°	Miter angle	57.5°	42.2°	33.4°	27.6°	23.6°	20.6°	18.3°	16.4°	14.9°	13.6°
	Bevel angle	68.5°	72.6°	75.6°	77.8°	79.4°	80.7°	81.7°	82.5°	83.2°	83.7°
30°	Miter angle	56.3°	40.9°	32.2°	26.6°	22.6°	19.7°	17.5°	15.7°	14.3°	13.1°
	Bevel angle	64.3°	69.3°	72.9°	75.5°	77.5°	79.0°	80.2°	81.1°	81.9°	82.6°
35°	Miter angle	54.8°	39.3°	30.8°	25.3°	21.5°	18.7°	16.6°	14.9°	13.5°	12.4°
	Bevel angle	60.2°	66.1°	70.3°	73.3°	75.6°	77.3°	78.7°	79.8°	80.7°	81.5°
40°	Miter angle	53.0°	37.5°	29.1°	23.9°	20.2°	17.6°	15.6°	14.0°	12.7°	11.6°
	Bevel angle	56.2°	63.0°	67.8°	71.3°	73.8°	75.8°	77.3°	78.5°	79.6°	80.4°
45°	Miter angle	50.8°	35.3°	27.2°	22.2°	18.8°	16.3°	14.4°	12.9°	11.7°	10.7°
	Bevel angle	52.2°	60.0°	65.4°	69.3°	72.1°	74.3°	76.0°	77.4°	78.5°	79.5°
50°	Miter angle	48.1°	32.7°	25.0°	20.4°	17.2°	14.9°	13.2°	11.8°	10.7°	9.8°
	Bevel angle	48.4°	57.2°	63.2°	67.5°	70.6°	73.0°	74.8°	76.3°	77.5°	78.6°
55°	Miter angle	44.8°	29.8°	22.6°	18.3°	15.4°	13.4°	11.8°	10.6°	9.6°	8.7°
	Bevel angle	44.8°	54.6°	61.2°	65.8°	69.2°	71.7°	73.7°	75.3°	76.7°	77.8°
60°	Miter angle	40.9°	26.6°	20.0°	16.1°	13.5°	11.7°	10.3°	9.2°	8.4°	7.6°
	Bevel angle	41.4°	52.2°	59.4°	64.3°	67.9°	70.6°	72.8°	74.5°	75.9°	77.0°
65°	Miter angle	36.2°	22.9°	17.1°	13.7°	11.5°	9.9°	8.7°	7.8°	7.1°	6.5°
	Bevel angle	38.3°	50.1°	57.8°	63.1°	66.8°	69.7°	71.9°	73.7°	75.2°	76.4°
70°	Miter angle	30.6°	18.9°	14.0°	11.2°	9.4°	8.1°	7.1°	6.3°	5.7°	5.2°
	Bevel angle	35.5°	48.4°	56.5°	62.0°	65.9°	68.9°	71.3°	73.1°	74.6°	75.9°
75°	Miter angle	24.1°	14.5°	10.6°	8.5°	7.1°	6.1°	5.4°	4.8°	4.3°	4.0°
	Bevel angle	33.2°	46.9°	55.4°	61.1°	65.2°	68.3°	70.7°	72.6°	74.2°	75.5°
80°	Miter angle	16.7°	9.9°	7.2°	5.7°	4.8°	4.1°	3.6°	3.2°	2.9°	2.7°
	Bevel angle	31.5°	45.9°	54.6°	60.5°	64.7°	67.9°	70.3°	72.3°	73.9°	75.2°
85°	Miter angle	8.6°	5.0°	3.6°	2.9°	2.4°	2.1°	1.8°	1.6°	1.5°	1.3°
	Bevel angle	30.4°	45.2°	54.2°	60.1°	64.4°	67.6°	70.1°	72.1°	73.7°	75.1°
90°	Bevel angle	30.0°	45.0°	54.0°	60.0°	64.3°	67.5°	70.0°	72.0°	73.6°	75.0°

USING THE MITER AND BEVEL ANGLE CHART ON PAGE 104

The miter angle given in the table is the amount that the cut deviates from a square cut. For example, as shown here, the miter gauge is set at 35.3°, correct for a 4-sided construction with sides that have a 45° pitch. Most miter gauges are marked to read this way.

The bevel angle given in the table is the angle between the saw table and the blade, not the tilt as shown on the saw's tilt scale. In the sample drawing here, the bevel angle is 60°, correct for a 4-sided construction with sides having a 45° pitch.

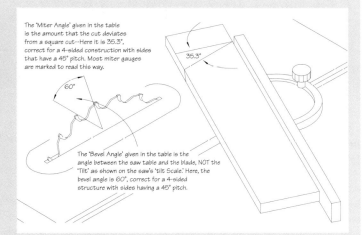

The 'Miter Angle' given in the table is the amount that the cut deviates from a square cut--Here it is 35.3°, correct for a 4-sided construction with sides that have a 45° pitch. Most miter gauges are marked to read this way.

The 'Bevel Angle' given in the table is the angle between the saw table and the blade, NOT the 'Tilt' as shown on the saw's 'tilt Scale.' Here, the bevel angle is 60°, correct for a 4-sided structure with sides having a 45° pitch.

crown moldings of modest width. If you're familiar with good, old-fashioned miter boxes, you'll recognize this as a table saw application of the same principle. To use the direct method on the table saw, first bevel-rip the front face of an auxiliary fence for your miter gauge to the desired tilt angle. By holding the face of the stock against this tilted fence face, you can miter the ends of the stock using the same miter angles as for a frame with no tilt. When setting up the saw and making the cuts for crown molding, I find it easier to keep track of just what I'm doing if I constantly remind myself that the saw table corresponds to the ceiling, the room is upside down and the fence is the wall. In the case of a picture frame, I remind myself that the picture is face up on the saw table.

The Bevel-Miter Method

The bevel-miter method avoids the need for a tilted miter gauge fence face and allows you to saw the correct angles on much wider stock lying flat on the saw table. On the other hand, it requires that you adjust both the miter angle and blade tilt quite precisely to angles for which the saw has no stops, and may not even have an accurate scale. While the direct method "found" the correct bevel and miter angles by mimicking the relationship between parts in the real world, the bevel-miter method "finds" the correct angles first by some rather involved trigonometry, then by some computer calculation and finally by looking up the angles in a good table saw book.

Since the stock lies flat on the saw table when using the bevel-miter method, the maximum blade height of the saw is usually not a limiting factor as it is with the direct method. So you can use the method for items such as wastebaskets, hoppers and lampshades in addition to smaller, shallower items such as picture frames and serving trays. The secret to success is keeping track, in your mind, of what you're doing.

I find it easiest to keep things straight by keeping in mind that all of these shapes are just parts of a pyramid. A pyramid can have many sides, it can be tall and slender or short and squat, it can be right side up or upsidedown and the pointed end can be (and usually is) cut off.

Grooves, Dadoes and Rabbets

Unlike the rip, crosscut and miter cuts I've discussed so far, dadoes, grooves and rabbets do not separate a workpiece into two parts. Instead, these cuts are two- or three-sided channels in the board. A channel across the grain of a board, away from the edge, is called a dado and is often used to house a crosspiece such as a shelf or a partition. This channel is called a groove if it is with the grain. When a groove or dado is along the edge or end of the workpiece, it's a rabbet and is most often used to help align two parts at a corner and to hide the edge of one.

The table saw is an excellent machine for making these cuts quickly and accurately because it usually has good power and because the action of the dado cutter is similar to a saw blade. To produce a splinter-free, flat-bottomed cut of consistent depth and width, you'll need a sharp, high-quality cutter, a close-fitting throat plate, adequate hold-downs and a steady feed rate. Because the workpiece remains whole after passing over the cutter, you will have to remove a standard blade guard and antikickback system when you make these cuts.

SETTING UP A DADO CUTTER

Before installing the dado cutter on the saw, double-check that the arbor is accurately set to 0° of tilt. After unplugging the saw, turn the saw's tilt-adjustment crank until the arbor carriage is against the zero-tilt stop. Crank the blade all the way up and check it against a right-angle drafting square. If the angle is off, reset the stop. When you're satisfied, lock down the carriage and remove the blade. It's better to check with a saw blade than with the dado cutter because the dado cutters for 10"

saws are usually only 6" or 8" in diameter. The larger saw blade makes it easier to see any misalignment.

Now, if your dado cutter is the stack type, follow the manufacturer's instructions for setting up the chippers and outside cutters. Be sure that the teeth of the cutters and chippers are staggered so none of them touch the teeth of adjoining cutters or chippers. You may have to use shims to get the exact width you want. The saw should, of course, remain unplugged while setting up the dado cutter.

Adjust wobbly and variable-stack dadoes by turning the cam hub as directed by the manufacturer. You can speed up the width-setting process by using the gauge shown on the next page to tell you which combination of chippers and shims or hub settings produces a certain width of cut.

You obviously can't use a saw blade's throat plate with a dado cutter because it just won't fit. Saw makers will sell you a plate for cutting dadoes, but you'll be better off making your own. To help get a splinter-free cut, especially when working with hardwood veneer plywood, make a fresh throat plate for each particular width of cut. Create a splinter-resisting, zero-clearance plate by making the opening in the plate with the dado cutter set to the desired width (see the sidebar on making throat plates). Label and save the throat plate for the next time you need to make that dado width.

There's another feature you might want to include in your throat plates for dadoes. To keep the depth of cut consistent over the full length of the dado, incorporate a slight hump in the throat plate alongside the dado cutter. As shown in the illustration, this subtle hump ensures that the board, even if slightly

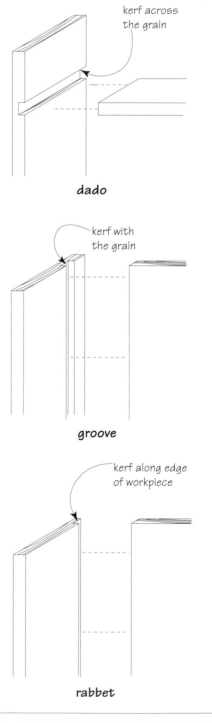

kerf across the grain

dado

kerf with the grain

groove

kerf along edge of workpiece

rabbet

DADO, GROOVE, RABBET IN TYPICAL USAGE

WIDTH GAUGE FOR DADO CUTTER

On your dado cutter width gauge, label your chipper and washer combinations required as well as the kerf application. Make your kerfs first in scrap to test fit, then cut into gauge, making note of the chipper and washer combination. Also label your washers "a", "b", etc. Then, seal your gauge with a coat of shellac to preserve the writing.

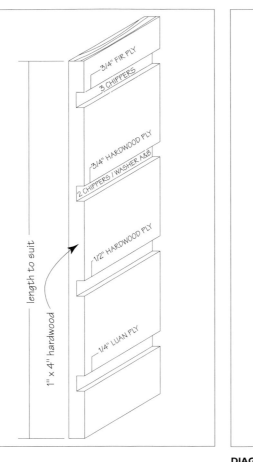

3/4" FIR PLY
3 CHIPPERS

3/4" HADKWOOD PLY

2 CHIPPERS / WASHER A&B

1/2" HARDWOOD PLY

1/4" LUAN PLY

length to suit

1" x 4" hardwood

workpiece touches throat at location of leading edge of blade

feed

workpiece

throat plate

cross section of throat plate (exagerated)

make hump about 1/8" higher than rest of plate (maximum) -- top of hump should occur at leading edge of blade (when set at typical cutting depth (1/4" to 1/2")

shape plate from 3/4" solid wood, belt sand ends to create hump

DIAGRAM OF A HUMPED THROAT PLATE FOR DADOES

bowed, will touch the throat plate in the proximity of the dado cutter instead of elsewhere on the table surface.

The next step in the basic setup process is to set the depth of cut. I sometimes use a commercial gauge that reads the height as I crank the cutter. I then make a test cut in scrap, adjusting the setting as necessary. More frequently, however, I use a shop-made gauge that includes the heights I most often use. For example, I often make dadoes and rabbets ¼" deep. To set the cutter height to ¼", I position the gauge over the cutter so the ¼" ledge will contact the top of the cutter at its highest point. I raise the cutter until it just touches this ledge.

If the material to be cut is dense, or the cut is deep, you may want to make the cut in a series of passes. This relieves strain on the motor and drive assembly of your saw, and it reduces the chances of kickback. The chart on the next page shows the recommended maximum depth of cut for hard- or softwoods for various widths of cut. For example, in hardwood cut a ¾" wide dado in three ¼" deep passes.

I always make test cuts in scrap to

assure myself I am making the exact width and depth of cut I need. I test the fit by pressing in the actual workpiece the dado or groove is to receive. The fit should be snug, but not so tight that pounding is required to fully assemble the joint.

CUTTING GROOVES

Cutting grooves with a dado cutter on the table saw is comparable to ripping, as you use the rip fence to guide the workpiece

over the dado cutter. Set up the cutter by adjusting it to the desired width and height. The next step is to set the rip fence.

To make it easy to set the rip fence, draw index lines on the throat plate that show you exactly where the dado cutter is going to make its cut at that width setting. It's a surprisingly simple procedure: Find a flat piece of plywood scrap about 1 square foot. Lock down the rip fence

SAFE DADO CUTTER DEPTH-OF-CUT

Cut Width	Softwood Cut Depth	Hardwood Cut Depth
1/8"	1 1/4"	5/8"
1/4"	1"	1/2"
3/8"	7/8"	7/16"
1/2"	3/4"	3/8"
5/8"	5/8"	5/16"
3/4"	1/2"	1/4"
13/16"	3/8"	3/16"

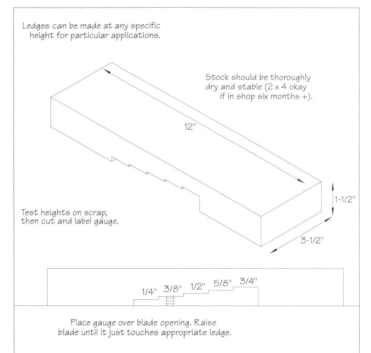

BLADE HEIGHT FIXTURE

Ledges can be made at any specific height for particular applications.

Stock should be thoroughly dry and stable (2 x 4 okay if in shop six months +).

12"

1-1/2"

3-1/2"

Test heights on scrap, then cut and label gauge.

1/4" 3/8" 1/2" 5/8" 3/4"

Place gauge over blade opening. Raise blade until it just touches appropriate ledge.

about 4" away from the cutter. Now hold one edge of the scrap tight to the rip fence and make a short cut in one end. You need only run it in an inch or so. Pull the scrap back, wait for the cutter to stop turning and then mark the edges of the cut just ahead of the cutter with a fine-tipped pen as shown in the photo to the right. I make these index marks on a strip of masking tape so they show up better and can be instantly removed when I'm finished with the dado cutter.

Once these index marks are in place, set the rip fence by one of several methods: to a dimension measurement read from a tape measure or other rule, to a story stick or to a component part. If you want precision to within 1/64", test the fence setting by making a test cut in a piece of scrap. Otherwise, you can put your faith in these index marks and save yourself some time.

You're still not quite ready to cut. For both safety and a cut of consistent width and depth, you must set up hold-downs to keep the workpiece tight to the fence and flat to the table. To do this, I use a gang of featherboards. Take the time to adjust the bearing pressure of the hold-downs to hold the work snugly, but not so tightly that they raise feed pressure to an uncomfortably high level.

Feed the work smoothly into the cutter, and be aware of your speed. Go fast enough to keep the cutter from burning the shoulders of the kerf, but not so fast that the teeth can't do their job. Experimenting with feed rate and a piece of scrap will teach you the optimal speed for the particular material and width of cut. If you experience splintering along the edges of the kerf at any speed, and

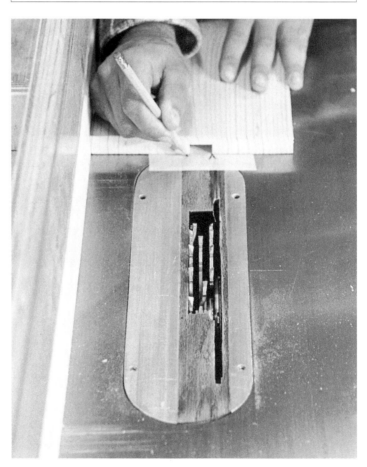

MARKING DADO CUT LOCATION
To mark a dado cut location, find a flat piece of plywood scrap about 1 square foot. Lock down the rip fence about 4" away from the cutter. Hold one edge of the scrap tight to the rip fence and make a short cut in one end. Pull the scrap back, wait for the cutter to stop turning and then mark the edges of the cut just ahead of the cutter with a fine-tipped pen.

you know the cutter is sharp, see if the rip fence is parallel to the cutter. Even a small deviation can cause the edges of delicate materials to split out.

Cutting Grooves Into Edges and Ends

Cutting grooves in edges presents a situation similar to resawing or sawing bevels on edges, and the solutions to the problems are basically the same. If the work-

WOBBLY CUTTER SETUP

An alternative way to set up for a cut with a wobbly-type cutter is to mark the groove's center line rather than its outside edges. This strategy saves time when making cuts of varying widths with the wobbly because, unlike a stack-type dado cutter, the center line of the wobbly's cut remains the same at any width setting.

To mark the center line, set the cutter for its maximum width and make the cut in a piece of scrap. Turn off the saw, pull the scrap back and lightly mark the sides of the cut ahead of the cutter on the throat plate (or strip of masking tape). Now measure to find the center line between the two shoulder marks and make a mark.

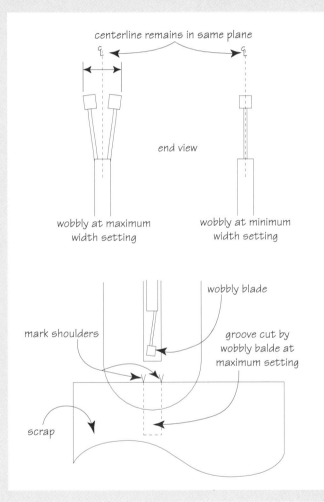

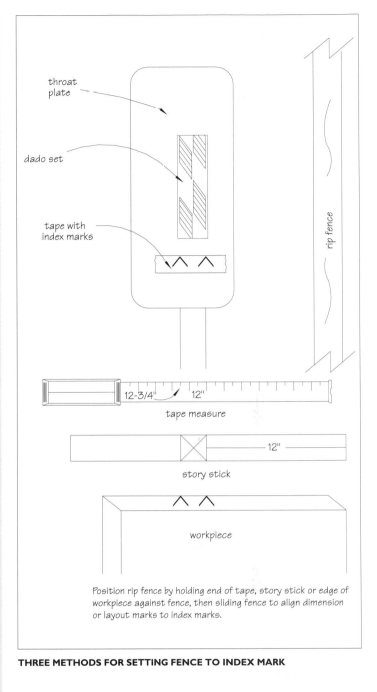

THREE METHODS FOR SETTING FENCE TO INDEX MARK

piece is wide, install the tall Universal Fence Fixture auxiliary fence and the featherboard fixture for resaw work. These fixtures ensure that the groove will run straight and square to the edge. To cut a groove in the end of a narrow board (less than 12"), use my rip fence sled fixture mounted on the universal rip fence fixture.

Locate the groove in the edge by setting the rip fence the same way you would for cutting a groove in the face of the stock. The simplest way to center a groove in an edge is to lay out the cut and set up the saw from center lines rather than from the edges. If you use a wobbly dado cutter, you probably already have the center line of the cutter marked on your throat plate. If you use a stack-type dado cutter, mark the edges of the cut on the throat plate and then measure to find the center. Mark the center line of the groove on the end of a scrap the same thickness as your workpieces, and adjust the rip fence so the center line on the scrap aligns with the center line of the cutter. Now cut the groove the full-length of the board into the edge of the scrap. Turn the scrap end-for-end and run the opposite end into the cutter. If the setup is correct, the cutter will enter the groove without cutting into either side.

To ensure an accurate end groove, I use my sliding rip fence fixture to carry the board through the blade. The fixture's clamps hold the board flat, the vertical

HOLD-DOWN SETUP FOR GROOVING
This drawing shows use of rip fence-mounted fixture with adjustable comb-type featherboards and use of table-mounted featherboard fixture exerting side pressure.

EDGE GROOVE SETUP
Using the vertical featherboard fixture for resawing ensures a perfect edge groove.

stops hold the board perpendicular (or at an angle if the end of the board is angled) to the table and the runner system controls the board as I slide it with the fixture along the universal fence fixture.

CUTTING DADOES

Just as cutting grooves is comparable to ripping, cutting dadoes is comparable to crosscutting. Depending on the length and width of the stock, I guide it with either a miter gauge equipped with an auxiliary fence or a sled. Used properly, these fixtures guide the stock safely and accurately. But, once again, beware of the dado cutter when it emerges from under the stock.

Not just any crosscut sled will give you splinter-free dadoes in materials with a brittle surface. To minimize splintering, the sled accommodates a removable kerf plate in the sled's base in the area of the cutter. I use a new kerf plate whenever I cut a dado of a width that I haven't cut before. I cut the aperture with the dado cutter set to the width of the dado. I keep

a stash of uncut kerf plates on hand for just this purpose. When using the miter gauge as the dadoing guide, I install a fresh, uncut throat plate on the table saw to provide zero clearance. Other ways of reducing splintering are described in Reducing Splintering (see page 111).

The next step is to mark the cut line on either the miter gauge or sled fence. Since the best way to do this is to cut into the fence with the cutter set to the width and height of the dado, I install a removable backing board on the fence in the cutter's target area. That way I can replace it with a fresh, uncut backing board for different cutter settings and haven't cut up my auxiliary fence. With a sharp pencil or fine-point pen and a combination square, extend the edges of the cut up the face of the backing board. Now you can align layout marks on the workpiece with the marks on the backing board. I usually slide a stop block against the end of the workpiece and clamp it firmly to the backing board. The block not only prevents the work from shifting but allows me to quick-

ly make multiple cuts. If the workpiece is wider than a few inches, I clamp the work securely to the backing board and fence. For workpieces wider than about a foot, I use the sled.

SPECIAL TECHNIQUES

Life in the woodworking shop would be boring if all we did was straightforward cuts. Sooner or later, probably sooner, you will need to cut dadoes at an angle to the edge of the board, grooves or dadoes that stop before they reach one or both ends of the board, and grooves and dadoes wider than the maximum width of your dado cutter. Eventually you will

---

SAFETY *tip*

USE A PUSH STICK!

Always use a push stick on the workpiece in the vicinity of the throat plate—never your hands. When cutting a groove or dado, you can't see where the cutter will exit the end of the workpiece.

need to make a series of equally spaced dadoes. Finally, you may occasionally have to dado an awkward-shaped workpiece. The special techniques that follow show how to successfully approach these dadoing adventures.

Cutting Grooves and Dadoes at an Angle

To cut a groove that isn't parallel to the long edge of the board, use a taper jig fixture to carry the workpiece over the cutter. The advantages of this fixture are threefold: The integral clamps hold the workpiece securely to the fixture, eliminating the need for push sticks; the guide system ensures an even, accurate cut; and the handle provides a safe place to push the fixture through the saw.

If the board or panel is too large for your taper fixture, you can temporarily screw a guide board to the workpiece. Because the side of the workpiece away from the rip fence is at an angle, the use of side hold-downs is impossible. So be especially careful to keep the edge of the fixture or guide board tight to the rip fence throughout the cut. I use the shoe-type push stick I made for gang saw work to enable me to exert a heavy down and side force.

Cutting a dado at an angle with a miter gauge setup requires little more than setting the gauge at the desired angle and making the cut. Remember, though, that the side forces of an angled dado cut will be signicantly greater than when cutting with a single blade. Use the open miter position if possible so that the workpiece tends to be forced against the end stop. If you have to use the closed position to gain support for the workpiece on the table, extend the fence so you can fix a stop to the right end of the board. Also clamp the work securely to the gauge's auxiliary fence. If you want to cut a mirror image of the angled dado—perhaps to make shelf housings in a pair of side boards that will support an angled shelf—see Making Angled Dadoes.

To use a sled to cut an angled dado, install a second fence at the desired angle. If the workpiece is too large to fit the sled at this angle, or you are going to make a lot of these cuts, consider making a sled specifically designed to cut at this angle.

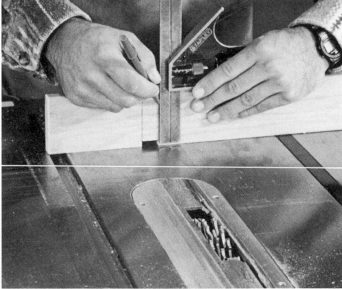

CLOSEUP OF DADO CUTTER, KERF PLATE AND SLED This photograph shows a dado blade protruding up through the kerf plate in a crosscut sled. The uncut portion is to the rear of blade. This is the process of creating an aperture for a new dado setting.

MITER GAUGE SETUP FOR DADO WORK Here's a closeup view that shows extending the lines from a dado cut on the backing board with a combination square to create reference lines.

REDUCING SPLINTERING

Finely veneered plywoods, laminate fiberboards and highly figured hardwoods often splinter along the edges of a dado. As a first line of defense against this splintering, attempt these cuts only with a high-quality, well-sharpened cutter. This will prevent the problem in most cases. But in especially splintery stock, or when the cutter loses its edge, you can employ these additional tricks:
- Double-check that the cutter is set at precisely 90° to the table and parallel to the rip fence.
- Make a throat plate or carriage sled base plate specific to the dado width so there is zero clearance around the sides of the cutter.
- When working with especially fragile plywood veneers, prescore the veneer at the shoulder lines with a razor blade or sharp utility knife.
- Make the cut in two or more passes.
- Slow the feed rate.
- Prevent tear-out at the end of the board where the cutter exits by using a backing board. To provide zero clearance, be sure to use a fresh fence insert or backing board for each dado cutter setting.

CUTTING A DADO WITH A SINGLE BLADE

It probably won't come as any surprise to you that a dado cutter is not the only way to cut a dado. Of course the dado cutter makes quick work of the cut by producing most dadoes in one pass. But you can also make a dado of any width with a standard blade by first cutting each side of the dado and then cutting away the waste in between with multiple passes. The bottom of the groove will likely be somewhat corrugated, but you can easily clean this out with a hand tool such as a router plane.

If you need to cut several dadoes of the same width and want to do it with a single blade, set up a stop for cutting one side of the dado and use a spacer between the stock and the stop when cutting the other side. Here's the process:

1. Make a spacer block the width of the dado minus the width of the kerf made by the single saw blade.
2. Clamp a stop block to the fence to position the stock, and make the first cut.
3. Insert the spacer block between the stock and the stop block, and make the second cut.
4. Remove the spacer block, and cut out the remaining waste with a series of passes, each one a kerf closer to the first cut. The first stop block prevents you from accidentally cutting the dado too wide.

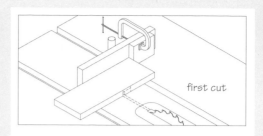

first cut

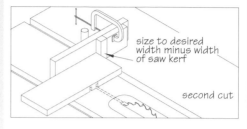

size to desired width minus width of saw kerf

second cut

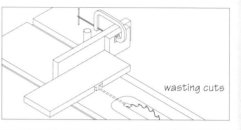

wasting cuts

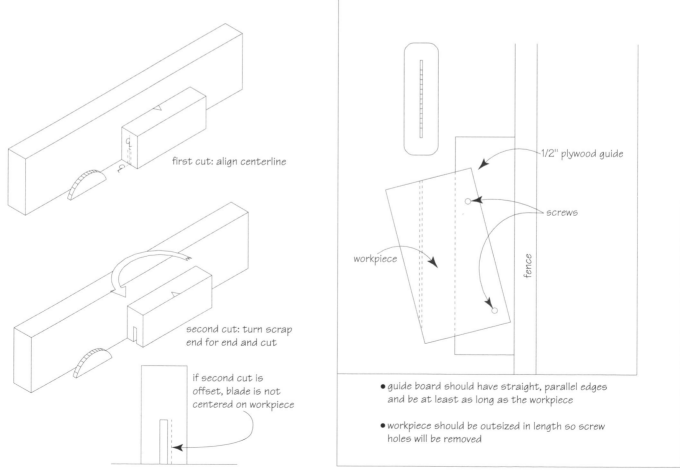

first cut: align centerline

second cut: turn scrap end for end and cut

if second cut is offset, blade is not centered on workpiece

1/2" plywood guide

screws

workpiece

fence

• guide board should have straight, parallel edges and be at least as long as the workpiece

• workpiece should be outsized in length so screw holes will be removed

CENTERING AN EDGE GROOVE

CUTTING TAPER WITH GUIDE BOARD

Cutting Stopped Grooves

If you don't want a groove to show at one or both ends of the board, you need to make a stopped, or blind, groove. Begin the setup for this cut by constructing and installing a long auxiliary fence on the rip fence. The need for length, and just how much length, will become apparent as you read this section. You'll mark the fence to show the fore and aft extent of the dado cutter at the desired height setting, you'll slide and clamp down one or two stop blocks to it to control the length of the cut and you'll install featherboards on it to hold the stock flat to the table.

To set the stops, first set the cutter height, and then, using a plastic drafting triangle, mark the location of the front and back of the dado cutter on the auxiliary fence. Draw vertical lines square up the face of the fence from the marks.

Next, lay out the location of the groove on the workpiece, and extend the layout marks to the edge of the stock and then around the edge to the opposite face so they'll show on the surface that will be visible when cutting the groove.

To set the end block for the groove, lower the cutter, place the workpiece against the fence and slide it forward until the layout mark indicating the near end of the groove on the workpiece aligns with the mark on the fence indicating the near extent of the cutter. Clamp the sliding block to the auxiliary fence so it butts against the far end of the workpiece. This is the end block.

To set the start block for the groove, align the layout mark on the workpiece that indicates the far end of the groove with the mark on the fence that indicates the far extent of the cutter. Clamp the block down so it butts against the near end of the workpiece.

If the groove needs to be blind only on one end, you need only one of these blocks of course. In that case, try to arrange the cut so that the start block is not needed.

To cut a single-blind groove (with an end block but no start block), reset the cutter height, make sure the fence position is correct, install hold-downs as you would for any grooving operation, turn on the saw and run the workpiece along the fence until its far end bears against the

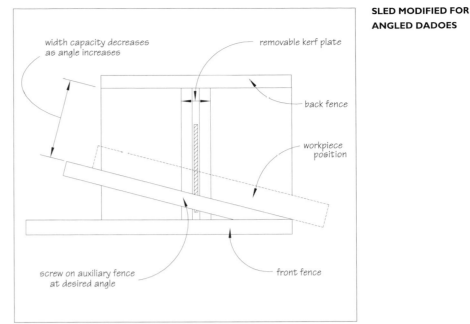

width capacity decreases as angle increases

removable kerf plate

back fence

workpiece position

front fence

screw on auxiliary fence at desired angle

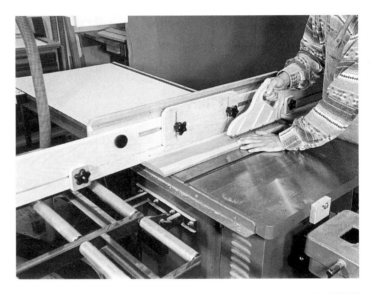

STOPPED GROOVE SETUP ON RIP FENCE This overview of the stopped groove fixture bolted to the universal fence fixture shows a workpiece in place, with the stops in place as well.

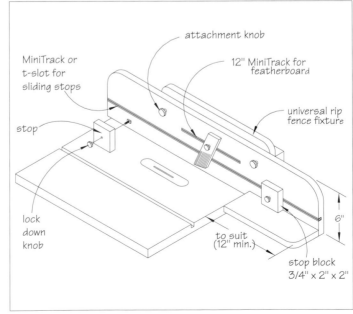

EXTENSION FENCE WITH T-SLOT FOR SLIDING STOPS

attachment knob

MiniTrack or t-slot for sliding stops

12" MiniTrack for featherboard

universal rip fence fixture

stop

lock down knob

to suit (12" min.)

6"

stop block 3/4" x 2" x 2"

MAKING ANGLED DADOES

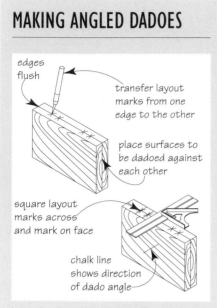

edges flush

transfer layout marks from one edge to the other

place surfaces to be dadoed against each other

square layout marks across and mark on face

chalk line shows direction of dado angle

Laying out paired boards for angled dadoes

Begin by clamping together the two boards that are to receive the dado cut, the surfaces to be dadoed against one another. Align their edges evenly. Lay out the position of both edges of the dadoes across both edges of the stock, and put tick marks on the faces of the boards. Draw a chalk line on the outside faces of the boards to indicate the angle of the dado cut. Set up the dado cutter to the required width and height, and set up the miter gauge with an auxiliary fence. Adjust the gauge to the desired angle, and then cut into the fence with the dado cutter to mark the exact position of the cutter. Extend the lines up square on the face of the fence. Next, line up the dado layout marks on the first board to the index marks on the fence and slide a stop against the end of the board. Double-check that the chalk line indicates the correct angle. Make the cut.

The first photo shown here illustrates the left-hand cut in progress, while the lower photo shows the right-hand cut in progress.

SETUP FOR MIRRORED ANGLES

To cut the mirror-image dado, set the miter gauge in the right-hand miter slot and reset it to the same, but opposing, angle. Note that this angle setting must be precise; if not, the board held between these two housing dadoes will be warped. To insure accuracy, make an angle setup jig as shown in the drawing. Again dado into the fence and draw the index lines. Line up the layout marks on the second board with the index lines, check that the chalk mark is oriented properly. Clamp the stop in place and make the cut.

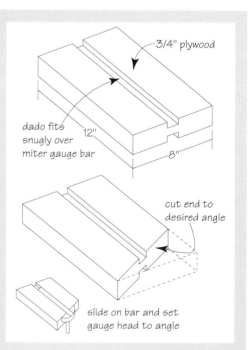

3/4" plywood

dado fits snugly over miter gauge bar

12"

8"

cut end to desired angle

slide on bar and set gauge head to angle

stop block. Turn off the saw, wait for the cutter to come to a complete stop and either lower the cutter out of the groove or carefully lift the stock off of the cutter.

To make the double-blind cut (or a single-blind cut using a start block), you must begin with the cutter lowered below the table. This gets a bit involved because you have to crank the running cutter up into the overlying board and have no way to measure its height. To get it right, first mark the crank wheel and then mark the saw cabinet directly opposite the mark on the wheel. Count the number of turns of the crank as you lower the cutter below the saw table. You are now able to return the cutter to its previous height by cranking the cutter up the same number of turns until the marks are aligned again.

With the cutter down, you're ready to make the cut. Slide the board against the fence, under the featherboards and against the start block. Turn on the saw and slowly crank up the cutter, counting the turns and lining up your marks on crank and cabinet. Then push the board along the fence until the far end bears against the stop block. Turn off the saw, lower the cutter and remove the board. The first time you do it, the setup and process can be a bit confusing and time-consuming, but doing it once will dissipate the confusion.

With all stopped cuts, as you probably realize, the blind end of the groove will taper up to the surface of the stock, reflecting the curve of the cutter. You can deal with this in either of two ways: You can chisel the groove square, or you can cut a matching curve in the workpiece that will be housed in the groove. I prefer the latter because it's faster and has little effect on the overall strength of the joint.

Cutting Stopped Dadoes

Many woodworkers find themselves cutting stopped dadoes more often than stopped grooves. For example, a stopped dado is commonly called for where fixed shelves join the sides of a cabinet. Stopping the dado short of the visible edge usually provides a cleaner-looking joint, especially if the dado is cut with a wobbly-type dado cutter.

A simple way to set up a stopped dado is clamp a board to the table saw surface

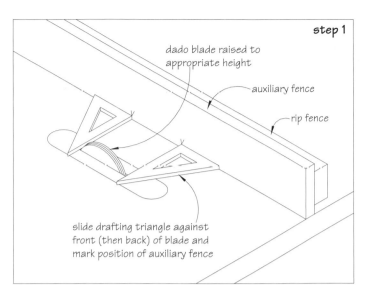

step 1

dado blade raised to appropriate height

auxiliary fence

rip fence

slide drafting triangle against front (then back) of blade and mark position of auxiliary fence

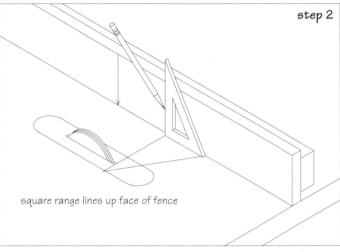

step 2

square range lines up face of fence

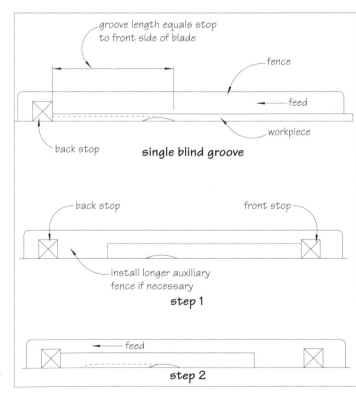

groove length equals stop to front side of blade

fence

feed

workpiece

back stop

single blind groove

back stop

front stop

install longer auxiliary fence if necessary

step 1

feed

step 2

MARKING FRONT AND BACK OF DADO CUTTER ON FENCE
To mark the dado blade range on the fence, first slide a drafting triangle against the front (and the back) of the blade and mark the position on the auxiliary fence, as shown in step 1.

Then, raise the triangle to transfer the lines to the face of the fence, as in step 2.

ALIGNING STOPS ON RIP FENCE
The first of these three schematics shows how to align for a single-blind groove.

The bottom two schematics illustrate how to set up your aligning stops for a blind groove in two steps.

to limit the travel of the workpiece into the cutter. Center the board directly over the miter gauge slot to avoid dangerously torquing the workpiece when it comes to bear against the board. Make a shallow groove in the bottom of the clamped board to prevent friction against the miter gauge guide bar.

If the workpiece is large, use the crosscut sled rather than the miter gauge to make dado cuts. Sled-guided dadoes are more accurate and safer to cut. To make a stopped dado, use an adjustable stop with an all-purpose crosscutting sled. The long slotted hole allows you to quickly adjust and set the stop setting.

While it's possible to cut a double-blind dado on the table saw using a process similar in principle to cutting double-blind grooves, it gets so cumbersome that it isn't really practical. If your design calls for double-blind dadoes, I suggest that you reach for your plunge router—or change the design.

Cutting Wide Dadoes and Grooves

There may be times when you need to make a dado or groove wider than the $\frac{13}{16}$" maximum width of most dado cutters. You may, for example, need to house the ends of strong bookshelves a full inch thick. The obvious way to enlarge the cut is to move the workpiece over and run it through the cutter at least one more time. The trick is to move it over exactly the right amount quickly and easily. I do it with a spacer.

When enlarging dadoes, the spacer technique is similar to the one presented in Cutting a Dado With a Single Blade. The spacer is sized to equal the distance you must move the stock to make the second cut. The process is simple but not a complete no-brainer—you have to make sure you're moving the stock the right direction for the second cut. Keep in mind that when you move the stock to the right along the fence of the miter gauge the next cut will be to the left along the stock.

Assuming you're working with the miter gauge or sled in its usual position to the left of the cutter, align the layout mark of the dado's right edge with the right side of the dado cutter as marked on the guide fence. Clamp a stop block to the fence at the left end of the stock and make the

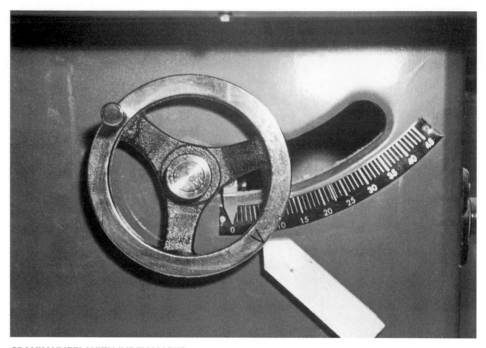

CRANK WHEEL WITH INDEX MARKS
Closeup shows mark on crank wheel aligned with mark made on masking tape on saw cabinet.

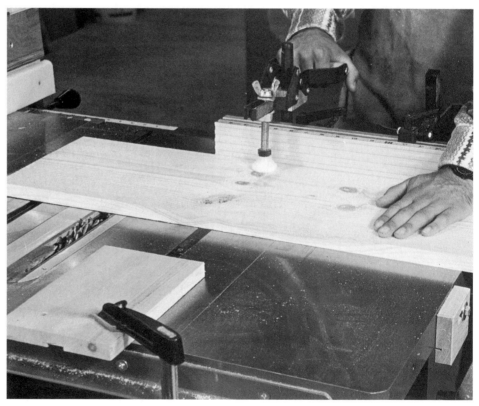

BOARD AS A DADO STOP
Shows saw table set up with board clamped in place. Dado in board (relief for miter gauge) visible.

first cut. Now insert your spacer between the stock and the stop, moving the stock to the right, and make the second cut, enlarging the dado to the left. Bingo! You've produced a dado that is the width of the dado cutter plus the spacer. If a test cut indicates that you need to make some

fine adjustment, you can adjust either the spacer or the width of the dado cutter, whichever is easier.

The same concept works for enlarging a groove but is a little less convenient because the spacer must be the full length of the rip fence and cannot be allowed to

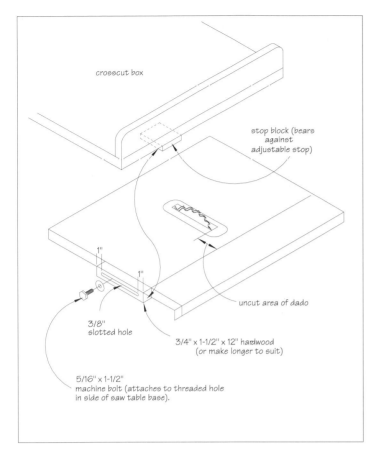

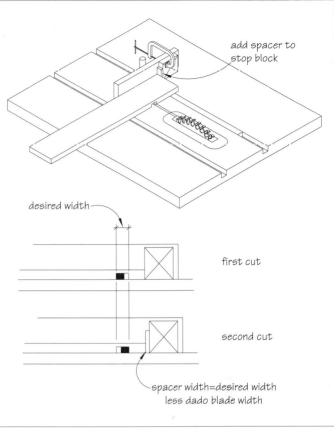

ADJUSTABLE STOP BLOCK FOR CUTTING STOPPED DADOES WITH THE CROSSCUT SLED

SETUP TO CUT OVERSIZE DADO

slide along the rip fence during the cut. With the fence to the right of the dado cutter, adjust the fence to align the left side of the cutter with the left side of the groove and make the first cut. Next, stick your spacer to the fence with double-sided tape, moving the stock to the left, and make the second cut, enlarging the groove to the right. If you'll have to repeat this cut often, consider making the spacer a few inches longer than your rip fence, adding a block to the near end of the spacer to prevent it from sliding along the fence, and adding a judiciously placed magnetic catch to the far end to keep the spacer up against the fence.

SETUP TO MAKE OVERSIZE GROOVE

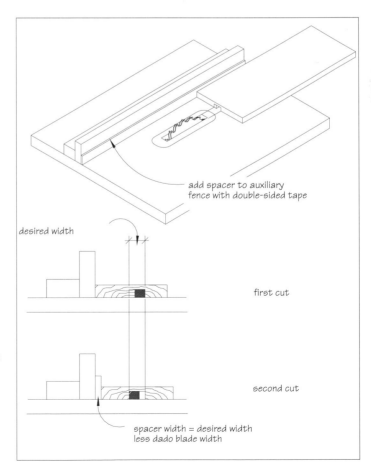

Cutting a Series of Spaced Dadoes

What do you do if a bookcase you want to build has many shelves and you don't feel like spending the rest of your golden years squinting at layout marks to align a series of dadoes in the side-support boards? The key is a shop-made fixture you can attach to your miter gauge (see drawing for Simple Dado-Spacing Fixture) that accurately positions and securely holds the stock for a series of dado cuts. It works by means of a key that engages the previous cut to position the stock for the next cut. If you intend to cut a lot of spaced dadoes, consider making the adjustable dado-spacing fixture for your crosscut sled as shown on page 119. This fixture attaches quickly and securely to the sled with two knobs and adjusts from side to side (changing the dado spacing) along a length of MiniTrack. Precut sockets for a variety of keys allow you to quickly set the jig for other dado sizes.

Cutting Dadoes in Odd-Shaped Workpieces

If your workpiece is an odd shape that is difficult to hold securely, don't risk your body parts or time invested in the workpiece by trying to somehow clamp it harder against the guide fence. Not only might the clamp disfigure the work, but vibration could shake the clamp loose, allowing the workpiece to shift and get thrown off the saw.

To make it safe, take the time to build a fixture that holds the oddball workpiece in the securest way possible. For example, a simple V-shape cut into a thick piece of stock often provides a secure carriage for a round post. Clamp this V-block to the guide fence, or, better yet, clamp the workpiece to the guide fence sandwiched under the V-block, as shown in the photo at right.

In many situations you have to invent fixtures that can only be used for the specific task at hand. Analyze the situation, anticipate every possible direction that the dado cutter could push the workpiece and provide solid stops to prevent the movement. I often fit a piece of ¼" plywood snugly between the front and rear guide rails of my crosscut sled and screw blocks to it from the underside. For example, to hold a curved chair leg in position to receive a dado cut, I've screwed pairs of blocks to the sheet and driven in wedges to secure the leg. If only one side of the workpiece will show, you can screw the workpiece directly to the plywood—but keep the screws away from the location of the dado cut.

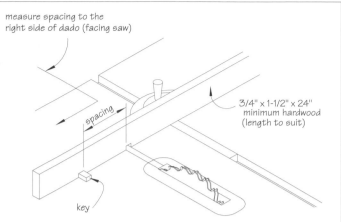

measure spacing to the right side of dado (facing saw)

spacing

3/4" x 1-1/2" x 24" minimum hardwood (length to suit)

key

(do not glue in key: press fit or screw from below)

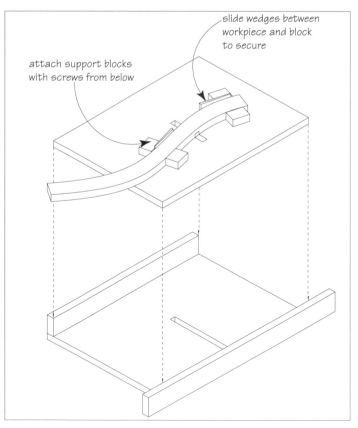

V-CARRIAGE HOLDING POST
View of fixture clamped over round post workpiece and to fence face of crosscut sled.

FIXTURE FOR CURVED WORKPIECE

slide wedges between workpiece and block to secure

attach support blocks with screws from below

MAKING AND USING AN ADJUSTABLE DADO-SPACING FIXTURE

Make the fixture from a 2"-wide by 8'-long strip of ¾" maple plywood. Run the dado to accept the MiniTrack for a length of 2' into one end. Round the edges of the strip, sand and coat it with shellac. Now lay out and drill holes in the fence of the small crosscut sled to accept the pair of ¼" bolts that will install the fixture to the MiniTrack. Space these holes about 4" to either side of the dado blade location. To create a key, set up a dado blade to a specified width and height and bolt the fixture in place (slide it as far as it will go to your left along the MiniTrack). Cut the dado in the fixture's bottom edge (it will be about 4" from the end) and fit a hardwood block to the socket. You can either screw or carpet-tape it in place. Size the key to protrude about ½" in front of fixture face. Note: You may have to readjust the crosscut sled stop mounted on the side of the extension wing to allow more forward movement of the sled because the dado blade is a smaller diameter than a regular blade.

To set a dado spacing, measure from the inside edge of the key to the edge of the dado kerf cut in the replaceable throat plate of the crosscut sled. This spacing will be the distance between dadoes in the workpiece. Make the first dado cut in the workpiece to its layout position. Index the next dado by setting the just-cut dado over the key and then making the cut. Continue in this way until all the dadoes have been cut. If the design calls for a change in spacing, loosen the attachment knobs and readjust the fixture by sliding it sideways to key in a new distance measurement.

FIRST CUT WITH ADJUSTABLE DADO-SPACING FIXTURE
This photo shows the workpiece in place against fixture fence face, dado entering edge.

SEQUENTIAL CUT WITH ADJUSTABLE DADO-SPACING FIXTURE
This photo shows the third dado being cut. Note that the dado just cut is indexed over the key.

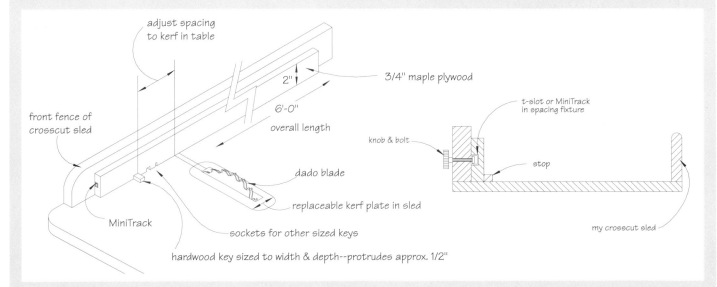

adjust spacing to kerf in table

2"

3/4" maple plywood

6'-0" overall length

front fence of crosscut sled

MiniTrack

dado blade

replaceable kerf plate in sled

sockets for other sized keys

hardwood key sized to width & depth--protrudes approx. 1/2"

t-slot or MiniTrack in spacing fixture

knob & bolt

stop

my crosscut sled

CUTTING RABBETS

There are two good ways to cut a rabbet on the table saw: Make two intersecting cuts with a saw blade as shown in the drawing to the right, or make a single wide cut with either a dado cutter or a chisel-shaped molding head cutter. At first glance, the two-cut method may not seem as efficient as the single-cut method, but in reality you can often make both saw cuts in less time than it takes you to set up a dado set or a molding head cutter. Also, if you're cutting a large rabbet in dense wood, you will likely have to make at least two passes with the dado cutter to avoid overloading the saw motor, and probably three or more with the molding head. The method you choose depends on the width and depth of the rabbet, the power of your saw and the total length of rabbets in all of the pieces you need to cut. I find that I most often make two passes with a saw blade, but when I need many yards of rabbets, I use the dado to make the cut. I'll cover these two procedures now and leave cutting with the molding head to a later chapter.

Saw Blade Rabbets

Cutting a rabbet in two passes with a saw blade is quicker for short runs and produces a much smoother cut than you can expect from most dado cutters. For rabbets with exceptionally smooth sides, use a blade designed for smooth ripping when sawing rabbets with the grain, and use a smooth-cutting crosscut blade for rabbets sawn across the end of your workpiece.

Set the blade height to the appropriate depth and the rip fence to cut the rabbet's width. Remember to account for the kerf produced by the blade itself. Make a test cut to check your settings. Begin by cutting the shoulder of the rabbet, using featherboards or push sticks in both hands to hold the workpiece tight to the fence and flat to the table. Next, readjust the height of the blade to cut the bottom of the rabbet to the shoulder cut line, and adjust the fence as necessary. Now slide the workpiece on edge against the fence, cutting the bottom of the rabbet as the waste falls to the outside (the side away from the rip fence) of the blade.

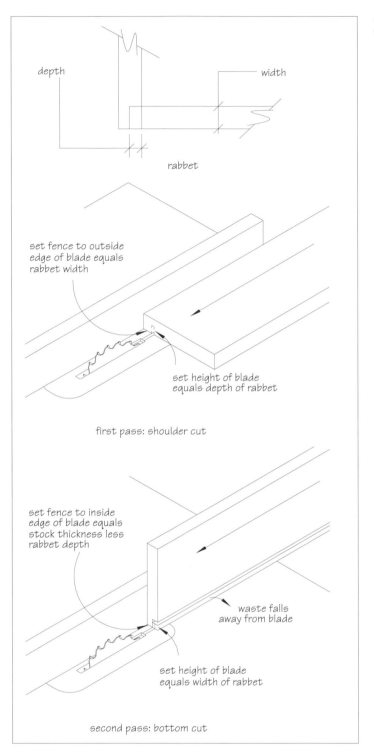

CUTTING RABBET WITH DOUBLE PASS

depth

width

rabbet

set fence to outside edge of blade equals rabbet width

set height of blade equals depth of rabbet

first pass: shoulder cut

set fence to inside edge of blade equals stock thickness less rabbet depth

waste falls away from blade

set height of blade equals width of rabbet

second pass: bottom cut

Dado-Cut Rabbets

Prepare to cut an edge rabbet with a dado blade by building this specialized rabbet fence, which bolts to the universal fence fixture. The fixture's T-slot accepts bolts to secure comb-type hold-downs as needed to hold the stock flat to the table. The cavity in the fence lets you "hide" a portion of the dado blade within the fence itself, allowing you to adjust the width of the dado by setting the position of the

---

SAFETY *tip*

LOCATING THE RABBET

Never make a rabbet along the edge of the workpiece away from the rip fence. This is dangerous because of the potential for severe kickback if the work wanders away from the rip fence, plus any deviation from the fence shows up as a deviation in the run of the rabbet.

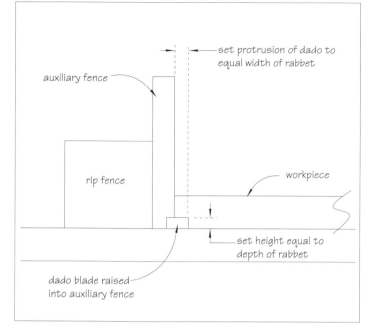

set protrusion of dado to equal width of rabbet

auxiliary fence

rip fence

workpiece

set height equal to depth of rabbet

dado blade raised into auxiliary fence

RABBETING WITH DADO BLADE

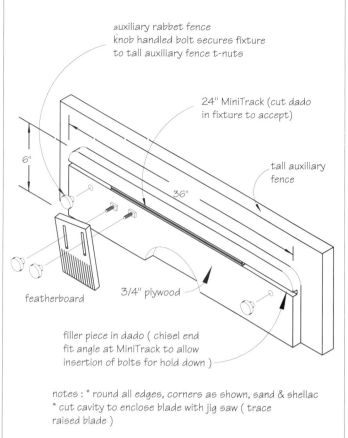

auxiliary rabbet fence knob handled bolt secures fixture to tall auxiliary fence t-nuts

24" MiniTrack (cut dado in fixture to accept)

6"

36"

tall auxiliary fence

featherboard

3/4" plywood

filler piece in dado (chisel end fit angle at MiniTrack to allow insertion of bolts for hold down)

notes : * round all edges, corners as shown, sand & shellac
* cut cavity to enclose blade with jig saw (trace raised blade)

RABBET FENCE FIXTURE WITH INTEGRAL T-SLOT HOLD-DOWN

RABBET FENCE IN USE
Overall view of fixture, hold-downs in place, cavity visible above workpiece.

CLEANING UP BOTTOM OF RABBET WITH HAND RABBET PLANE

fence rather than changing the width of the dado blade. With the cutter height adjusted to the depth of the rabbet, you need only run the workpiece against the fence to produce the finished cut, and you don't need to worry about what the waste is doing because it's all sawdust. Be sure the hold-downs are secured firmly in place, as any movement of the stock away from the table will cause the rabbet to fluctuate in depth. This is also a good time to use the humped insert to ensure an even depth. When finished, clean up the bottom of the rabbet with a hand rabbet plane.

Cutting an End Rabbet

To cut an end rabbet, make the shoulder cut by guiding the workpiece through the dado blade with either the miter gauge or my rip fence sled fixture. With the former, you can use the rip fence as an end stop. To set the rabbet width, measure from the face of the rip fence to the outside (away from the rip fence) of the dado blade. The height of the blade cuts the depth of the rabbet.

To use the sled, clamp the workpiece flat to the fixture, supporting it upright between the two adjustable stop blocks. Using the fixture method ensures an extremely accurate cut, even if the workpiece is slightly cupped or warped.

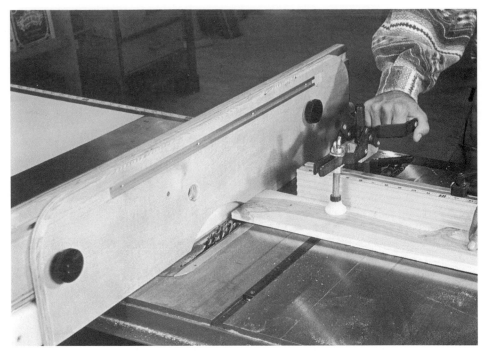

END RABBET WITH MITER GAUGE WITH RIP FENCE AS STOP
View from back shows dado blade entering workpiece, creating cut at desired width and depth of rabbet.

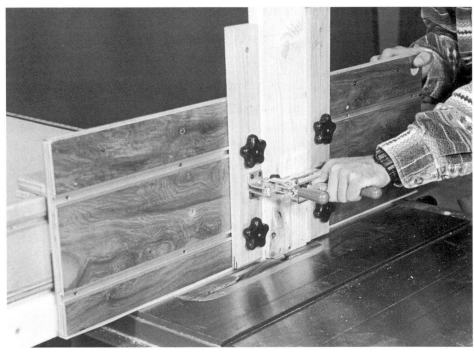

RIP FENCE SLED FIXTURE IN USE FOR END RABBET BOTTOM CUT
This overview photo shows the setup involved for the rip fence sled fixture.

S A F E T Y *tip*

BEWARE OF THE WASTE!

The small size of the waste from cutting a rabbet may not seem threatening, but propelled lengthwise at the speed of the saw teeth, it can hit you like a stab from a pencil. Always make sure that your second cut, which clears the waste from the board, leaves the waste free to move away from the blade, not trapped between the blade and the fence.

Sheet Stock and Small Parts

When you are working in the macro- and micro-ranges on the table saw (full-size sheet stocks on one end and tiny, down to less than 1"-square miniature workpieces on the other) you're faced with tasks that challenge a table saw's standard guidance systems. In this chapter, I'll present specific techniques, many utilizing specialized fixtures, that will help you get the best and safest performance out of your saw when working in these ranges.

SAWING PANEL STOCKS

If you intend to cut a full sheet of panel stock into numerous component pieces, take the time to set up your saw to do the job right. Putting on the appropriate blade and installing a zero-clearance throat plate will make for a clean and efficient cut. Setting up accessories, such as an extended auxiliary rip fence and additional stock supports, will help you handle the more cumbersome materials with added ease and safety. Always run veneered sheet goods with the good side up—any tear-out will occur on the bottom surface.

Saw Setup for Cutting Panels

I keep an all-purpose blade on my saw (a thin-kerf ATB) so that I don't have to change blades every time I want to cut a piece of plywood or other panel stock with a face veneer. If the blade is sharp and clean, it will cut most sheet stock with minimum tear-out on the bottom surface and will handle most solid stock cuts. But if I want absolute insurance against tear-out on a pricey veneer plywood, or if I'm faced with cutting man-made materials such as dense particleboard, then I install a blade specifically designed to handle these materials.

Be aware that the height setting of the blade affects the quality of the cut: The higher the blade, the less tear-out on the top surface of the sheet. You must, of course, balance this against the hazard of a more greatly exposed blade. I raise the blade just enough to eliminate top surface tear-out.

Throat Plate

You can help a specialized panel blade—or even your all-purpose blade—make a splinter-free cut by installing a fresh, zero-clearance throat plate. Because the plate supports the stock's veneer right up to the cutting edge of the teeth, the surface of the plate can act as a fulcrum against which the material is sheared away from the underlying substrate. The geometry of the cutting action prevents splinters from forming and makes for a clean bottom cut.

There are at least three ways to come up with this zero-clearance throat plate: You can make a fresh throat plate (see chapter one), install a new wood sleeve in a commercially made throat plate or cheat. In the drawing on the next page, I illustrate how a piece of hardboard (white melamine-faced Masonite is ideal) can serve as a quick and clean way to provide zero clearance around your cutting blade. Size the hardboard to the dimensions of your table saw surface. If you are cutting large panels, add more width so the board can rest on your external side-support system (otherwise your table surface will be the thickness of the hardboard above the support).

To inaugurate the hardboard as a zero-clearance throat plate, simply run it into the blade to create the kerf until the plate's stop bears against the front of the saw table, as shown in the drawing. To prevent the board from shifting under the workpiece, hold the plate in place with a 1" to 2" strip of carpet tape under each

CHOOSING BLADES FOR SHEET STOCK

ATB
A good choice for cutting plywoods is the ATB blade. The shearing cut of beveled alternating teeth reduces splintering. Top bevels are 10° to 20° with hook angles of 6° to 15°. The ATB can be left on the saw for general crosscutting and light-duty ripping of solid woods.

ATB-HIGH BEVEL ANGLE
The ATB with high bevel angle (25° to 40°), which usually has a lower hook angle than a standard ATB (from maximum of 10° to a negative hook angle), is best for cutting plywoods with fragile veneers. This blade won't tear out bottom veneer (including fragile, thin hardwoods and melamines), thus eliminating the need for scoring the blade ahead of the primary blade or using other tricks for reducing tear-out. Disadvantage: Teeth with high bevel angles dull faster than with lower angles. The high-angle ATB is not as efficient as the low-angle ATB for solid woods.

TC-TRIPLE CHIP
The unusual tooth pattern of the TC blade features two grinds on alternating teeth: one with chamfered edges and the other with a flat, chisel shape. The first tooth cuts the center of the kerf while the flat tooth cuts the edges clean and square. Bluntness of tooth edges relative to ATB-type blades means it resists dulling more, making it the blade of choice for man-made, glue-saturated sheet stocks such as particleboards.

back corner. You can, of course, use this same piece of hardboard for other rip fence settings by making a fresh kerf. After a while, however, you will likely have to replace the board.

Fence Setup

When cutting sheet stock, there is no need to worry about reactive wood closing around the kerf and binding against the blade. The construction of most plywoods (the layers alternate grain direction perpendicular to one another) and the composition of man-made sheet materials (devoid of grain direction) prevent this phenomenon from occurring. Therefore, use your standard fence (you won't need a short auxiliary fence) when ripping sheet goods. Better yet, for a safer and more precise cut, build and use my shop-made long-extension fence (shown on the next page). If the sheet goods are thin and pliable—for example, ⅛" door skins or plastic laminates—use another type of shop-made fence fixture shown later in this chapter.

This extension fence, which I designed to be compatible with my tall auxiliary fence, features an extralong guide fence to offer large workpieces more guidance ahead of the blade, ensuring a more accurate cut. The horizontal support ahead of the table offers additional guidance and support when and where you need it most. You'll find that this fixture allows you to get the panel situated level to the table and tight to the fence before you push it into the blade. No more worrying about hitting the front edge of the panel against the spinning blade while you are struggling to get the panel aligned to the rip fence. I have not included any specific provisions for hold-downs with this fence (you can clamp featherboards to it if you wish) because I find that the weight of the panel stock helps keep the fence flat to the table. Large workpieces also provide plenty of leverage to help you manipulate them and keep them tight to the rip fence.

I suggest making this extension fence from straight, hardwood veneer ¾" ply. Add the ¾"- or ½"-thick plywood horizontal support with screw and plate biscuit joinery or with Ready-to-Assemble (RTA) fasteners. Notice how this fixture sandwiches around the tall auxiliary fence: This

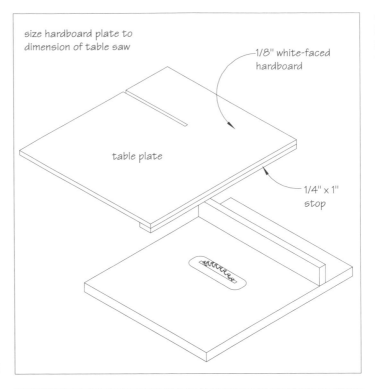

size hardboard plate to dimension of table saw

1/8" white-faced hardboard

table plate

1/4" x 1" stop

My shop-made extension auxiliary fence, which bolts conveniently to the universal fence fixture, supports and guides the sheet stock well ahead of the blade, easing handling and ensuring a more accurate rip. Another shop-made fixture, the jointer-mounted support, features ball bearings that support the sheet to the side of the saw.

provides additional stiffness for the portion of the fence extending past the front of the saw. Round all exposed edges of the fixture, sand and shellac to make the edges smooth and splinter-free. I add a strip of Ultra High Molecular Weight (UHMW) plastic or teak to the fence to provide a low-friction bearing surface. The strip also allows me to subtract an even inch when reading the rip fence cursor, making for quicker setups. This fixture fastens to my tall auxiliary fence with studded knobs screwed to the fence's existing T-nuts.

Stock Supports

Because sheet stocks are invariably large and unwieldy, especially when making the initial cuts into the full-size sheets, you need all the handling help you can get. Unless your work space is crawling with eager shop buddies who have little else to do with their time, it's up to you to provide some form of support to the front (infeed), sides and back (outfeed) of the sheet. Simple, flat-surfaced tables, even and level with the table saw, work fine as the outfeed and right-side supports and can be left up permanently. To the left side and in front of the saw, it's best to use temporary supports featuring unidirectional ball rollers. I generally avoid bar-type rollers with unfixed supports because if they shift away from being perpendicular to the direction of feed (or better, about 2° toward the rip fence), they can throw off the cut and potentially cause a kickback.

In my shop, I set my 8" jointer immediately to the left of the table saw, which twenty-five years of shop experience have convinced me is the most efficient location for this tool. This setup allows me to use the jointer as the base of a temporary side-support system. Built of ¾" plywood, this fixture features box-beam construction to ensure rigidity and straightness, a long length (6') for ample support, and easy dismount. Other features include a stop to prevent forward motion and a gang of unidirectional roller balls placed every 8" (this spacing is the maximum; closer spacing doesn't hurt and gives better support for narrow workpieces and crosscutting sled fixtures). There is an important setup factor with this support system: Your jointer table must be parallel with the saw table. Shim the jointer's base as necessary to make it so. (Directions for making this fixture are in chapter three.)

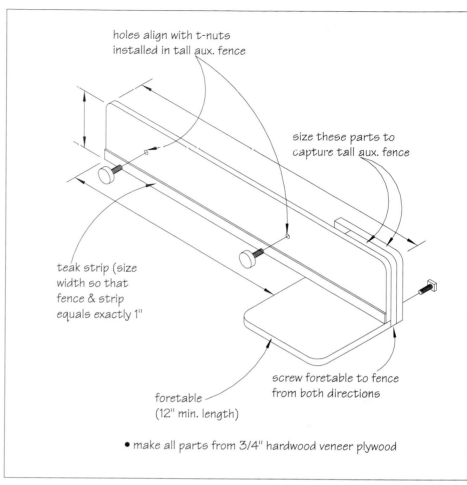

holes align with t-nuts installed in tall aux. fence

size these parts to capture tall aux. fence

teak strip (size width so that fence & strip equals exactly 1"

screw foretable to fence from both directions

foretable (12" min. length)

• make all parts from 3/4" hardwood veneer plywood

CONSTRUCTION DRAWING OF EXTENSION FENCE FOR SHEET GOODS

SUPPORTING PANEL STOCK ON SAWS WITHOUT A SIDE EXTENSION TABLE

If your saw does not have a side extension table and you are trying to cut out a wide strip of thin panel stock, you may be in trouble. It is possible (approaching probable with stock ¼" thick and under) that the strip might slip under the fence. Not only will this throw off the cut, it might also throw the panel off the saw—not a pretty picture. To prevent this from happening, make a support fixture that you can temporarily clamp (or bolt) to the rip fence (see the drawing shown here for construction details).

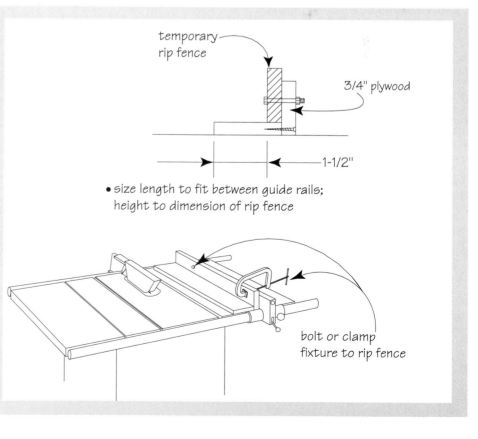

temporary rip fence

3/4" plywood

1-1/2"

• size length to fit between guide rails; height to dimension of rip fence

bolt or clamp fixture to rip fence

Off Switch Access

Because full-size sheets cover the on/off switch on most table saws, it is imperative to provide some kind of hands-free panic stop. If a sheet starts to bind in the cut, you'll need both hands to keep the sheet under control while you turn off the machine. You can install a commercially made oversize panel switch (see chapter three) or make your own panic bar, as shown in chapter one. Either of these setups will turn off the machine with a bump of your hip or a stab of the foot. As an added convenience, I mount the dust collector's remote switch on the top of the panic bar with a strip of self-adhesive Velcro.

Layout and Prep Work

Now that your table saw is set up to handle sheet goods with efficiency and safety, it's time to learn about the actual cutting processes. Before you make a cut, however, it's important to your back (not to mention your pocketbook) to learn how to cut up the sheets in the most efficient way possible. A good cutting layout will allow you to get the sheet into manageable-size pieces as quickly as possible as well as organize the component pieces to get the most out of the panel's surface area.

Begin the component layout process on the sheet area by checking the stock for defects. Look for damaged edges, blows (voids in the laminations under the surface that cause cracking in the surface veneer) and cosmetic blemishes. Mark the defects with a crayon or piece of chalk so that you will notice and avoid them. Now comes the challenge: laying out the component parts to allow you to cut the sheet into manageable chunks while getting the most use out of the available surface area.

Hopefully, you will have given yourself a head start during the design phase by planning the component dimensions, as much as possible, around the numeric realities of a 4'x8' sheet of material. In other words, do the pieces' measurements relate to whole fractions of 48" and 96"? For example, do parts fall under 24", 16" or 12" in width and 64", 48", 32" or 24" in length?

One trick I use to ease the drain on my brain is to begin the layout with the largest components. Once these pieces

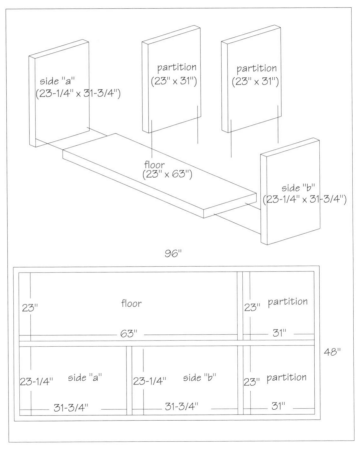

A bump with my leg against this shop-made "panic bar" turns the saw off.

RELATIONSHIP OF CABINET'S COMPONENTS TO EFFICIENT CUTTING LAYOUT ON SHEET STOCK

are accounted for, I work my way through the smaller parts, grouping them whenever possible to create a series of easy-to-handle strips of material, which I will later cut to length.

Presquaring and Straightening Edges of Sheets

In an ideal world, the factory edges of the panel stock would always be straight and true and square to the ends of the panel. Then you could use the existing edge as a reference against the rip fence or crosscut sled fence. But it's not an ideal world and you can't always trust the edges to be straight or square to one another. Panels may also have rough edges because of void fillers, warehouse "rash" and even staples. You should also be aware that some sheet stocks are oversize; for example, industrial-grade particleboards are often 49"x97".

I use one of two methods to trim sheet stock's factory edges clean and straight (after removing the staples, of course): a jointing fixture on the table saw or a tem-

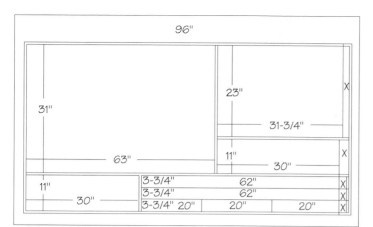

EXAMPLES OF EFFICIENT SHEET LAYOUTS

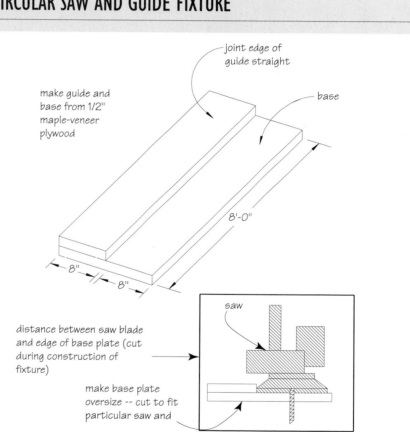

GEOMETRY OF THE JOINTING SETUP ON THE TABLE SAW

plate-guided router. To gain a square end, I use a shop-made square/template with the router.

Jointing on the Table Saw

Yes, you really can joint the edge of a board or length of sheet stock on the table saw. In practice, I use this trick primarily for cleaning up the rough factory edges of plywood to create a reference edge free of bumps or other imperfections. The principle is simple (as is the actual procedure): The rip fence, equipped with a special fixture, guides the edge of the stock into the blade so that the blade removes a shaving rather than cutting a kerf. On the outfeed side of the blade, the fence fixture is offset the thickness of the shaving to catch and guide the outfeeding edge of the stock. The drawing on page 128 shows the geometry of this setup as well as an illustration of the fixture.

Make the fixture from a straight-edged strip of hardwood veneer plywood cut at least as long as your rip fence or to a minimum of 16" past the back of the blade. As with a standard jointer, the longer the surface, the more accurate the jointing action. Cut a half-circle opening to clear the saw blade. (I prefer to cut the clearance semicircle rather than creating it by raising the spinning blade into the fixture. There are two reasons: The full-depth cavity allows side adjustment of the fixture without bearing on the blade, and the extra clearance prevents overheating the blade when it's defected sideways under stress.) I build out the outfeed section of the fixture with a ¹⁄₁₆"-thick plastic laminate.

SIZING SHEETS TO MANAGEABLE SIZES WITH CIRCULAR SAW AND GUIDE FIXTURE

Construction drawing of circular saw guide fixture for cutting panel stock.

If you are working with a small table saw (9" or smaller) with limited rip fence width capacity and/or your shop has limited space around the saw itself, you will likely find it easier to precut the full-size panels into more manageable pieces off the saw. Use this simple-to-make guide fixture with a circular saw to size down the sheets quickly and with a surprising degree of accuracy.

After jointing the edges straight, you can then use the sawn edges as the reference edges for ripping to final width on the table saw. Be sure to support the panel well when making the circular saw cuts. I use three to four 2x4s set across a pair of sawhorses.

To set up the fixture for use, clamp it directly to your rip fence or attach it with two handled bolts to the universal tall auxiliary fence. Next, adjust the rip fence position so that the blade removes a shaving the exact same size as the outfeed build-out (the 1/16" laminate). Test cut scrap until you get it right. Now run the stock by the blade using side push sticks to keep it tight to the jointing fixture. Important: Apply slightly more pressure against the outfeed portion (where the laminate strip is) of the fence to ensure that the edge joints straight.

Jointing With a Router

An alternative method for cleaning and straightening the edge of sheet stock is to clamp a straight-edged board to the sheet stock and use it as a guide template for a router set up with a shank-mounted bearing, pattern-following bit. Clamp the guide board parallel to the stock's edge and inset about 1/8" (or more if there is need to cut out a damaged section). The board should be wide enough to allow the router base to clear the clamps and long enough to extend at least 6" past either end of the stock. To make the cut, hold the router in position on the overhanging portion of the guide board, turn it on and run it from left to right. Keep the shank bearing running against the guide board throughout the cut. Make a second clean-up pass to ensure a perfect replication of the guide board's straight edge.

To cut the end of the sheet square to the straightened edge, clamp a squaring template to the sheet, aligning the stops of the template to the sheet's edge and insetting the crossarm about 1/8" in from the end. Run the router as before, this time across the end of the sheet. If your squaring template is true, the sheet stock will be too. You can now use this edge and end as reference surfaces for making subsequent sizing cuts.

Panel-Cutting Procedures

When sizing components from sheet stock, the basic procedure usually involves three steps: Rip strips to width, crosscut the components to finished length, then rip them (if necessary) to their finished width. In general, offer sheet stocks good side up to the table saw

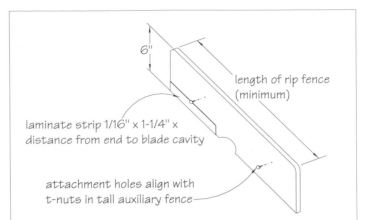

JOINTING FIXTURE FOR RIP FENCE

6"

length of rip fence (minimum)

laminate strip 1/16" x 1-1/4" x distance from end to blade cavity

attachment holes align with t-nuts in tall auxiliary fence

This shop-made fixture, bolted to the universal fence fixture, turns the table saw into a jointer by allowing the blade to skim off the edge of the workpiece.

To make the end of a sheet perfectly straight and perpendicular to the side edge, rout the edge with a pattern-following bit. A shop-made square clamped to the sheet stock guides the cut.

so any roughness from the blade will appear on the less desirable (and hopefully unexposed) bottom face.

Note the terminology: I use "ripping" to mean sawing with the long dimension of the sheet—usually, though not necessarily, with the grain of the surface veneer. "Crosscutting" means sawing across the short dimension. As a general rule you'll use the rip fence when sizing the long

dimension to width and a crosscut guide (a sliding table or sled) to size the strips to length.

Ripping

Prepare to cut with the grain or long dimension of the sheet stock by setting up infeed and outfeed supports (be sure they are level with the table saw surface) and by installing a fence extension. You can do without these accessories, but you put both the quality of the cut and your body at risk. Take the time to give yourself a hand when working with these awkward-size, heavy workpieces.

I follow this basic ripping procedure: I check the factory edge for defects and straightness, removing any staples or other foreign objects. Then, if I feel it's too rough to serve as is, I joint the edge. Next, I set the fence to the strip width dimension indicated on my graphic representation of that sheet, adding about ¼". I then cut the strip, reset the fence to the exact width dimension and then recut it a second time using the first ripped edge as a reference against the rip fence. The strip now has two parallel long edges and is ready for crosscutting.

Ripping at an Angle

What do you do if the rip cut is not to be parallel to the reference edge? If the workpiece is relatively small, you may be able to guide it through the cut with a taper jig or a hold-down sled (see chapter five) to create the wedge-shaped component. If, however, you are working with a full-size panel, these fixtures are way out of their class. Your best option is to employ a special guide system that uses the edge of the saw table rather than the rip fence as a guide.

To construct this guide system, begin by cutting a runner from a 4' length of stiff hardwood (I use hard maple) or two strips of ½" maple ply glue-laminated together. This runner must be straight and have slightly rounded or chamfered edges (to prevent catching on the panel) and a polished finish (to reduce friction). I found I had to notch my runner to fit over my rip fence system's front guide bar. To make installation and removal quick and easy, I drilled and tapped the cast iron extension wing to receive a pair of ⁵⁄₁₆" machine bolts. If your table's wing is sheet metal, use through bolts and wing nuts.

Here's how to use the system: Install the runner and set up your side and infeed supports. Draw the cut line directly on the face of the panel stock. Now measure the distance from the blade to the edge of the runner (record this dimension as you will use it again in future setups), and tranfer this distance dimension onto

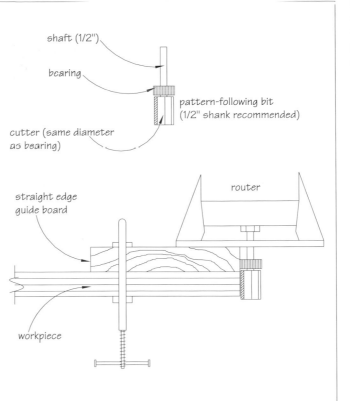

shaft (1/2")

bearing

pattern-following bit
(1/2" shank recommended)

cutter (same diameter as bearing)

straight edge guide board

router

workpiece

PREVENTING TEAR-OUT ON FRAGILE VENEERS

Some sheet goods have fragile veneers (wood or plastic laminate) that can easily tear out where the saw blade's teeth exit the kerf, especially if the blade is dull or not designed to cut that specific material. The problem is particularly acute when crosscutting hardwood veneer plywood and melamine-laminated fiberboards. If you are stuck with the blade at hand, try using one or more of these techniques to reduce the amount of tear-out:

- Use a freshly cut, zero-clearance throat plate.
- Prescore the cut line with a sharp utility knife. When setting up for the cut, orient the score line to the blade's alignment mark on the throat plate. Don't pull the stock back through the blade after making the cut.
- When crosscutting strips to length with a crosscut sled, you can precut the veneer on the bottom of the workpiece

to minimize tear-out by employing the climb cut—a procedure in which you feed the stock in the same direction as the rotation of the blade. Here's how to do it: Set the blade about ¹⁄₃₂" above the sled surface. Lock the fence stop to dimension. Now slide the sled past the back of the blade, set the workpiece securely in place against the fence and stop, turn on the saw and draw the sled to the front until the blade has passed the back edge of the workpiece. Turn off the saw and adjust the blade height to cut all the way through the stock. Recut, this time in the usual fashion from the front to the back (against the rotation of the blade). Safety note: This climb cut technique requires extra caution. Prepare to keep back pressure on the sled. Keep your hands away from where the blade will exit the back end of the stock.

SAFETY *tip*

Never use the rip fence as a guide to crosscut a component piece with a short dimension of less than 18".

the panel by squaring over from the cut line at the front and back. Now you are ready to clamp a guide—a straight-edged board about 6" wide (for stiffness) and at least 1' longer than the workpiece—under the panel at the layout marks.

Time for the cut. Turn on the saw, place the panel on the infeed and side supports and align the guide against the runner bolted to the saw. As you run the panel through the blade, keep the guide tight against the runner throughout the cut. You can cut more than one panel at a time up to about 1" of total thickness by clamping the guide to several layers of panel stock. If the panels are each less than ½" thick, I suggest carpet-taping the sheets together in the area of the rip cut to prevent them from fluttering and tearing out on the underside of the cut.

Trimming Bandings

When working with sheet stocks, it's often part of the program to cover the exposed edges with a solid-wood banding. To do this efficiently I make the bandings oversize in width. This allows me to trim the banding flush to the stock rather than having to plane or sand the sheet stock surface flush to an undersized banding—a tricky proposition considering how thin the veneers are. I've discovered that the quickest way to bring the bandings nearly flush (leaving just enough protrusion for sanding) is to trim the banding on the table saw. The fixtures shown on the next two pages ensure accuracy and impressive speed.

If the workpiece is narrow, I use the guide fixture shown in the drawing on page 131 to trim off the protruding ends of the banding. The fixture is simply a rectangular-shaped scrap of ¾" maple plywood about 6"x12" (the measurements are not critical, though the two long edges must be parallel). I apply a strip of sandpaper to one edge with spray adhesive or carpet tape to provide a high-friction surface for the workpiece. Setup and use is easy: Raise the blade high enough to cut off the banding. Now hold the scrap against the rip fence and slide them both toward the blade until the outside face of the blade (the face away from the rip fence) is even with the outside edge of the guide fixture. After locking down the

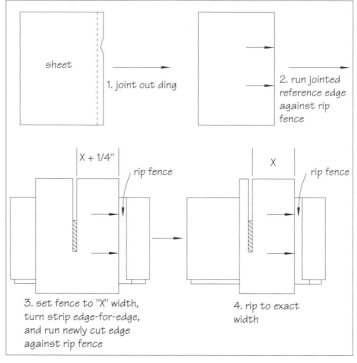

SEQUENCE GRAPHIC OF BASIC SHEET STOCK RIPPING PROCEDURE

sheet

1. joint out ding

2. run jointed reference edge against rip fence

X + 1/4" rip fence

X rip fence

3. set fence to "X" width, turn strip edge-for-edge, and run newly cut edge against rip fence

4. rip to exact width

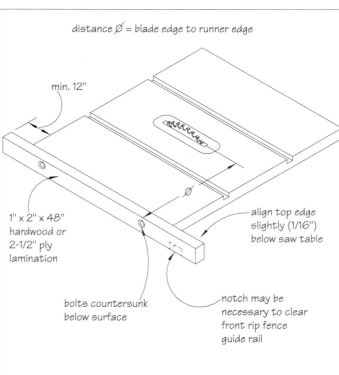

EXTENSION WING RUNNER SYSTEM

distance Ø = blade edge to runner edge

min. 12"

1" x 2" x 48" hardwood or 2-1/2" ply lamination

align top edge slightly (1/16") below saw table

bolts countersunk below surface

notch may be necessary to clear front rip fence guide rail

rip fence and turning on the saw, hold one edge of the workpiece firmly against the sandpapered edge of the guide and feed them both into the blade, stopping when the blade has cut off the protruding edge band. Flip the workpiece edge for edge (and then end for end if necessary), and repeat the process.

To trim banding along the edges of a workpiece, I add a pair of runners (as

SAFETY *tip*

The clamps must be secure as shifting of stock during the cut could cause a kickback. A more fail-safe alternative to clamping is to screw the guide board to the panel. The screw holes should, however, fall in a waste area of the workpiece, as they will show on the top surface of the panel.

shown in the drawing on page 132 to my rip fence sled. These runners—strips of 2"-wide ¾" plywood—are quickly installed to the sled fixture with knobs (into bolts from the MiniTrack) at their far ends. The knobs at the front of the sled also secure a clamp carriage in place. This accessory provides both backing support and hold-downs for the workpiece.

To set up the cut, slide the rip fence with sled installed toward the blade until the face of the lower runner is even with the outside face of the blade. Lock down the rip fence. Raise the blade just high enough to trim off the banding. Now pull back the fence sled, set the workpiece in place against the clamp carriage and clamp it down. Be sure to allow at least 1" of clearance between the front edge of the workpiece and the blade. Turn on the saw and slide the fixture forward until the blade cuts through the full length of the banding.

Crosscutting

The basic procedure for crosscutting strips of sheet stock using a crosscut sled or miter gauge fence is a simple three-step process: First, oversize the length of the first cut in the strip by about ½" (unless you have already template-routed the end of the sheet square). Second, set the fence stop to the exact length distance (consult your sheet-cutting graphic) and recut the first panel to length by reversing it end for end and placing the fresh-cut end against the stop. Third, make the subsequent cuts in the remainder of the strip.

Cutting Small Panel Components With a Square-Template Fixture

Here's a trick for quickly cutting out a square or rectangular-shaped component from a scrap of sheet stock. The neat thing about this trick is that the scrap need only have one straight edge. Another advantage is that you don't have to get down a cumbersome crosscut sled for just one component. All you need are this square-template fixture and the rip fence to guide the scrap through the blade.

Make the fixture from a scrap of flat panel stock (¾" hardwood-faced plywood is first choice) that you have cut to a perfect rectangle with your crosscut fixtures.

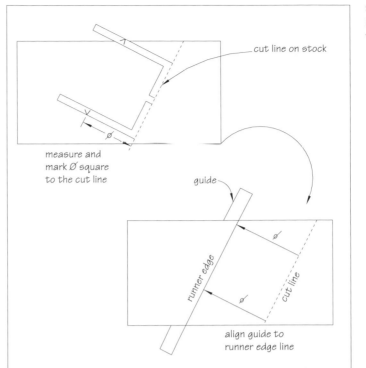

cut line on stock

measure and mark Ø square to the cut line

guide

runner edge

cut line

align guide to runner edge line

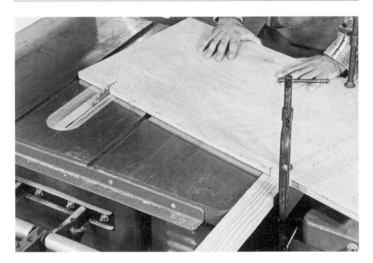

With a straight stick bolted to the side of the saw table and a straight board clamped to the workpiece, I create a guide system that accurately makes angled crosscuts across boards too wide to guide with the miter gauge.

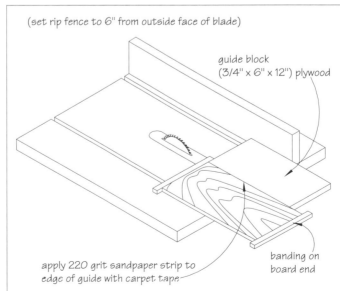

TRIMMING BANDING AT ENDS OF NARROW WORKPIECES

(set rip fence to 6" from outside face of blade)

guide block (3/4" x 6" x 12") plywood

apply 220 grit sandpaper strip to edge of guide with carpet tape

banding on board end

(Test it by measuring its diagonals—they should be equal.) I sized mine to cut pieces from about 4"x12" to about 16"x24". Shape the fixture as shown, and add a front stop to the bottom and a strip of teak or UHMW plastic to the indexing edge. I shellac the entire fixture, then coat the bottom with paint to which I have added a nonslip additive (fine silicon sand).

Before using the fixture, be sure the rip fence is parallel with the saw blade (see chapter two). This alignment is critical or you will not be able to create a figure with even diagonals (four square corners). To use the squaring fixture, follow these steps: Lay the fixture over the scrap, aligning the scrap's straight edge against the front stop. Be sure there is at least a 1" clearance between the front edge of the workpiece and the blade as the side of the fixture indexes against the rip fence—if not, the workpiece is too wide for this trick. Also be sure that the end of the scrap doesn't protrude past the fixture's index edge. Set the rip fence so that the blade cuts off about ¼" from the far end of the scrap. Next, set the rip

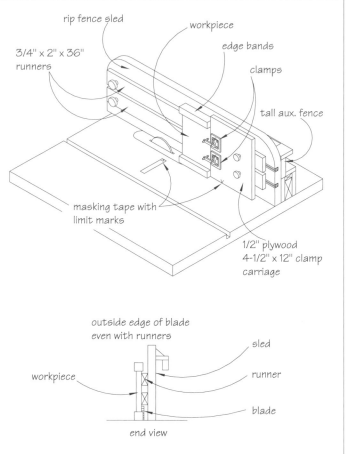

TRIMMING BANDING ALONG THE EDGE OF A WORKPIECE

Adding two strips and a clamp board to my sliding rip fence fixture turns it into a fast and accurate banding trimmer.

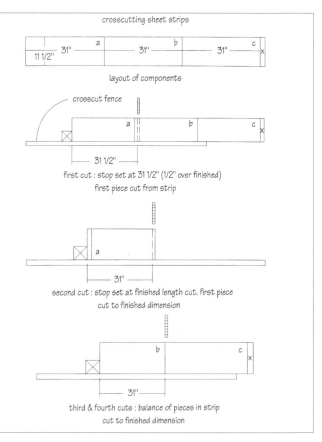

SEQUENCE GRAPHIC FOR CROSSCUTTING SHEET STRIPS

fence to the desired length, reverse the scrap end for end and then align the fresh-cut end flush with the index edge of the jig (and thus against the rip fence). Now guide the assembly through the blade. The component is now cut to length with two perfectly square corners. Finally, set the rip fence to the desired width and run the component through with its original straight edge against the rip fence. You now have a product with four square corners.

Cutting Laminate and Other Thin Sheet Stocks

Thin sheet stocks, such as plastic laminates, wall paneling, door skins and hardboards, pose specific challenges when cut on a standard table saw. A common problem is the difficulty in handling the frustratingly flexible sheets. Not only are they hard to maneuver onto the saw, they can be difficult to keep against the rip fence (laminates in particular tend to slip under it) and flat to the table surface.

There is, however, a good solution for dealing with these sheet stocks, beyond providing adequate side and infeed support, that makes them easier to handle and to guide through the saw blade: a specialized, shop-made, thin-sheet auxiliary rip fence that controls slippage and curling as you push the sheet across the saw and through the blade. This fixture captures the edge of the sheet in a slot, keeping the panel flat, stiff (it can't buckle on you) and under control. You can see to keep the reference edge tight to the fence, and the slot prevents the sheets (especially the thin laminates) from fluttering as the uprising back of the blade encounters the stock.

Make the fixture from a strip of hardwood veneer ¾" plywood cut at least as long as your rip fence (or a minimum of 36"). The sheet stock will be controlled between two guide surfaces: a thin bottom strip of plastic laminate and a strip of clear Plexiglas. I use a sandwich construction technique to make construction simple and strong, edge-gluing together the vertical plywood component, the Plexiglas strip, the spacer strip and the laminate strip (the bottom support). I make the spacer strip of teak for strength and slickness, sizing it to exactly 1" in width to

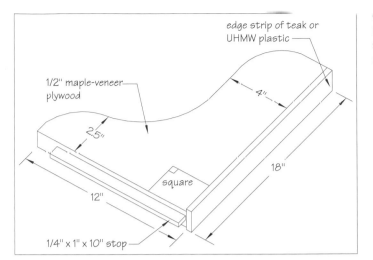

edge strip of teak or UHMW plastic

1/2" maple-veneer plywood

2.5"

4"

square

18"

12"

1/4" x 1" x 10" stop

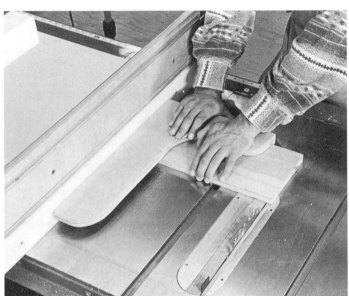

This simple jig—nothing more than a square piece of plywood with a stop under the front edge—runs against the rip fence to cut off the end of a small workpiece perpendicular to its edge. Lightweight and easy to use (it's preset to cut 90°), I tend to reach for this jig rather than the miter gauge when I need to trim or square up an odd piece of wood.

make it easier to set the rip fence with the cursor.

When it's time to cut up some thin sheet stock, pull the fixture off the wall and secure it to the rip fence. Designed for use with my tall auxiliary fence, this fixture attaches in seconds with two star-handled bolts. (You can also clamp it to a standard rip fence.) When setting the fence to width, remember that the cursor index of your rip fence will be off by the thickness of the fixture's spacer strip-make it exactly 1" and the calculation is easy. Feed the thin sheet between the guide strips, being careful to keep pressure against the fence in front (your side) of the blade throughout the cut. Cut sheet stock good side up whenever possible to reduce the impact of any tear-out. Note: I generally cut laminate oversize to allow final trimming to its substrate with a bearing-guided router bit.

RIPPING STOCK TO NARROW STRIPS

If you've worked around the table saw a while, you've likely run into situations where you need to rip narrow strips of wood: making edge banding for plywood, runners for drawer guides and decorative inlay strips to mention a few. As you've no doubt discovered, the narrower the strip you have to rip, the trickier the process gets. A standard fence and guard system doesn't leave any room for the blade guard between the rip fence and the blade under a certain dimension. When you remove the guard to get it out of the way, you not only lose protection, but also the splitter. Also, a standard throat plate with its large opening lends poor support to the strips and may even catch the end of one, causing kickback. Finally, your poor push stick, if it's wider than the strips being cut, will eventually become shredded and dangerously ineffective.

So what can be done to make ripping narrow strips a less anxiety-ridden process? One foolproof strategy is to rip the thin strip(s) in a thick board where the blade need not pass all the way through the stock. Though you'll have to remove the splitter, you won't need it because the uncut stock captures and controls the strips. To release the strips, you simply lay the stock on its side and rip them off all at once to the outside of the blade (away from the rip fence). Another method, which allows the splitter and guard to stay on the saw, is to simply rip off the strip on the outside of the blade. But as you have no doubt surmised, there is a price to pay for the security of these methods: The fence must be reset for each strip. If you want to cut multiple narrow strips with efficiency, read on to learn about some shop-made fixtures that will make it so.

Accessories for Ripping Narrow Stock

When I set up for ripping narrow stock, I install a sharp, thin-kerf carbide blade with ATB teeth. Such a blade will take away a minimum amount of material (sometimes gaining an additional strip from the stock) while providing a smooth-edged cut that needs no surfacing (which can be tricky with thin stock). In addition, I always use a shop-made throat plate with zero clearance and an integral splitter as described in chapter three to provide ample support and control for the narrow strips.

If the narrow strips are to come out of a board about 8" to 16" long, use the simple fixture shown in the drawing on the next page to push the board past the blade. To rip lengths shorter than 8" with safety and precision, you can employ the sled fixture designed for working with small parts, shown later in this chapter.

This notched push fixture provides a secure carriage for the stock and allows ample room for my hand and the guard system between the blade and the rip fence. I make the fixture from a scrap of ¾" hardwood-faced plywood, installing a separate backstop that can be unscrewed and adjusted, or replaced entirely, as it wears from usage. A strip of teak or

UHMW plastic added to the index edge and a polished shellac finish eliminate most of the sliding friction from the fixture itself.

To use the fixture, first set the rip fence to width—a simple matter of setting the cursor to the desired thickness of the strip plus the width of the fixture. Adjust the backstop to protrude about ⅛" past the edge of the fixture plus the thickness

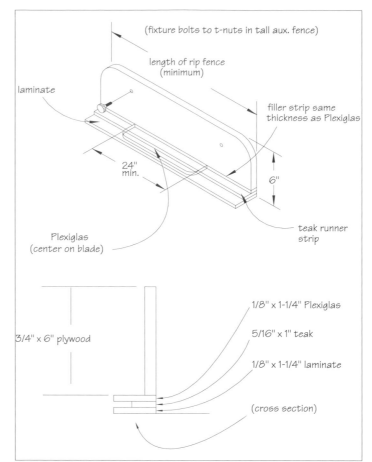

THIN-SHEET AUXILIARY FENCE

(fixture bolts to t-nuts in tall aux. fence)

length of rip fence (minimum)

laminate

filler strip same thickness as Plexiglas

24" min.

6"

teak runner strip

Plexiglas (center on blade)

3/4" x 6" plywood

1/8" x 1-1/4" Plexiglas

5/16" x 1" teak

1/8" x 1-1/4" laminate

(cross section)

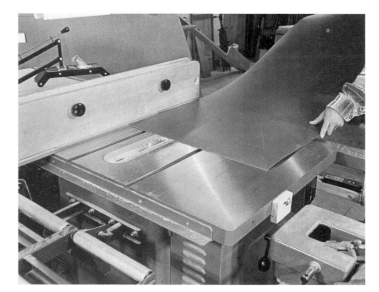

This accessory mounted to the universal fence fixture captures thin sheet goods between two guide surfaces, ensuring the sheet rides against the fence to produce a safe and accurate cut.

SAFETY *tip*

Check the stock carefully for defects before ripping it into thin strips. Avoid cross grain and knots, as these are weak points that can allow a narrow strip of wood to shatter during the cut.

of the strip. Set a board against the side of the fixture and to the backstop, turn on the saw and move the fixture forward into the blade. Use a V-notched side stick (see chapter three) to hold the board firmly against the side of the fixture, being careful to apply pressure only against the area ahead of the blade. When the board passes behind the front edge of the blade, back off on the push stick and with your right hand continue to push the fixture until it clears the back of the blade. Push the fixture and narrow strip onto the outfeed table (or until the strip drops off into a box set against the back of the saw).

If I need strips longer than I feel comfortable cutting with the notched fixture, I install a shop-made low rip fence as shown on page 136. This fence fixture provides ample guidance for the longer strips, plenty of room for the guard system and room (and visibility) to use a push stick against the end of the strip. Designed to integrate with the auxiliary tall fence, which is usually left on the rip fence, it installs in seconds with two star-handled bolts. The slotted attachment holes allow this low rip fence accessory to also be used as a guide fence for pattern cuts.

If I'm ripping long, narrow stock without the low fence, I use a specialized shoe-type push stick to push the stock through the blade. Because this pusher is designed to straddle the rip fence, it is much easier to keep under control when the pusher encounters the blade along with the narrow stock. I attach the stop with screws (in slotted holes so the depth of the stop is adjustable) so I can easily replace it when it becomes too mangled to provide a secure footing for the stock. Notice how I've drilled out ¾" holes in the side of the ½" plywood pusher, filling the holes with ¾" dowel stock to offer a more secure purchase for the screws. (Plywood tends to lose its screw-holding power after several removals and reinsertions.) To ensure a tight, but still slippery, grasp on my tall auxiliary fence, I temporarily clamp the parts of the pusher together and test the fit. I plane the center spacer down if the fit is too loose, or add sandpaper shims if too tight. When satisfied, I glue and screw the assembly together.

NARROW STRIPS FROM THICK STOCK IN THREE STEPS: STRIP CUT, CONTINUED CUTS, FREEING CUT

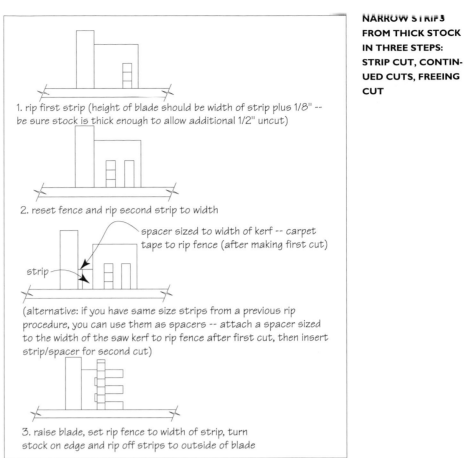

1. rip first strip (height of blade should be width of strip plus 1/8" -- be sure stock is thick enough to allow additional 1/2" uncut)

2. reset fence and rip second strip to width

spacer sized to width of kerf -- carpet tape to rip fence (after making first cut)

strip

(alternative: if you have same size strips from a previous rip procedure, you can use them as spacers -- attach a spacer sized to the width of the saw kerf to rip fence after first cut, then insert strip/spacer for second cut)

3. raise blade, set rip fence to width of strip, turn stock on edge and rip off strips to outside of blade

THE VACUUM FENCE: A SPECIALIZED ACCESSORY FOR RIPPING THIN SLICES

When cutting tall, thin slices of flexible materials such as balsa wood (I often make my own sheet stock for model airplane construction), I find that as the slices leave the front cutting edge of the blade, they start fluttering from blade vibration and probably the tiny, though swift, wind currents generated by the blade tips. The results range from a rough-cut, slightly scorched surface to a complete shattering of the slice if it jams against the splitter.

This fixture, which uses the powerful suction of a Shop Vac to hold the slice against the rip fence, not only eliminates the need for a pusher against the thin slice cut, which is highly problematic at these dimensions, but also allows the slice to separate from the workpiece (between the blade and fence) without moving into the blade or down into the throat plate opening. The strong hold-down force from the vacuum also ensures that the slice is

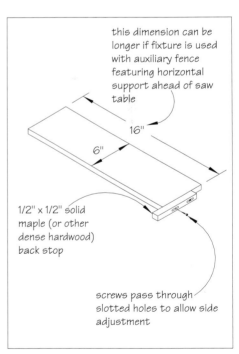

this dimension can be longer if fixture is used with auxiliary fence featuring horizontal support ahead of saw table

16"

6"

1/2" x 1/2" solid maple (or other dense hardwood) back stop

screws pass through slotted holes to allow side adjustment

NOTCHED PUSH FIXTURE FOR RIPPING NARROW STOCK

cut at a uniform thickness over the full length of the stock.

This vacuum fence fixture coordinates with the universal rip fence fixture, easily installing with two knob-handled bolts. Build the vacuum fence fixture from maple plywood and a length of pegboard stock. The joints are glued and screwed together. Cut the hole in the cap board before assembly, sizing the hole to fit the end of your shop vacuum hose. I use a jig-saw, though a hole saw (if you are fortunate enough to have the right size) makes for a quicker, cleaner job. Round all exposed corners and edges of the fixture and coat with shellac or other sealer.

Setting up and Using the Vacuum Fence

Use this fixture in conjunction with a zero-tolerance throat plate with integral splitter. Bolt the fixture to the universal rip fence and then slide the fixture to the blade to be sure the blade is parallel with the face of the fixture's fence. For an absolutely precise setup, hold a .01" feeler gauge between a tooth at the top of the blade and the fence, and adjust the fence until the blade of the gauge slides smoothly between the tooth and the fence face.

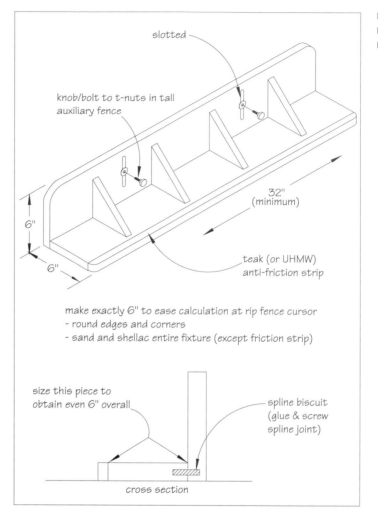

LOW FENCE FOR RIPPING LONG, NARROW STRIPS

slotted

knob/bolt to t-nuts in tall auxiliary fence

6"

6"

32" (minimum)

teak (or UHMW) anti-friction strip

make exactly 6" to ease calculation at rip fence cursor
- round edges and corners
- sand and shellac entire fixture (except friction strip)

size this piece to obtain even 6" overall

spline biscuit (glue & screw spline joint)

cross section

I use this simple fixture to safely cut narrow strips from the edge of a board. The backstop is adjustable side to side so it will not be cut off with the strip.

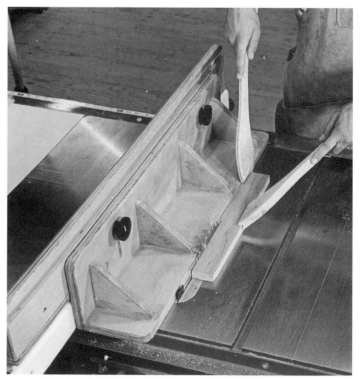

I use this fixture for cutting long narrow strips. Because the guide fence is low and is brought away from the rip fence, there is plenty of room for both push sticks and the guard system—and for seeing what you are doing.

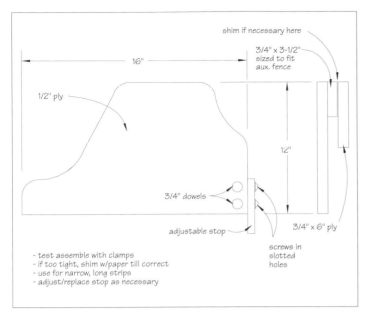

shim if necessary here

3/4" x 3-1/2"
sized to fit
aux. fence

16"

1/2" ply

12"

3/4" dowels

adjustable stop

3/4" x 6" ply

screws in
slotted
holes

- test assemble with clamps
- if too tight, shim w/paper till correct
- use for narrow, long strips
- adjust/replace stop as necessary

STRADDLE-TYPE PUSHER FOR LONG NARROW STOCK

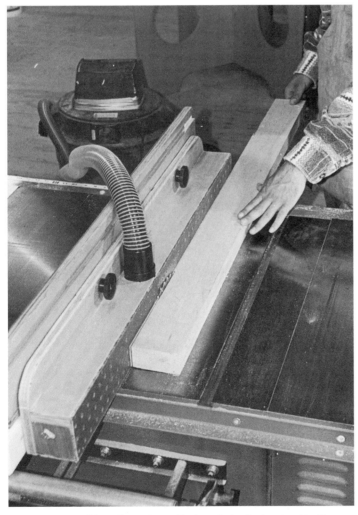

A vacuum-actuated fence fixture is an effective solution for keeping thin slices under control during the ripping operation. When hooked up to a portable Shop Vac, the resulting negative pressure forces the just-cut slice tight against the fence, free from flutter or the potential of encountering the splitter.

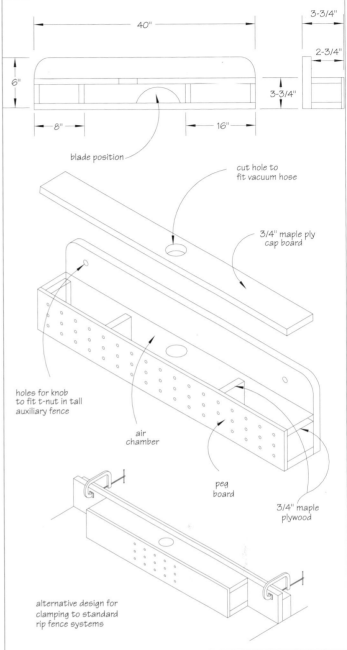

40"

3-3/4"

2-3/4"

6"

8"

16"

3-3/4"

blade position

cut hole to
fit vacuum hose

3/4" maple ply
cap board

holes for knob
to fit t-nut in tall
auxiliary fence

air
chamber

peg
board

3/4" maple
plywood

alternative design for
clamping to standard
rip fence systems

VACUUM-ACTUATED RIP FENCE

SAFETY *tip*

Never reach over the blade to remove the strip from the fixture, and never push against the side of the board once the stock moves past the front of the blade.

Now rotate the tooth to table level and try the gauge again. If there is a difference in fit, adjust the arbor angle. When satisfied, set the rip fence for the desired thickness of cut. A sharp blade on a wobble-free arbor (within tolerance) in conjunction with the stock-controlling power afforded by the vacuum within the fence will ensure a smooth slice with consistent, uniform thickness.

Turn on the vacuum and the table saw, and feed the stock into the blade using a push shoe. Because of the holding power of the fence, you need not push against the portion of the stock that will be sliced to dimension. When the offcut is freed from the sliced cut, set the offcut to one side, stand to the right side of the rip fence and pull the slice along the face of the fence with your right hand until it clears the back of the blade.

SAWING SMALL, ODD-SHAPED PARTS

A typical table saw is designed to work efficiently with stock that is at least 1' long and has at least one straight edge. This is what these machines' standard guidance systems (the miter gauge, the rip fence and even the standard throat plate) are scaled to handle. When workpieces get smaller than this or are oddly shaped, procedures get tricky. It becomes nearly impossible to guide and hold onto the stock securely. Your fingers can come perilously close to the blade in some cases, and it's even possible to lose the smallest-size pieces to the throat plate opening.

My secret weapon for working with small and odd-shaped workpieces is this diminutive carriage sled made from a flat piece of ¾" hardwood veneer plywood. This fixture fully controls the workpieces, no matter their shapes or sizes, without requiring your fingers to come near the blade. Because the sled table presents zero clearance around the blade, there is no chance a tiny piece will be lost to the saw. Also, waste cuts are carried safely away from the blade. To further help ensure a clean, accurate cut when working with small parts, I always use a fine-cutting, sharp blade (a 60-tooth ATB) outfitted with a stablizer. I also check to be sure that the arbor is locked down at

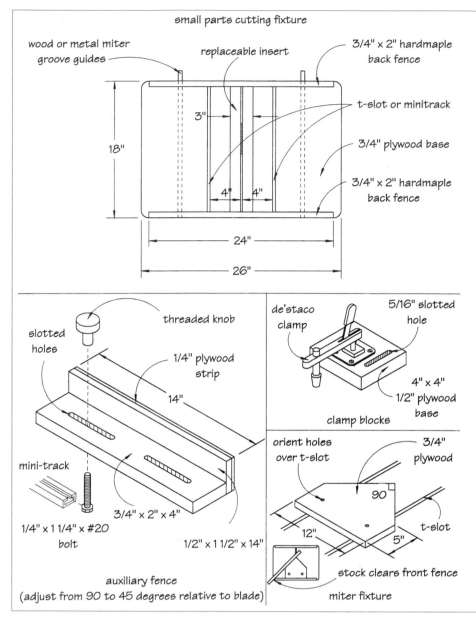

SMALL PARTS CUTTING FIXTURE

precisely 90° to the table.

Studded knobs run through slotted holes in the sled's separate guide fence to secure the fence to a pair of aluminum extrusions (MiniTrack) inset into a dado in the tables. This setup allows the fence to adjust from 90° to more than 45° to the blade. A replaceable strip on the face of the fence—covered with a strip of sandpaper applied with carpet tape to provide plenty of friction—offers a solid backing for the workpieces, preventing tear-out. This highly versatile fixture also has shop-built accessories for mitering small-size moldings, for precisely cutting triangular shapes, and for making odd cuts, such as the chord line of a circular workpiece.

To set up for a typical crosscut, index the guide fence perpendicular to the blade by inserting a parallel-edged spacer 2" to 3" wide between it and the sled's support fence. Squeeze the spacer between the fences, and lock down the guide fence with the knobs. The presence of the spacer brings the fence forward toward the center of the sled, allowing more visibility and room for your hands.

To make a cut, hold the workpiece against the face of the guide fence with your fingers and slide the fixture into the blade. The sandpaper strip provides friction to resist shifting. For more security, you can clamp a stop to the guide fence at the far end of the piece. I hold the smallest pieces (less than 3" long) to the fence with a sharp awl to keep my fingers away from the blade.

To make an angled cut, set the internal fence to the desired angle by holding it against the blade of a bevel gauge with its heel oriented to the saw-kerf in the sled base. If you are cutting a standard angle, such as 45° or 30°, you can set a drafting triangle between the guide fence and the sled's fence to establish the precise angle.

Outfitted with clamping blocks that slide along the integral tracks, this fixture easily handles offbeat cutting tasks, such as creating triangles or cutting the chord of a circle. But why stop there? The addition of scrap wood blocks, held in place with carpet tape or screws, allows you to perform such tasks as securing a curved or oddly-shaped workpiece in position for making a cut across its end.

PATTERN SAWING

Pattern sawing on the table saw offers a surprisingly quick and absolutely accurate way to create duplicates of a prototype. There are two different types of pattern sawing: The first uses the low auxiliary fence as a runner to which you can index a template attached to a workpiece. I use this technique when I'm duplicating a complex form or creating a straight-line rip along the edge of a board or panel. The second type of pattern sawing technique—the spacer system—offers a way to rip a workpiece to the exact width of the prototype without having to remove an auxiliary fence or rely on the accuracy of a rip fence cursor when resetting the fence. I'll start with the pattern fence; it will offer about the most fun you can have on a table saw.

Template Cutting to a Pattern Fence

Start by making an exact prototype/template of the shape you want to reproduce.

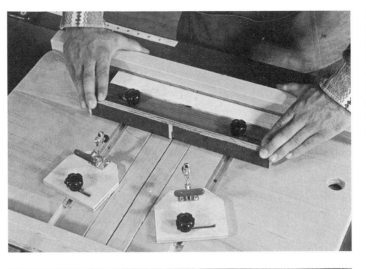

I set the internal guide fence of my small-parts fixture to a precise 90° by inserting a parallel-edged strip of wood between the back of the auxiliary fence and the face of the sled's front fence.

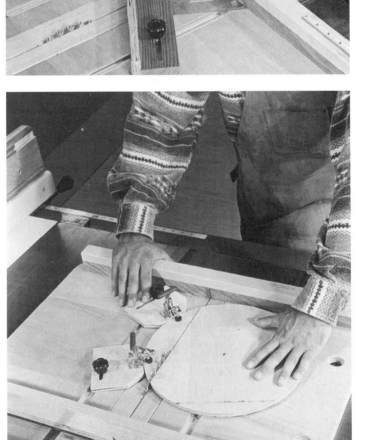

I quickly and accurately set the internal guide fence to a standard angle by inserting a drafting triangle between the back of the guide fence and the face of the sled fence.

The movable clamps allow me to hold odd-shaped objects, such as this circular workpiece, in place as I make the cut.

SAFETY *tip*

Never rip any board less than 8" long without a specialized fixture. The safest approach is to simply cut long lengths of the narrow strips and crosscut them to size later.

Be sure to get it right because all its off-spring will be its clone. I usually add a handle to the template to provide a more secure grasp. The next step is to rough-size the workpiece(s) within 1" of its finished shape. Avoid a larger waste margin as the offcuts might get trapped between the blade and the rip fence.

Now attach the template to the work-piece with protruding pins (brads) or screws if their hole marks are not going to show on the finished workpiece. If both sides must be good, use a vacuum clamp system if you have one or go with double stick tape. The latter will last for five to six cuts before it needs replacement. To help the tape stick better, sand the bottom of the template and brush or spray on several coats of shellac or other sealer. To ensure a good grab to the carpet tape, tap the template onto the workpiece with a rubber-faced mallet.

To set up for the cut, raise the low fence on a scrap of stock the same thickness as the workpiece, then add another ¼" (use a piece of ¼" ply as a spacer). Now move the fence system over until the outside reference edge of the low fence comes flush to the outside of the blade. Set the height of the blade to just a fraction below the fence base—it should almost touch. Note the cursor reading on the rip fence for future reference.

You're now ready to perform the magic: Index one facet of the template against the fence ahead of the blade and, with a steady motion, move the template (with the rough-cut workpiece below) forward through the blade. Keep the edge of the template tight to the fence. Now rotate counterclockwise to the next facet and cut again. Repeat this process until you have cut all around the template. As you will discover, you have created a perfect replica of the template in the attached workpiece. If you've used carpet tape, remove the template by tapping the side it with a light hammer.

The pattern fence system is also an excellent way to gain a straight edge on a board of any length. Just attach a straight-edge to the board precisely along the cut line. On any work more than 1' long, I recommend screwing (rather than carpet-taping) the guide in place. If the guide board is wide enough (the longer the

Here I'm cutting a miter in the end of a curved workpiece. A scrap block of wood carpet-taped or screwed to the sled table helps secure the workpiece in position.

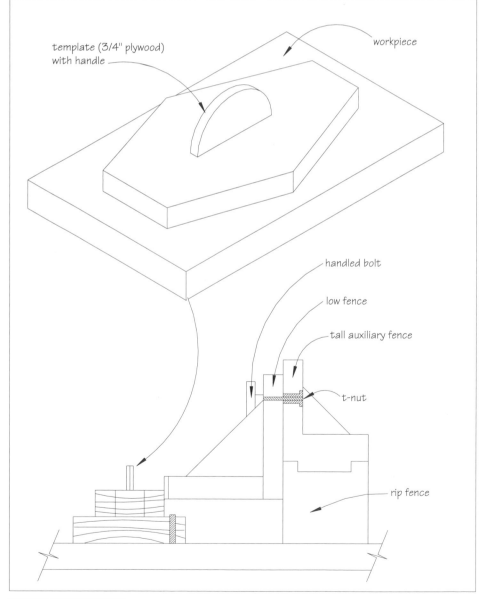

template (3/4" plywood) with handle

workpiece

handled bolt

low fence

tall auxiliary fence

t-nut

rip fence

PATTERN FENCE SETUP

SAFETY *tip*

If the template is too small to comfortably be held with both hands, add a handle. Be sure the template is securely attached to the workpiece, the pattern fence is tightly locked to the rip fence and the rip fence is secured to its guide rail(s). Double-check to be sure there is ample room for the waste cuts between the blade and the rip fence (under the base of the low fence). If unsure, recut the workpiece closer to the shape of the template. Finally: Never reach under the low fence base to clear offcuts, and never look under the fence while the blade is turning.

board the wider: about 1" per 2½' of length), you need only screw at the ends. If your guide board is perfectly straight (check it against a known straightedge) and you are careful to keep the guide against the pattern fence, you will come up with an edge as true as one you would gain from a jointer.

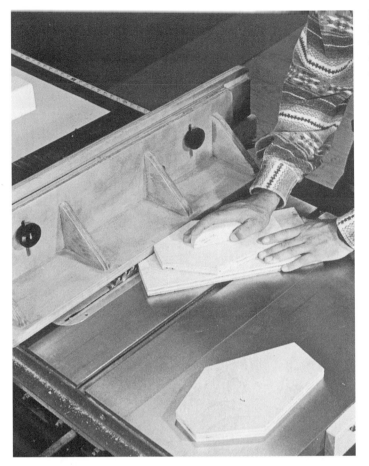

In combination with a low fence system, a template quickly creates clones of any straight-edged workpiece. Carpet tape holds it in place, and a handle makes the operation comfortable and safe.

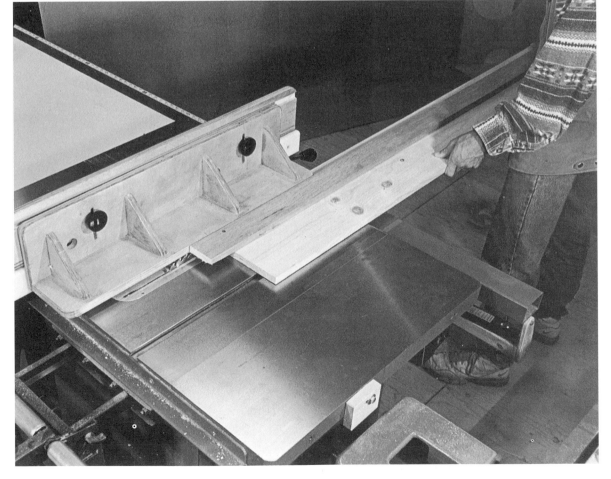

With a straightedge screwed to a board, I can quickly cut a straight edge anywhere and at any angle along the length of the board.

Making Duplicate Cuts With a Spacer System

This system is the essence of simplicity: To make any number of duplicate cuts to an original prototype (the template), you merely create a spacer that indexes the cut. You don't have to remove an auxiliary fence from the rip fence or worry about setting the fence to a precise cursor setting. Note, though, that your template, which will index the rip cut of the spacer, should be precisely made, with its edges parallel to one another and perpendicular to the face.

The drawing at right illustrates the process: First, move the rip fence to allow about a 2" gap between the prototype template and the saw blade. Now fix the template to the saw table with several strips of carpet tape. Align the template's leading end 1" past the front edge of the blade; its edge should be tight to the side of the rip fence. The template becomes a temporary auxiliary rip fence for cutting the spacer strip. (Note that the spacer strip can be longer than the template to offer better cutting control when it, in turn, becomes a ripping guide.) After producing the strip, remove the template and then, with the rip fence left locked in the same position, carpet-tape the spacer strip in place. Also orient its leading end to about 1" behind the front edge of the blade. When you run stock through the saw against the spacer, you create a workpiece with exactly the same width dimension as the original template.

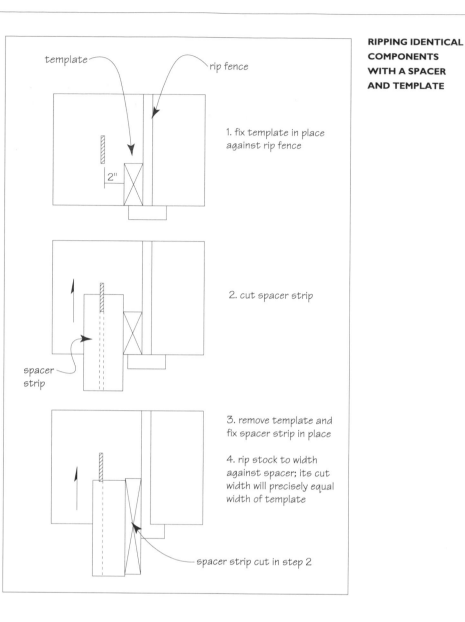

template — rip fence

1. fix template in place against rip fence

2. cut spacer strip

spacer strip

3. remove template and fix spacer strip in place

4. rip stock to width against spacer; its cut width will precisely equal width of template

spacer strip cut in step 2

Curves and Moldings

It may come as a surprise to many of you that you can indeed cut moldings, curves and even circles on the table saw. Using the proper fixtures, these cuts are safe, efficient and accurate. In fact, you may find it easier and faster to cut large-size curves and circles with the table saw than with the band saw (the typical choice). You're about to discover that the table saw is also the tool of choice for creating certain molding patterns and deep cove cuts, outperforming most shaper systems. Additionally, you'll learn how to convert your table saw into a high-performance sanding machine, expanding the usefulness of this already highly versatile woodworking tool.

SAWING CURVES AND CIRCLES

I was happy to discover that you can cut a curve on the table saw—up to ¾" per foot arc in ¾"-thick stock. (I do not recommend cutting curves in stock thicker than ¾", as the forces involved become huge.) I discovered the use of the table saw for curve cutting when I set out to cut planks for a small boat from 4'x10' sheets of plywood. I found that I could cut these planks nearly four times faster on the table saw than with a jigsaw or circular saw. I also discovered that the table saw produced such an accurate cut that no trimming other than a bit of hand planing was necessary to make the planks fit precisely to one another.

The trick to making curved cuts is to use a curved-edge template or batten, which is fixed to the stock, in conjunction with my auxiliary pattern fence (see chapter five) and a 40-tooth combination blade (don't use a thin-kerf blade). If you keep the curves shallow (no more than ¾" change per foot), the kerf cannot bind on

the blade because the offset of the carbide tips keeps the concave side of the kerf away from the blade plate. The saw blade doesn't care that the kerf line curves, as long as you carefully control the stock so it can't back into the blade. This is where the pattern fence comes in.

Using the Template and Pattern Fence

The first step to making a curved cut is to lay out the curve. At this point you have two procedural options: You can fix a batten in place to station points directly on the workpiece (which leaves little nail holes to fill but is remarkably fast), or you can lay out and then cut out a curved template in a piece of sheet stock. The latter procedure is preferable if you intend to make a number of pieces to this particular curve.

I draw a shallow arc using a simple stick system or trammel points, as shown in the illustration and photo on the next page. A curve with changing radius (most boat plank edges, for example) must be laid out to station points and connected with a flexible batten.

With the template or batten fixed to the workpiece, your next step is to set up the pattern fence as described in chapter eight. If the offcuts of the stock will be too big to fit between the blade and the rip fence, cut off any oversize areas. Mark the location of the front of the blade on the top of the pattern fence as a visual reference. This is where you must keep the template or batten guide in contact with the fence as you proceed through the length of the cut. Feed the stock smoothly and steadily through the spinning blade, keeping the guide tight to the pattern fence at the blade range mark. Be sure to set an outfeed table to catch the stock. If

SAFETY *tip*

If you intend to cut solid wood to a curve, be sure the wood is highly stable; otherwise you are risking kickback. Do a sample straight rip cut to observe any reactivity, especially if the stock exhibits much cross grain or is highly figured. Sheet stock is the ideal choice for curve cuts because the saw-kerf remains absolutely consistent, even if the surface veneer grain indicates otherwise.

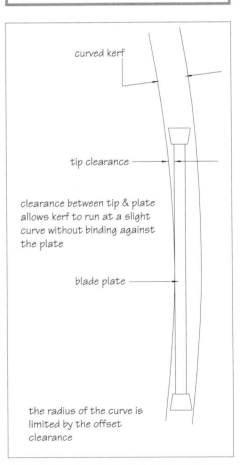

curved kerf

tip clearance

clearance between tip & plate allows kerf to run at a slight curve without binding against the plate

blade plate

the radius of the curve is limited by the offset clearance

GEOMETRY OF THE CURVED CUT RELATIVE TO A SAW BLADE

you encounter resistance and/or see wisps of smoke, the curve is too tight for your blade. Stop feeding immediately, lower the blade and remove the board. Try another blade with greater tip clearance. If this isn't available or doesn't help, you'll have to use another cutting method.

Cutting a Circle

Though cutting a workpiece to a full circle is quicker on a band saw (with the right fixture), you can also cut circles on the table saw with just as much, if not more, accuracy—though the process is a bit more tedious because of the need to cut off a series of ever-smaller corners before making the final spinning cut that trues and smooths the perimeter. Decided advantages of cutting circles on the table saw include the ability to make a perimeter rabbet (you can't do that at all on a band saw) and a broad support surface that allows you to more easily cut larger-size circles.

Circle-Cutting Fixture

The design of my fixture ensures safe circle cutting because the focus of the workpiece pivots on a through bolt capped with a lockdown knob. Also, the base of the fixture locks securely to the saw table (in the miter gauge slot) for the final spinning cut. Because the pivot bolt slides along a section of MiniTrack, an infinite adjustment of radius is possible—limited only by the length of the fixture table and the track extending to the left of the blade. These features provide a rigid support to ensure an accurate circular cut and to help prevent the workpiece from shifting and potentially kicking back. You can also use this fixture to hold the circular workpiece for rabbeting and edge-sanding its perimeter.

There is, however, one disadvantage to this fixture design: The center bolt requires that you drill a ¼" hole in the center of the circle. (Some other jig designers suggest that you can use a screw point protruding from the base of the fixture into the bottom of the workpiece, but I consider this unsafe and don't recommend it.) If the focus hole is to show in the finished workpiece, you can camouflage it to near invisibility by inserting a ¼" tapered bung of the same material.

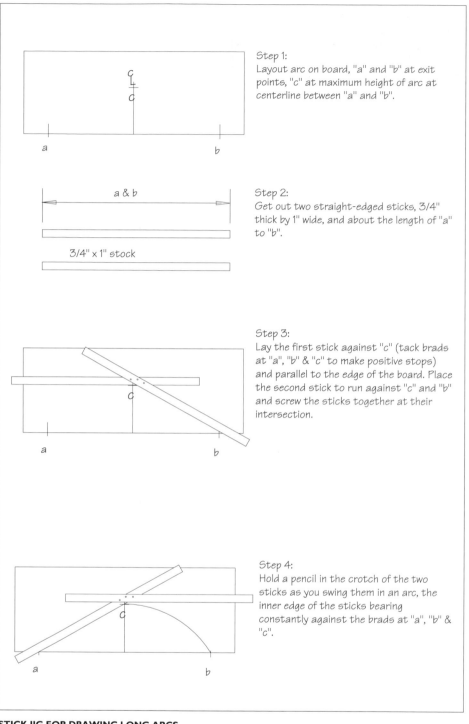

Step 1:
Layout arc on board, "a" and "b" at exit points, "c" at maximum height of arc at centerline between "a" and "b".

Step 2:
Get out two straight-edged sticks, 3/4" thick by 1" wide, and about the length of "a" to "b".

3/4" x 1" stock

Step 3:
Lay the first stick against "c" (tack brads at "a", "b" & "c" to make positive stops) and parallel to the edge of the board. Place the second stick to run against "c" and "b" and screw the sticks together at their intersection.

Step 4:
Hold a pencil in the crotch of the two sticks as you swing them in an arc, the inner edge of the sticks bearing constantly against the brads at "a", "b" & "c".

STICK JIG FOR DRAWING LONG ARCS

Making the Circle Cut

Before beginning the circle cut, find the center point of the square or rectangular workpiece blank (which I cut about ¼" larger in diameter than the finished circle) by drawing diagonals from corner to corner and marking their intersection. Drill a ¼" hole here, using a drill press if possible to ensure the hole is perpendicular to the face and will thus produce a true circle. (If you are hand-drilling, use a fixture to guide the drill square.) Now set the pivot point at the desired radius by sliding the bolt along the track. Measure from the edge of the fixture, which is even with the edge of the blade, to the center of the bolt with a rule measure or a story stick. Lock the pivot bolt in place by tightening the nut to the MiniTrack rail. You are now ready to cut.

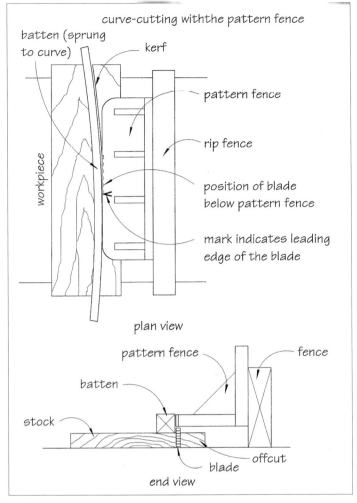

curve-cutting withthe pattern fence

batten (sprung to curve)

kerf

pattern fence

rip fence

position of blade below pattern fence

mark indicates leading edge of the blade

workpiece

plan view

pattern fence

fence

batten

stock

blade

offcut

end view

PLAN VIEW OF CURVE-CUTTING OPERATION

Here's a trick: With the batten tacked to the workpiece (allow at least 6" to 8" of surplus material at either end to ensure a fair curve), run the board through the saw using the pattern fence as a guide. The saw cuts flush to the outside edge of the batten.

Using a pair of trammel points (one of which holds a pencil), and a length of stick, you can draw a perfect circle of any diameter. Be careful, however, to keep the focal point (the pin) from moving off center.

DRAW A CHANGING-RADIUS CURVE TO A BATTEN

If the curve is not a portion of a circle, use a batten set to a table of station points. Begin by drawing the desired curve to scale on a sheet of quadrille paper (6 squares to the inch is ideal) or full size if possible. Measure to the curve from a baseline at 1' intervals, and create a table as shown in the drawing. Refer to this table when laying out the curve on the workpiece or template stock. Draw a baseline on the stock, mark 6" intervals, square up to the station point given on the table and make a mark.

Now all you need is a flexible batten to connect the dots. The ideal material for batten stock is a piece of ½"x¾" straight-grained spruce—though any clear, straight-grained hardwood, such as ash or oak, will do. Make the batten at least 1' overlength to ensure it pulls to a fair curve at the extremities of the bend.

Begin at the middle station point, temporarily tacking the batten in place with a brad against either edge. Do not tack through the batten; you may split the wood. Work your way toward either end, tacking the batten at each station point. If the curve is fair, the batten will tend to fall naturally at each station point. If you find yourself forcing the batten to a point, look down the length of the batten to see if there is an unsightly hump. You may find it better to go with your eye rather than the marked points (unless the station points were marked relative to an existing object to which the curve is to be fitted). Draw a pencil line along the outside edge of the batten onto the underlying template stock. If the batten is to serve as the cutting guide, tack it in place at each station point.

Tacking a flexible batten to station points marked on the face of the workpiece, my helper connects the points to create a smooth curve. Scraps of wood provide tack points beyond the board to ensure the batten continues in a fair curve.

Set the workpiece on the pivot bolt, and lock it down with a corner projecting evenly off the right side of the fixture. Back up the fixture, and raise the blade ⅛" higher than the top surface of the workpiece. Turn on the saw and slide the fixture forward, carrying the projecting corner of the workpiece through the blade. Continue to cut off the corners; after four cuts you will have an octagon. Continue to cut projecting corners to 16 sides and again to 32. At this point, the projecting corners are probably less than the thickness of the blade. If so, you are ready for the finishing spin cut that will make the workpiece perfectly round.

To make the final spin cut, turn off the saw, mark the position of the leading edge of the blade on the throat plate and lower the blade. Slide the fixture forward until the front edge of the MiniTrack is even with the front edge of the blade (oriented to the mark on the throat plate). Lock the fixture to the table by turning the runner lockdown screws. (Clamp the fixture to the saw table if the workpiece is so large it covers these knobs.) Also, lock the workpiece to the fixture by turning the pivot-bolt knob. Now turn on the saw, raise the blade to ⅛" above the workpiece, slightly loosen the pivot knob and rotate the workpiece slowly counterclockwise. The blade should skim off the edge. If tiny corner edges are still apparent, raise the blade a little higher, adjusting its position relative to the center of the circle, and spin-cut again. Finish the perimeter edge smooth by installing the table saw's sanding disc and using this same fixture.

Rabbeting the Perimeter of a Circle

You can use this same jig for creating a rabbet along the circular edge. Install a dado blade if the rabbet is to be wider than your single-blade thickness. You could, of course, step-cut the rabbet with a single blade, but this technique forces you to readjust the pivot point for each pass.

Here's the procedure: First, install the dado set, which you have stacked or adjusted to the desired rabbet width plus about ⅛". Set the pivot by locking down the pivot bolt at the radius of the inside edge of the rabbet (measure from the blade end of the fixture). Next, lower the blade and mark its top center on the throat plate. Slide the fixture forward, and lock it down to the miter slot when the center line of the MiniTrack aligns to the top-center mark. Set the workpiece on the fixture, clamp it down and then double-check that its projection over the end of the fixture is equal to the desired width of the rabbet. I use a depth gauge for this check.

If everything looks OK, you are ready to rabbet: Turn on the saw, and raise the arbor until the blade cuts the underside of the workpiece. Adjust the height until you reach the desired depth of rabbet marked on the edge of the workpiece. (If the depth is greater than ¼", it's best to make the cut in stages, a maximum of ¼" cut at a time.) Now, pressing down on the workpiece with your hand, slightly loosen the pivot knob and slowly and steadily turn the workpiece counterclockwise until the rabbet cut travels around the full circumference of the circle.

Kerfing

There are a number of different ways to get a piece of wood to go around a bend, though each has a drawback. For example, sawing the workpiece to the desired curve generally requires a wide board and can be weak and odd looking because cutting across the longitudinal run of grain creates ovular patterns; laminating thin strips to a form cut to the curve results in strong glue-lamination, but the process is also messy and time-consuming; Steaming the wood until it becomes flexible enough to take the desired bend requires a substantial time investment in equipment setup.

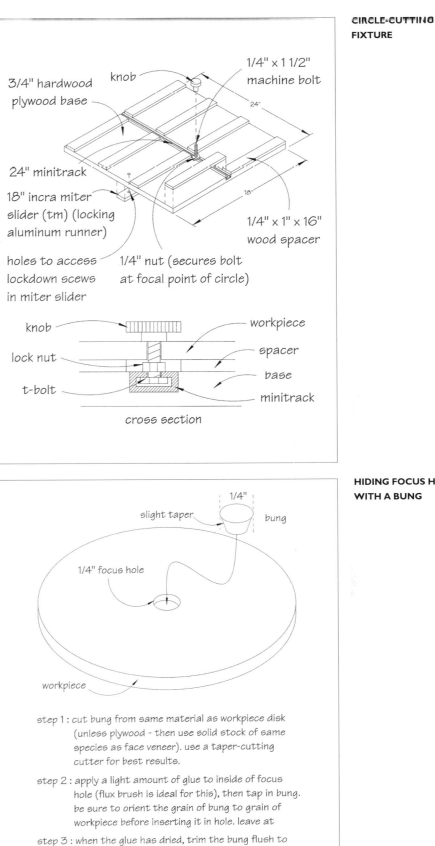

CIRCLE-CUTTING FIXTURE

3/4" hardwood plywood base
knob
1/4" x 1 1/2" machine bolt
24"
24" minitrack
18"
18" incra miter slider (tm) (locking aluminum runner)
1/4" x 1" x 16" wood spacer
holes to access lockdown scews in miter slider
1/4" nut (secures bolt at focal point of circle)

knob
workpiece
lock nut
spacer
t-bolt
base
minitrack

cross section

HIDING FOCUS HOLE WITH A BUNG

1/4"
slight taper
bung
1/4" focus hole
workpiece

step 1 : cut bung from same material as workpiece disk (unless plywood - then use solid stock of same species as face veneer). use a taper-cutting cutter for best results.

step 2 : apply a light amount of glue to inside of focus hole (flux brush is ideal for this), then tap in bung. be sure to orient the grain of bung to grain of workpiece before inserting it in hole. leave at

step 3 : when the glue has dried, trim the bung flush to the disc surface with a chisel followed by a cabinet scraper.
chisel

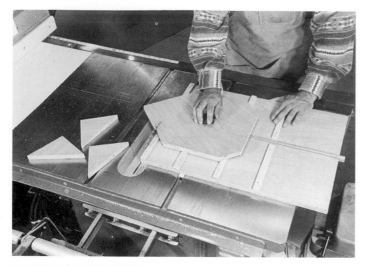

CREATING A CIRCLE: STEP 1

The first step toward creating a circle with my circle-cutting fixture is to cut off the four corners of the square workpiece. I keep one hand on the lockdown knob to ensure the workpiece doesn't spin during the cut as I slide the fixture forward.

CREATING A CIRCLE: STEP 2

Continue rotating the workpiece to project a corner and cut it off.

CREATING A CIRCLE: STEP 3

Prepare to make the final spin cut that skims the edge of the workpiece perfectly round by locking down the fixture to the saw table. To do this, access the expansion screws of this commercially made slider through the access holes.

CREATING A CIRCLE: STEP 4

With the fixture locked down (to position the front edge of the blade to the front edge of the MiniTrack), raise the blade above the workpiece and then spin it slowly counterclockwise. This allows the blade to skim off any projections, creating a perfect circle.

Having dissed these three methods, I'll offer what I feel is the simplest, the fastest and an acceptably strong way to bend wood: Kerf it to allow the board to flex to the desired radius. While the kerfed board will never be any good to fasten to, it will otherwise be sufficiently strong if you attach it to a structure or give it a longitudinal sheet backer.

How do you know how close or deep to make the kerfs? The drawing on page 150 shows a low-tech graphic technique to determine the minimum kerfing depth and spacing necessary to obtain a particular curve. This trick only gives you a starting point, however. I generally double the number of kerfs indicated in this way because additional kerfs significantly lower the visibility of flats—though an increased number of kerfs does tend to weaken the workpiece. Hold the kerfs back at least $\frac{1}{16}$" from the exposed surface to allow you to sand out any evidence of flats. With particularly flexible woods, such as oak or ash, it's OK to hold back $\frac{1}{8}$", which ensures you won't sand through the surface into a kerf.

Kerfing Fixture

The drawing on page 150 illustrates my fixture for indexing the kerf cuts to produce them on the table saw. It works on the same principle as the fixture shown in chapter seven for spacing dado cuts. Like the dado fixture, this kerfing jig quickly bolts to the front fence of my small cross-cut sled. The MiniTrack allows adjustment for various kerf spacings.

To prepare the fixture for use, make a $\frac{1}{2}$"-deep cut (with the blade you'll use to cut kerfs) in the bottom edge of the fixture, aligned to about the center line of the MiniTrack. Insert a piece of hardwood into the kerf to create the index pin. Sand the thickness of the pin to a friction fit so it will be easily replaceable as it becomes worn or damaged.

To set the kerf spacing, loosen the fixture's lock bolts and measure from the outside of the pin to the inside of the blade, which translates as the measurement from center line to center line, as you slide the fixture along the crosscut sled fence. Lock it down at the desired spacing. Make the first kerf cut, then set the kerf over the index pin and make the next cut, continuing along the length of the board. If the board is long and you feel you're losing support, move the fixture to the left, setting the index pin to the same distance to the left side of the blade. Then turn the board end for end, set the last-cut kerf on the pin, and work right-to-left toward the uncut section of the board.

SHAPING WITH THE MOLDING HEAD

Just what are the advantages of making moldings with the table saw? Let me count the ways:

1. It is economical: The table saw provides the motor—no need for another stand-alone machine; and because there is only one head assembly, the individual sets of cutting bits can be relatively inexpensive (though they are high-speed steel rather than carbide, you can resharpen them easily.

2. The relatively large arc of the cutters produces shallow mill marks, which are easier to sand out than those produced by the much smaller arc of shaper and router bits.

3. Consistent speed across the blade cut area makes it easier to find a feed speed that eliminates burning. Router and shaper bits produce a much wider range of cutting speeds—up to 100 mph compared to 30 mph—across portions of their cutting edges, which makes it difficult to prevent burning by adjusting the feed speed.

4. The table saw is easy to adjust: To change the depth of cut, you simply crank the saw's arbor wheel vs. fooling with trickier fence adjustments

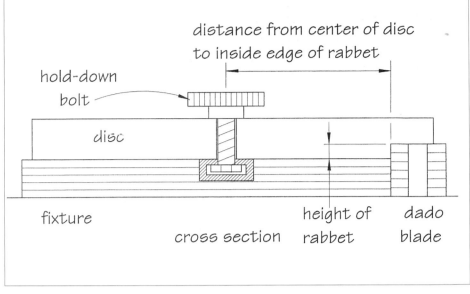

SETUP OF CIRCLE JIG FOR RABBETING

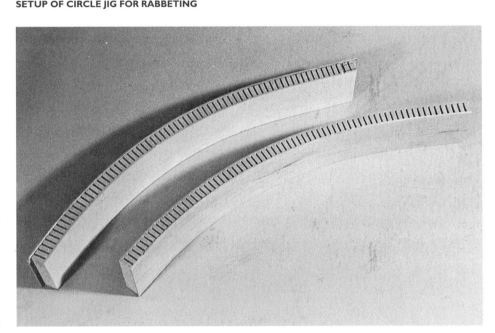

Kerfing produces both concave and convex bends. You can stiffen and build up the strength of the curved workpiece by gluing a longitudinal strip of ⅛" plywood to the workpiece.

of a router or shaper table. This characteristic is especially appreciated when you have to make a series of progressively deeper cuts.

5. The table saw cutterhead offers greater varieties of cuts than an equal number of router bit profiles might because unlike most router and shaper setups, you can tilt the arbor carrying the blade so that one bit can produce a variety of shapes. (This option is not available on all table saws, however. You must check your saw to be sure internal clearance allows tilting the arbor with a

cutterhead installed.) Also, you can use a series of cutters to create a unique shape.

Blade and Cutterhead Setup

Begin setup by inspecting the cutters: They should be equally sharp and free of nicks. Send them back to the manufacturer for a regrind if any are deeply nicked. Inspect the cutterhead, cleaning out any sawdust caught in the receiving grooves. Wearing gloves to protect your hands, install the cutters with the head off the saw. Snug the setscrews, but wait for a final tightening after you mount the head on the saw. Be sure the cutters are properly oriented to one another by laying the head on its side on a flat surface and checking that the sides of the cutters are even. If they look good, install the head on the saw arbor (read the cutterhead manual to check the procedure). Tighten the arbor nut, and then secure the cutters by tightening the setscrews, adding a little more torque this time.

Throat Plate Setup

I never use my saw's standard metal throat plate, even though its wide throat clears the cutters. Instead, I provide a reusable throat plate for each of the cutters. A blade-specific throat plate is safer because there is no chance of the stock jamming on the throat edge, and the cut is cleaner because of the zero clearance. The illustration on page 152 shows my throat plate for molding cutters. I use 9-ply ½" birch plywood to ensure a void-free, stiff support, finishing it with shellac and a buffed waxed coat to make it friction-free. (See chapter one for more information on making throat plates.)

Installing the Throat Plate

To install and set up the throat plate, begin by lowering the arbor and cutterhead all the way, being sure the cutters at top center won't touch the underside of the throat plate blank. Measure and mark the approximate predicted location of the cutter kerf opening on the plate's top surface, then place the blank plate in place, washer in back. To hold the plate down for the initial cut, bring the rip fence over, aligning it just to the right of the predicted kerf opening. Use a wood auxiliary fence with a cavity (I use the rabbet auxiliary fence) to ensure the metal portion of your rip fence won't contact the blade. Now plug in and turn on the saw, and slowly raise the cutters into the bottom of the throat plate blank. Be sure to stand to one side. Raise the cutters to the height that produces the full profile for that particular cutter set.

Fence Setup

Decide if the stock is to be fed flat or on edge to the cutters. Note that the profile is different depending on the orientation of the stock to the cutters. If the stock will

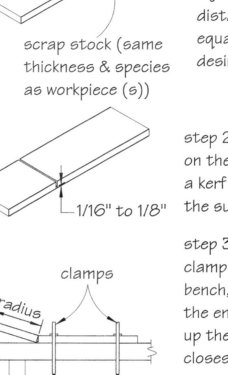

radius of bend

scrap stock (same thickness & species as workpiece (s))

1/16" to 1/8"

clamps

radius

spacing of kerf

step 1:
layout a kerf cutline at distance from one edge equal to radius of the desired bend.

step 2:
on the table saw, crosscut a kerf to 1/16" to 1/8" of the surface.

step 3:
clamp the workpiece to a bench, aligning its end of the end of the bench. lift up the end until the kerf closes and measure the amount of lift. this amount equals the spacing of kerfs necessary to achieve the desired radius of kerf.

DETERMINING KERF SPACING RELATIVE TO BEND RADIUS

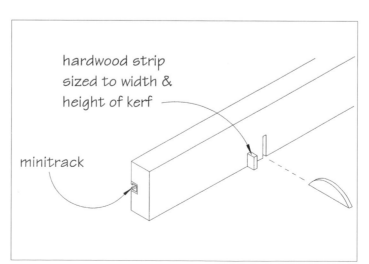

KERF INDEX FIXTURE FOR THE CROSSCUT SLED

hardwood strip sized to width & height of kerf

minitrack

feed flat, install the auxiliary fence for rabbeting (see chapter seven). The cavity over the blade allows you to adjust the fence side to side without interference from the cutters. Slide the fence toward the cutters, locking it down at the desired distance (determined by measurement or, better, by orientation to a profile drawn on the stock or to a story stick).

The large forces involved in these molding cuts require that the stock be held firmly and securely to the table surface. I use featherboards bolted to the MiniTrack of my universal tall auxiliary fence when running stock flat past the cutters. To set the featherboard, lower the cutters all the way, set the stock in place and push the featherboard down onto the top surface of the stock, and tighten the bolts. When running stock vertically on end against the rip fence, I use my rip fence sled with its backing boards and hold-down clamps to ensure a safe and accurate cut.

Stock Preparation

Before making any cuts, carefully inspect your stock. Do not attempt to shape wood with knots, splits, wild grain or a honeycombed interior. Not only will you get poor results, but defects create a high possibility that the stock could blow up on you during shaping.

As a general rule, shape only oversize workpieces, cutting them to width and length after the shaping process. For safety's sake, never shape pieces less than 12" long or 3" wide. For efficiency, make the shaping cut along both edges of a wide board where, when ripped, you will then obtain two molded workpieces. If the board is wide enough and the product narrow, you may get more than two pieces from the stock by repeating the process. There is an exception to this rule: In high-efficiency production work, you may want to shape stock that has been preripped to widths narrower than 3". You can run these narrow workpieces safely if you use a special feed fixture.

If you decide you will run the boards vertically (on edge) through the cutters, be aware that you may need to provide additional support to the workpiece if the cutter profile removes greater than two-thirds of the edge. The requirement is to

Setting the kerf spacing by measuring from the outside of the index pin to the close edge of the blade. The two knobs lock the indexing fixture to the crosscut sled fence.

SHARPENING MOLDING CUTTERS

You can quickly hone a molding cutter bit by rubbing the flat side of the cutter on a waterstone.

Unlike chisels and plane irons, which require that you sharpen their bevel—a procedure requiring a jig for best results—you can hone a molding cutter to a sharp edge by simply rubbing its flat side on a sharpening stone. I use a series of waterstones (1000, 1500 and 6000 grits) because the stones are easy to flatten and don't require messy oil.

always provide two surfaces for support. Note that you will not need to add support when end-cutting boards vertically if you are using my rip fence sled fixture, since the work is secured to the carriage and between two stop boards.

Standard Procedures

In addition to the featherboard hold-downs when flat feeding, I push stock through with a shoe-type push stick to help maintain down pressure. An end-type push stick is a second choice if the stock is relatively narrow.

How you feed the material into the cutters is important to safety and performance. You want a smooth, steady motion at the proper speed. Jerky motion is dangerous because the jump in feed speed can lead to kickback. To assess correct feed speed, be aware of these signs: Chattering and/or motor bogging means you're taking too fast and/or too deep a cut; a scorched cutting surface means you are going a little too slowly. Feeding stock for molding cuts is a prime candidate for a power feeder (see chapter three).

Never try to make any profile in one pass. The number of passes it takes is relative to the density of the material and the type of profile: The denser the material and the more material the profile demands be removed, the more passes required. In any case, figure on ⅜" as a maximum pass depth and down to ³⁄₁₆" for large profiles in dense hardwood, such as hard maple. In all cases, leave ¹⁄₁₆" for the final cleanup pass. If you are producing multiples, run all the stock through at one height setting, then reset and run again. To index the full height position of the cutters, you can mark masking tape placed behind your arbor's height crank.

Shaping Across the Grain or Short Dimension

I make shaping cuts across the grain of a board or the short dimension of a plywood strip using a combination of a miter gauge set up with an auxiliary fence and the rip fence set up with the rabbet fence and

Lay the cutterhead down on the saw table to see that the cutters are parallel with one another and thus properly locked in place.

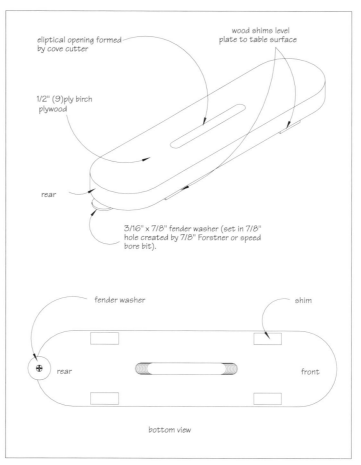

MAKING A THROAT PLATE FOR SHAPING CUTTERS

eliptical opening formed by cove cutter

wood shims level plate to table surface

1/2" (9)ply birch plywood

rear

3/16" x 7/8" fender washer (set in 7/8" hole created by 7/8" Forstner or speed bore bit).

fender washer

shim

rear

front

bottom view

hold-down. Never use the miter gauge head alone, even with an auxiliary fence. There is simply too much chance of shifting and kickback when large amounts of material are being removed. If I'm cutting the profile around the perimeter of the workpiece, I crosscut across one end of the board first, then continue around the perimeter. This strategy eliminates tearout because the lengthwise cut removes the tear-out at the edges of the board.

With the rip fence locked down over a portion of the new plywood throat plate, raise the spinning cutters into the plate to create a zero-clearance throat opening for that particular cutter set.

Eyeballing the drawn profile against the shape of a cutter is a quick way to align the fence. A test cut in scrap verifies the setting.

Shaping Boards in a Vertical Position

Understand up front that shaping boards fed on their edge or end tends to be more time-consuming than running the boards through flat on the table. I avoid this feed position if possible. But if I have no choice, perhaps the boards are slightly cupped or warped, I use my sliding rip fence sled fixture to carry the ends or narrow dimension of the workpiece through the cutters. The backing board stop, the front stop and the integral clamps hold the board flat and square to cutters and allow me to focus on feeding the stock smoothly through the cut. If the board is to receive edge treatment as well, I cut across the end grain first.

When cutting along the edge, I use the featherboard fixture designed for resaw work (see chapter five) to hold the board flat against the rip fence's tall auxiliary fence. If you are working without this fixture and the profile removes all the flat edge, be sure to carpet-tape a strip of wood to the workpiece to provide support along its bottom edge. This strip will support the wood on the outfeed side of the cutters, meeting the requirement to provide two support surfaces.

Shaping Narrow Stock

To shape preripped stock that is under 6" wide fed on edge, use a molding support fixture. Because it surrounds and supports the stock both on the infeed and outfeed sides, the fixture ensures a safe

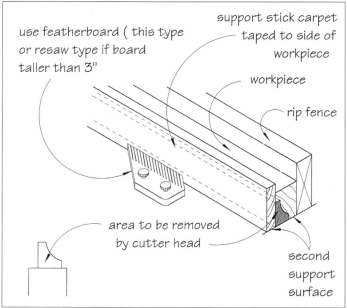

and highly accurate cut. Shaping narrow, presized stock saves considerable time when making long runs of moldings because the basic processes are grouped: ripping and joining all the stock to width and then shaping the profile. My fixture is adjustable to a variety of molding heights, from ½" to 5½". If the molding is thicker than the ¾"-thick upper support, I add premade shims as shown. Fine adjustments are made with scraps of sandpaper.

Setup and Use of the Molding Support Fixture

To set up the molding support fixture, first position the rip fence relative to the cutters, then lower the cutters out of the way. Set the stock in place along the

fence, and place the support fixture over it. Set the top support against the top of the molding, and bolt it to the MiniTrack in the tall auxiliary fence. Next bolt the side support in place to the top support, its bottom edge flat on the table. Insert sized shims if necessary. If the molding feels too tight, remove the side support and add scrap strips of sandpaper. Alternatively (and preferably), plane the molding stock to a thickness that works with your standard shims or the top support alone.

Now you're ready to work. Slide out the stock, turn on the saw and raise the blade to the first step cut. Depending on the profile, it may or may not cut into the side support. Run all the stock through (a test piece first is wise), using the next piece of molding stock as a push stick. Then raise the blade to the next step and repeat. Continue until you've cut the full profile on your full run of stock.

Shaping Along a Circular Edge

The adjustable fixtures shown in the drawing on page 156 allow you to shape a profile along the edge of a circular work-piece. By bolting the fixtures to the MiniTrack of the tall auxiliary fence, you can easily position them to guide the edge of the work as it rotates over the cutters. All you need do is slide the circular piece into the spinning cutters and turn the workpiece to create an edge profile around its circumference.

Setting Up and Using the Fixtures

Refer to the drawings for a step-by-step illustration of setting up the fixtures. Having completed the setup and made a test cut to ensure accuracy, you are now ready to make this magical cut: Raise the cutters to the first step cut, turn on saw, hold the workpiece against the front fixture and roll it toward and into the cutter until the workpiece touches the face of both fixtures' guide edges. Now turn the workpiece counterclockwise (into the direction of the spinning cutters) with the rim bearing against both fixtures as you make the cut around the full perimeter. Then back the workpiece away, raise the blade to the next step cut and repeat the procedure until you reach the desired profile.

SHAPING WITH A BLADE

You don't necessarily need a cutterhead system to cut molding shapes on the table saw. Instead, the single blade will cut a beautiful cove shape, both symmetrical and asymmetrical, if you use a specialized guide fence. This cove shape can, with further cutting and shaping, become sco-tia, ogee or other varieties of moldings. Other moldings, such as the brick mold-ing, can be made by simply cutting a series of kerfs or rabbets along the length of a face.

Cove Cuts

If you feed stock at an angle other than parallel to the blade, the resulting broad

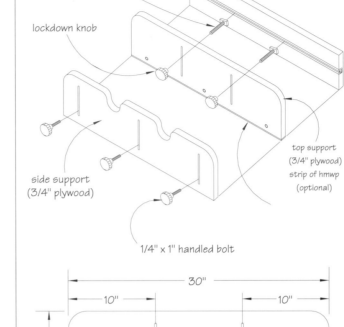

1/4" x 1-1/2" bolt (fits into MiniTrack on auxiliary fence)

lockdown knob

top support (3/4" plywood) strip of hmwp (optional)

side support (3/4" plywood)

1/4" x 1" handled bolt

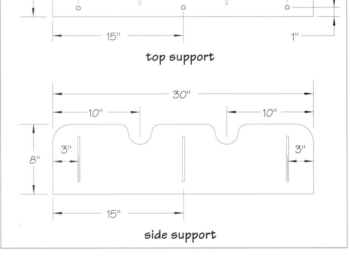

30"

10"

3"

8"

15"

1"

top support

30"

10"

3"

8"

15"

side support

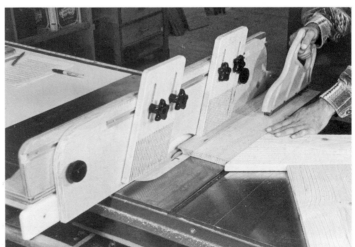

My setup for running a board flat through the cutters: rabbet fence with featherboards to guide and control the cut, featherboards clamped to the saw table to exert side pres-sure, and a shoe-type push stick to provide additional control and safety.

kerf becomes a section of an ellipse. The higher the feed angle, the wider and shallower the ellipse until at 90° to the blade it becomes a section of a circle. The drawing on page 159 illustrates how the change in feed angle affects the width of the cut. If the blade is tilted, the cove shape becomes an asymmetrical ellipse—an appealing and unique shape for many types of moldings.

Why create coves on the table saw? For one, because the table saw surpasses the ability of most shapers, even heavy industrial varieties, to make broad, deep cove cuts. And second, you are not limited to the arc of a particular cutterhead. Cove cutting doesn't hurt the machine or the blade if you do it properly. That means using an adequate, securely anchored fence, hold-downs over the stock and a slow feed speed in small height increments. The blade should, of course, be clean and sharp.

The Basic Setup

For most cove cutting, I use a 10" 40-tooth combination blade with a standard, not thin-kerf, plate thickness, finding it gives a relatively smooth, fast cut. I don't recommend a blade of fewer teeth because the cut will be much rougher and will require more sanding to remove the mill marks. I sometimes use a flute profile on a molding head for cove-cutting work. Though setup is a bit more tedious, the cut goes a little faster and produces a smoother finish

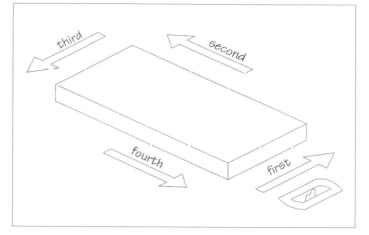

compared to the combination blade.

To make a cove cut, you need to guide the workpiece into the blade at an angle with a fence clamped securely to the saw table. You get more safety and better results if you use two fences to act as a channel.

I use a parallel-arm-type setup jig to determine and lay out the angle of feed for a particular width and height of cove cut. Basically, I set the arms to the desired width of the cove, place the fixture over the blade set to cut the full height of the cove and then angle the fixture until the edges of the front and back fences span the range of the blade at the table surface.

A neat thing about my setup jig is that it doubles as the fence system itself, making setup far more efficient. Since the swing arms lock down with knobs, I can remove them to convert from the layout jig to the guide fixture. Slots in the base of the fixture allow the front fence to bolt down to the saw table's miter groove, reducing setup time. For the greatest efficiency in making a particular cove cut that is commonly produced in my shop, I make a dedicated wedge-type fence as shown on page 159. I also use this type of fence for making a series of flutes.

Standard Cove Cut Procedure

Begin by carefully selecting the stock. Avoid knots, splits and internal honeycombing. Also be aware of the grain pattern that the cove will exhibit once cut. The pattern is determined by the orientation of the cove in the board, as illustrated on page 159.

Draw the cove shape on the end of a workpiece or make a full-scale rendering. Measure the width and height of the cove,

To shape across end grain, I use the miter gauge in combination with the rabbet fence setup. The clamp of this gauge system contributes to holding the board flat to the saw table as well as tight to the face of the gauge fence.

While using the sliding rip fence fixture to carry the stock on end through the cutters, the replaceable backing strip of hard maple on the vertical support closest to me prevents any tear-out where the cutters exit the board.

set the fixture to this width and raise the blade to height. I set the blade height by sighting the blade tips against the layout on the end of the workpiece. Next, mark the blade range on the throat plate, then lay the fixture over the blade, hold-down bolts protruding through the slots. From parallel to about 45° to the blade, I place both attachment bolts in the right-hand miter slot. From 45° to perpendicular to the blade, a bolt goes in each slot. Turn the fixture until the front and back fences are aligned to the marks on the throat plate. Note that my fixture is designed for feeding the stock from left to right. This is a bit awkward for me—a right-hander— it's necessary when I make asymmetrical cove cuts with the blade tilted.

The fixture, acting as a parallel arm layout device, has given you the correct feed angle for creating this particular width of cove. Now it's time to convert the fixture to a fence system to guide the workpiece. Draw a pencil line along the edge of the front fence on the throat plate and saw table. Loosen the knobs holding the arms, and open the fixture. Measure the spacing from the front edge of the workpiece to the cove as indicated on the end of the workpiece. Lock down the front fence at this distance from the pencil line. Lower the blade, insert the workpiece between the fences and lock the arms to hold the back fence at this spacing. Check to see that the workpiece is snug along its length but not resistive to sliding. When it feels OK, clamp the back fence securely to the saw table with large C-clamps or speed clamps. Finally, swing the arms out of the way (I lock them down on the back fence) and set the hold-down device. I use one wedge-shaped, single-direction wheel (see chapter three) located directly over the blade. If the stock disallows its use, I forgo the hold-down and use a shoe-type pusher in both hands.

Now you are ready to begin cutting. Start with the blade set for ⅛" cut. Turn on the saw and push the work through with a steady feed rate, using a push stick or the next workpiece to push the stock past the blade. Progress in ⅛" steps (learn your crank range—mine is ¹⁄₁₆" per half turn), reducing to ¹⁄₁₆" for the final finished depth cut. Make this last cut as slowly and

Bolted to the rabbet fixture, this specialized fixture captures predimensioned stock for controlled, production shaping. The fixture is adjustable in height and width to accommodate a wide range of stock sizes.

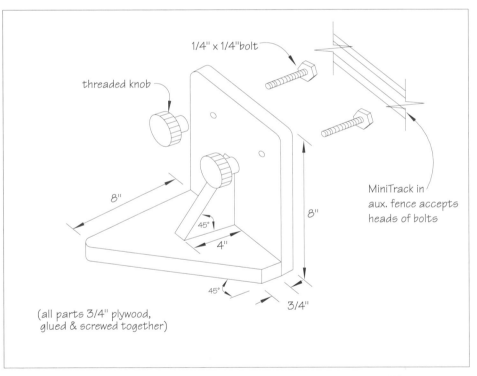

FENCE FIXTURES FOR GUIDING CIRCULAR WORKPIECES FOR PERIMETER SHAPING

smoothly as possible. Assuming a sharp blade, there should be little cleanup. Sand away the mill marks from the blade using a shaped sanding block. Shape a piece of softwood or dense foam to the negative of the cove, and apply sandpaper to the block with carpet tape.

Before you disassemble the setup, make an extra piece as a sample for the

next time you want to create this particular cove. Mark the feed angle in degrees on the sample for setting the fence system. You can also make an alignment template to keep with this sample, as shown in the drawing on page 160. To align the fence, you simply hold the stop of the template against the front edge of the saw table while holding the fixture's fence against the front edge of the template. Slide the template and fixture sideways until you obtain the desired relief setting.

Ogee and Scotia Moldings

To create an ogee molding, lay out the profile of the molding on both ends of the stock for reference. Set up and cut the cove portion, leaving a flat to one side. Shape this flat area to a convex shape with hand planes and a scraper, melding it smoothly to the concave cove. As you plane, test the shape with a template along the full length of the stock.

To create scotia molding quickly, cut a full cove and then rip it in half. This trick gives you two scotia moldings. If, however, you are working with stock already sized to the width and height of the finished molding, you need to add an auxiliary fence to the back fence to cover the back portion of the blade. Carpet-tape the fences together, holding down the auxiliary fence with a push shoe when you raise the blade to initialize the setup. Because you are creating only half a cove, the workpiece loses support on one side of its bottom. To provide the necessary two support surfaces, the design of the scotia must provide support flats, as shown in the drawing.

Asymmetrical Coves

As I mentioned earlier, you can create an asymmetrical cove by simply tilting the saw blade. The steeper the tilt for a particular feed angle, the more asymmetrical the cove. A booklet is available that illustrates a wide range of cove profiles with their feed and tilt angles: Cove Cutting by Klaus-Tech, P.O. Box 78, Pluckemin, NJ 07978, (908) 658-4396.

A crude way to determine the angles is to sight along a fence with one eye, changing both the blade angle and the feed angle until you see the shape you like. Do test cuts before committing to these angle settings. Record these angles on a

---

SAFETY *tip*

If you use only one fence, it must be set in front of the blade since the cutting action forces the workpiece against the fence, increasing control.

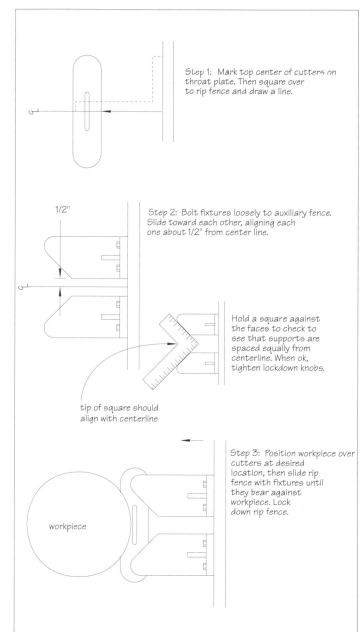

Step 1: Mark top center of cutters on throat plate. Then square over to rip fence and draw a line.

1/2"

Step 2: Bolt fixtures loosely to auxiliary fence. Slide toward each other, aligning each one about 1/2" from center line.

Hold a square against the faces to check to see that supports are spaced equally from centerline. When ok, tighten lockdown knobs.

tip of square should align with centerline

Step 3: Position workpiece over cutters at desired location, then slide rip fence with fixtures until they bear against workpiece. Lock down rip fence.

workpiece

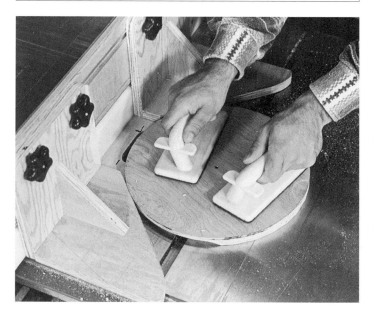

These shop-made fixtures bolt to the universal rip fence fixture to control a circular workpiece as it receives a shaping cut around its perimeter. The fixtures slide along the fence fixture to allow final positioning of the cut. I use shoe-type pushers—never my hands—to slowly spin the workpiece counterclockwise against the spinning cutters.

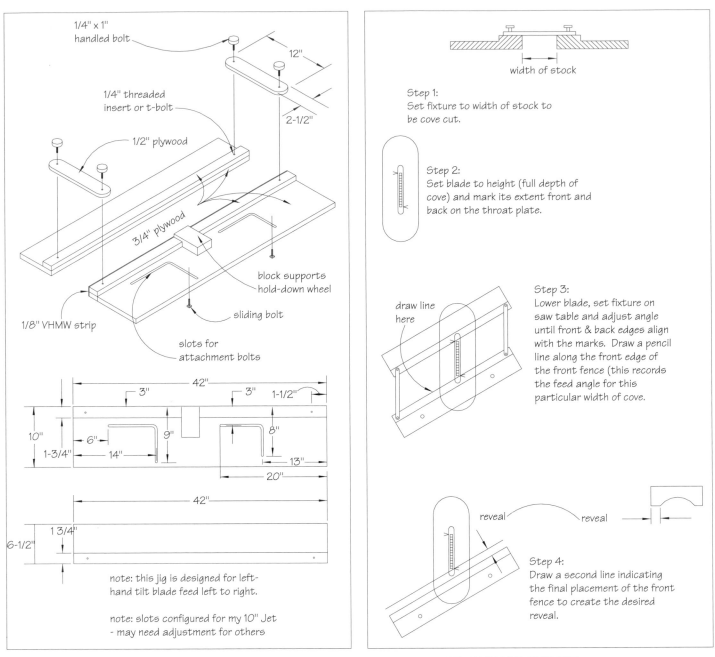

COMBINATION SETUP JIG AND GUIDE FENCE SYSTEM FOR COVE CUTTING

DETERMINING FEED ANGLE FOR COVE CUT

surplus piece and alignment template for future reference.

Making Multiple Narrow Flutes

An excellent application of table saw cove cutting is the creation of evenly spaced flutes along the length of a board to create a classic fluted pilaster molding. The dedicated fence for cove cutting takes only a minute to set up, allows for quick angle adjustment to fine-tune the width of the flute and uses a simple system to create perfect spacing between the flutes. The base of the fixture accepts the wheeled

hold-down fixture I designed to bolt to my rip fence. A turn of two knobs transfers it here.

To make the flutes, begin by laying out the flutes, determining their width and spacing. Make spacers whose width equals the flute width plus the width of the flat between the flutes. You'll need one less spacer than the number of flutes (i.e., N minus 1, where N equals the number of flutes). Now set up the fence fixture, bolting it to the universal rip fence fixture. Shim it as necessary to cut the desired

flute width. Shims set around the back attachment knob cause the fence to produce a narrower flute; shims to the front, a wider one. Note that my design is set up to cut a ⅜"-wide flute without shims. Move the rip fence into position so that the flat between the edge of the board and the first flute is as desired (it may or may not be the spacing between the flutes).

Now you are ready to make the series of flutes. Cut the first flute with all spacers in place between the rip fence and the stop block. Remove one of the spacers and cut the second flute, continuing in

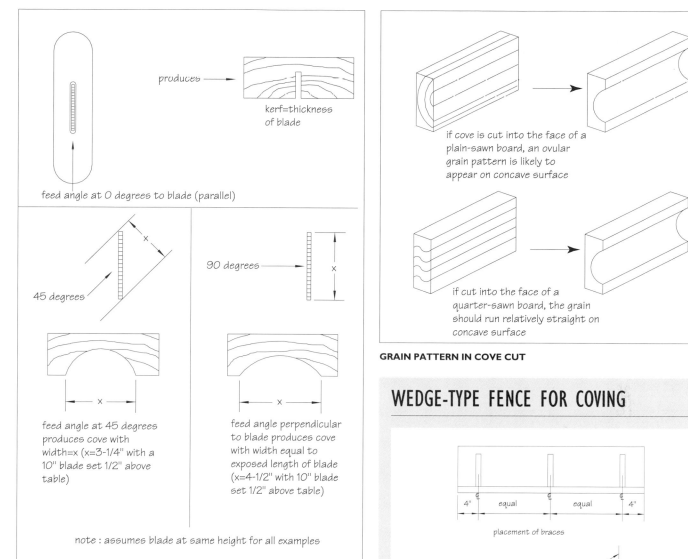

produces →

kerf=thickness
of blade

feed angle at 0 degrees to blade (parallel)

45 degrees

90 degrees →

feed angle at 45 degrees
produces cove with
width=x (x=3-1/4" with a
10" blade set 1/2" above
table)

feed angle perpendicular
to blade produces cove
with width equal to
exposed length of blade
(x=4-1/2" with 10" blade
set 1/2" above table)

note : assumes blade at same height for all examples

COVE CUTS AT AN ANGLE TO THE SAW BLADE

if cove is cut into the face of a
plain-sawn board, an ovular
grain pattern is likely to
appear on concave surface

if cut into the face of a
quarter-sawn board, the grain
should run relatively straight on
concave surface

GRAIN PATTERN IN COVE CUT

WEDGE-TYPE FENCE FOR COVING

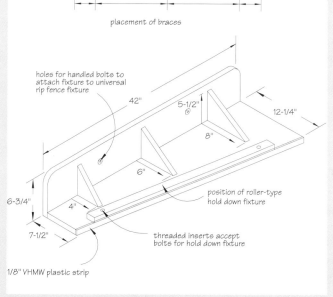

4" | equal | equal | 4"

placement of braces

holes for handled bolts to
attach fixture to universal
rip fence fixture

42"

5-1/2"

12-1/4"

8"

6"

position of roller-type
hold down fixture

6-3/4"

4"

7-1/2"

threaded inserts accept
bolts for hold down fixture

1/8" VHMW plastic strip

With the front fence locked down, set the back fence to the proper spacing by squeezing it against a sample of the stock. The clamps will secure the back fence to the saw table.

The advantage of this fence system for cove cutting is the ease of setup. Designed to bolt to my rip fence's tall auxiliary fence, it mounts in a matter of seconds. I need only install the removable hold-down board with a pair of knobs (the same board designed for use on my rip in chapter three) and adjust the blade height to be ready to create a particular cove cut.

this way until the last spacer is removed and you have cut the last flute. If your flutes are too deep to make in one pass (not likely because they are narrow, but may be necessary if the wood is particularly dense), cut all the flutes at the first height step then replace all the spacers and repeat the process with the blade lifted to final height. Clean up the flutes with two dowels sized to fit in the cove. Apply 80-grit sandpaper to one dowel and 120-grit to the other with spray adhesive.

SAWN MOLDINGS

You can also shape moldings on the table saw with straight-line cuts. A sequence of kerfs can create astragal and other casement-type molding profiles. Including a dado and angled cuts adds more interest to these profiles and can also create overlay and lipped door edging patterns. A repetitive sequence of dado cuts creates dentil-type molding. The possibilities are limited only by your imagination.

The drawing on page 165 illustrates some of the moldings I have created on the table saw and shows the sequence of cuts I used. Notice that the dentil-type molding makes use of the index fixture presented in chapter seven. It's important to choreograph the proper cut sequence for each type of molding to avoid cutting off a portion of stock needed to support the work through the other cuts in the sequence. I use a sharp ATB 60-tooth blade to produce smooth-faced rips, reducing cleanup time. I slightly round edges with a hand block plane, clean up in rabbet corners with a shoulder plane, and finish with sandpaper on a sanding block.

SANDING WITH THE TABLE SAW

Why would you want to sand on the table saw? It's not as odd as it sounds; after all, sanding is, in a way, just another form of cutting, something the table saw is extraordinarily good at. For starters, using the

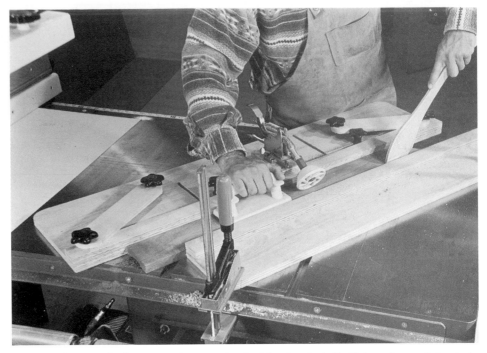

Using a combination of a shoe-type pusher, an end push stick and a wheeled hold-down, I can push the stock smoothly through the blade with great control and safety.

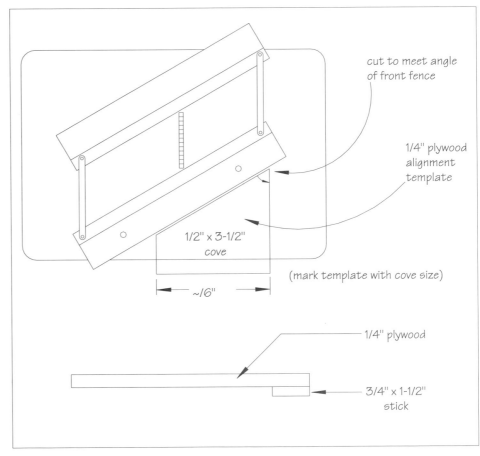

cut to meet angle of front fence

1/4" plywood alignment template

1/2" x 3-1/2" cove

(mark template with cove size)

~16"

1/4" plywood

3/4" x 1-1/2" stick

MAKING AN ALIGNMENT TEMPLATE

table saw for sanding is economical in terms of both money and shop space. The machine supplies the motor, eliminating the need for a stand-alone machine—with the added plus that you can use the existing dust collection system of the table saw. All you need is a special disc made for this purpose.

On the table saw, the sanding process is highly aggressive and thus efficient while providing excellent control of the process: The arbor crank quickly and precisely raises and lowers the exposed portion of the sandpaper while the miter gauge and the rip fence provide precision guide fixtures. You can even crank over the arbor to sand at any bevel angle up to 45°.

You have two choices of disc types: the standard flat disc and the improved tapered disc. I prefer the tapered disc for sanding edges because the sanding takes place only at the top of the arc, where the direction of sanding runs in the same direction as the grain. The standard disc is a good choice for sanding the ends of workpieces, where sanding takes place at the front of the blade. If you only want to own one disc, choose the tapered version; you will get the best of both worlds since one side is flat.

CORRECTING THE SHAPE OF COVE CUTS

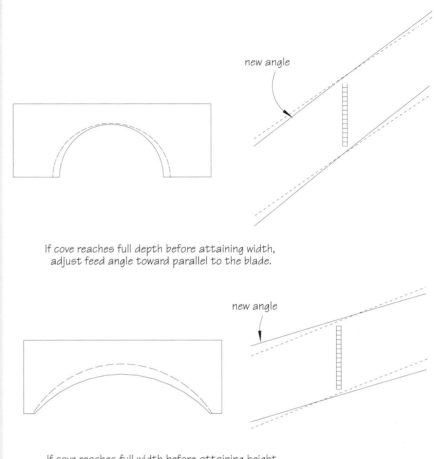

new angle

If cove reaches full depth before attaining width, adjust feed angle toward parallel to the blade.

new angle

If cove reaches full width before attaining height, move fence toward perpendicular to blade.

If the cove reaches full depth before reaching width, the feed angle is off. You can correct this by moving the fence toward parallel to the blade and continuing to cut. Likewise, if the cove reaches full width before it reaches full depth, move the fence toward perpendicular to the blade and continue cutting.

COVE CUTTING WITH FLUTED CUTTERS ON A MOLDING HEAD

There are two significant advantages to cutting coves with the fluted cutters of a molding head set: The cut goes more quickly as you can remove more material with each step pass, and the cutters make a cleaner cut because they do not score the wood as does a standard blade. There is some payback though: The fence setup is a little trickier to pull off because you have to approximate the cutterhead's fore and aft range when you set the alignment marks for the parallel rule jig. Also, most cutterheads will not cut as deeply as a standard 10" saw blade. My set will only produce a ¾"-deep cut.

The only difference in the cutting procedure is the amount of material you can remove with each pass: I take up to ¼"-deep cuts in softwood, though I back down to ⅛" in dense hardwoods. As with the regular blade, I make the last pass a ⅟₁₆" cut, going slowly to leave a surface that needs little sanding.

Basic Sanding Procedures

Always unplug the saw when installing the sanding disc or applying sandpaper. (It's easier to apply the paper when the disc is off the machine anyway.) Because the disc spins at a relatively high speed on the table saw, its action is highly aggressive, even at the finest grits. This means you will never need to apply anything but light pressure during sanding, always keeping a close eye on your progress. Keep the work moving or risk overcutting and/or burning. Choose the grits wisely: Don't use the finest grits to do shaping, and use the coarsest grits for rough shaping. In general, shape all your pieces first, then switch to a finer grit for finishing. If you intend to do a lot of shaping and sanding on your table saw, consider getting two or more discs, set up with different grits. You'll find it's much faster to change a disc than to change paper, and you can easily switch back and forth between discs.

On flat discs, always sand on the front portion where the rotation of the disc holds the workpiece to the table. Constantly move the workpiece to different areas of the front portion of the disc to avoid clogging. Clogged sandpaper causes burning because it burnishes rather than cuts the wood.

On a tapered disc, set the height so you are sanding only at the top of the disc. Note that you will have to adjust the arbor angle so that the taper (usually about 2°) is perpendicular to the saw table. With both types of discs, use shoe-type pushers to hold the work flat to the saw table and to guide the workpiece. Exercise this book's general admonition to keep your hands away from the area of the throat plate—remember that sanding is cutting and you don't need wasted fingers to remind you of that fact.

End Trimming

You can use the sanding disc to fine-tune butt and miter joints. The basic procedure

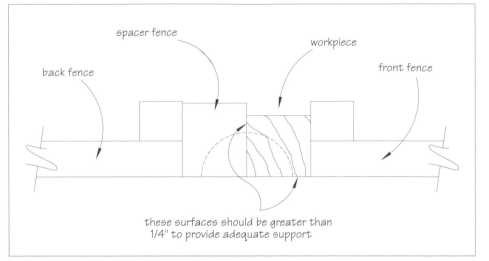

SCOTIA PROFILE PARAMETERS TO PROVIDE SUPPORT FLATS

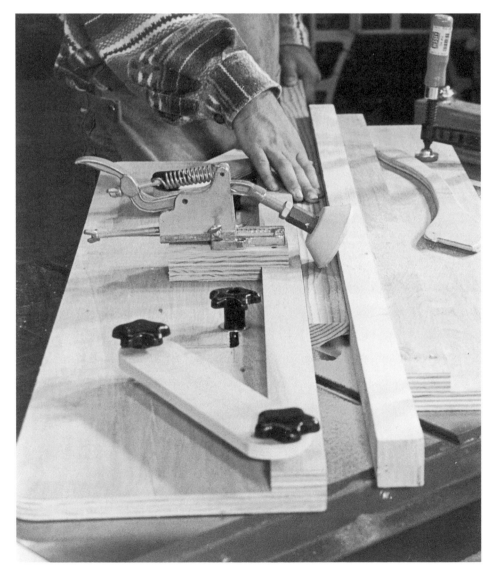

I add a second fence to the back fence of the cove fixture setup to control predimensioned stock being shaped to finished moldings—in this case a scotia.

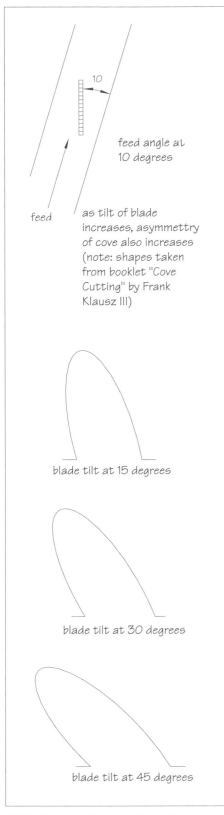

feed angle at 10 degrees

feed

as tilt of blade increases, asymmetry of cove also increases (note: shapes taken from booklet "Cove Cutting" by Frank Klausz III)

blade tilt at 15 degrees

blade tilt at 30 degrees

blade tilt at 45 degrees

ASYMMETRY OF COVE RELATIVE TO TILT OF BLADE

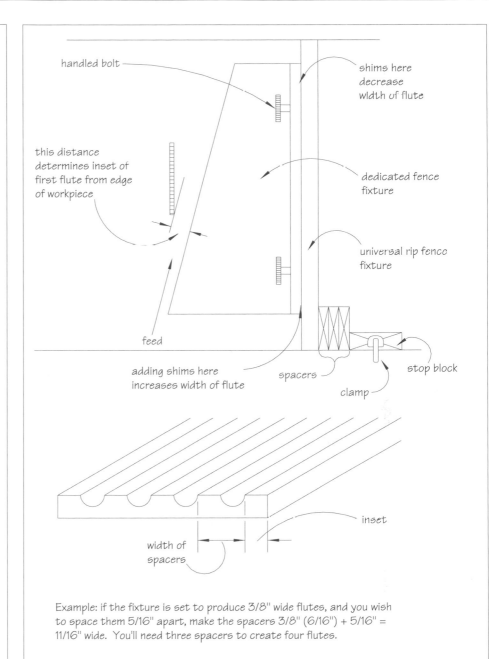

handled bolt

shims here decrease width of flute

this distance determines inset of first flute from edge of workpiece

dedicated fence fixture

universal rip fence fixture

feed

adding shims here increases width of flute

spacers

stop block

clamp

inset

width of spacers

Example: if the fixture is set to produce 3/8" wide flutes, and you wish to space them 5/16" apart, make the spacers 3/8" (6/16") + 5/16" = 11/16" wide. You'll need three spacers to create four flutes.

LAYOUT OF FLUTES AND SPACERS, SHIMS FOR WEDGE-TYPE FIXTURE

is to guide the end of the workpiece into the flat side of the spinning disc as you run the workpiece's edge along the auxiliary fence of the miter gauge. You can quickly find the correct angle at which to set the miter gauge by bearing the cut end against the disc (not spinning at this point!) and adjusting the miter gauge head to the correct angle. If the end cut is square, be sure the disc sits square to the table surface. Of course, you can tilt the arbor to accommodate compound angle cuts.

I like the open position for end trimming, as it places more of the workpiece on the table, ensuring it sits flat and square to the disc. I also like working from the left side of the blade, so I face the flat side of the disc this way for end trimming, placing the miter gauge in the left-hand miter slot. To make the trim-sanding cut, turn on the saw, then slide the butt or mitered end into the disc. Don't let it stay there, and don't slide the workpiece forward or backward. Instead, use a quick in-and-out motion. The sanding action works quickly, even at the finest grits. Test the fit and repeat if necessary. It usually only takes once or twice to trim a jointed end surface in this manner.

Jointing

The tapered disc works well for joint-sanding the edge of a workpiece. The process not only straightens the edge of the board (assuming it is not out of line by more than about ⅟₃₂" per foot) but it smooths the edge to a ready-to-finish surface. To guide the edge of the workpiece by the disc, I use the auxiliary fence I designed for rabbeting (see chapter seven).

To set up, I square the tapered surface of the disc to the table by raising the disc all the way up and adjusting the arbor angle. I then lower the disc to about ⅛" above the workpiece and slide the rip fence over until the auxiliary fence is flush with the sanding disc. A 24" straightedge helps me make the proper alignment. Turning on the saw, I feed the work past the disc, maintaining even pressure both in front and in back of the disc to keep the work bearing firmly against the auxiliary fence. Be careful not to press directly opposite the disc as this can throw the sanded edge out of line, especially near the end of the cut.

Edge-sanding a bevel uses the identical setup, except that you will, of course, adjust the angle of the arbor and disc to the desired bevel. Be aware, however, that the bearing surface of the edge against the fence is only a sharp corner. Be sure that your fence fits tightly to the table surface to prevent it from sliding under the fence, ruining the edge cut.

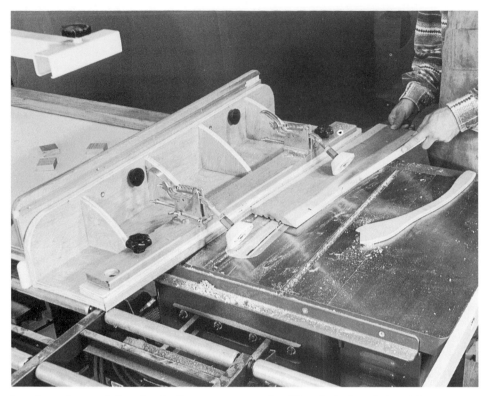

I use the wedge-type dedicated coving fixture to create a series of flutes in the face of a board. A spacer system indexes each cove in sequence.

Shaping

The sanding disc makes it extraordinarily easy to trim the curved end or edge of a workpiece to fit perfectly against a mating surface. It takes a little practice to gain the proper control, however, as sand shaping is quicker than you might think. It takes a light, quick, controlled touch. Since the surface is curved, you will not be using the miter gauge for support; in

> **SAFETY** *tip*
>
> Never feed the flat end of a workpiece freehand into a spinning disc; always use a support (the miter gauge fence). It is all too easy for the corner of the work to catch on the disc and careen out of your hands.

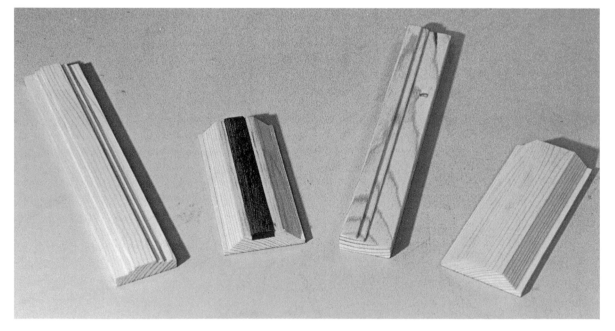

Here are some of the moldings you can make with a series of straight cuts: (from left to right) stepped astragal, inlaid astragal, brick, beveled astragal.

molding	cut sequence

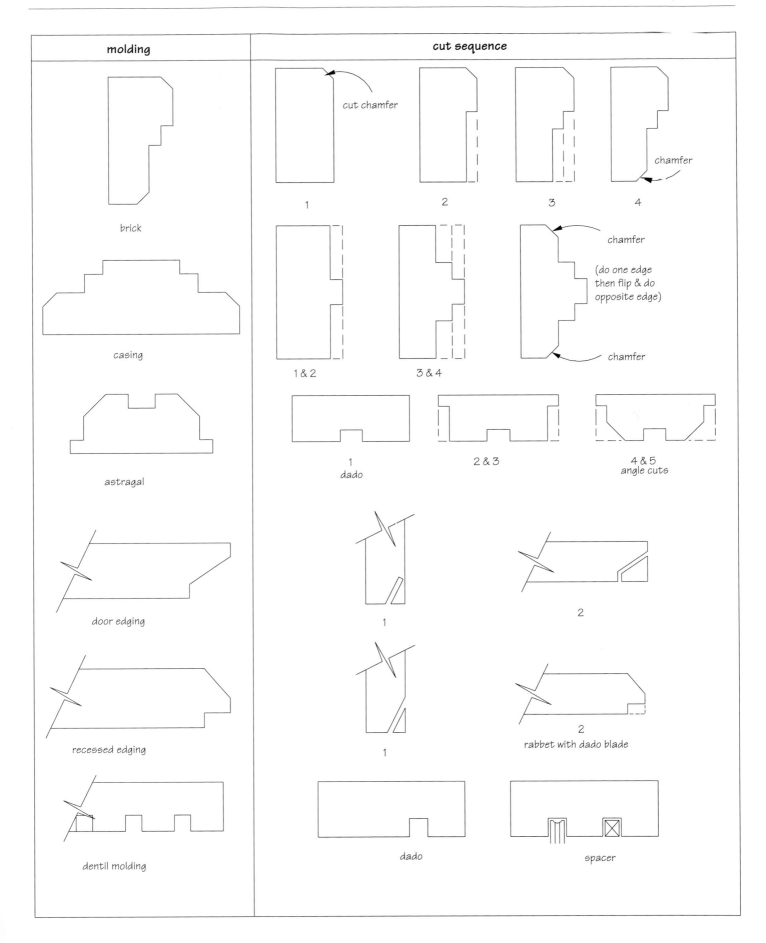

brick

1 — cut chamfer

2

3

4 — chamfer

casing

1 & 2

3 & 4 — chamfer (do one edge then flip & do opposite edge) — chamfer

astragal

1 dado

2 & 3

4 & 5 angle cuts

door edging

1

2

recessed edging

1

2 rabbet with dado blade

dentil molding

dado

spacer

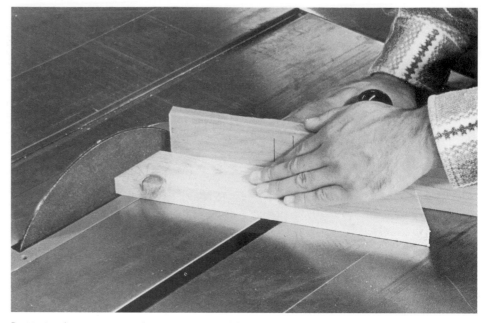

Positioning the miter gauge in the open position, I slide the end of the workpiece into the flat side of the sanding disc to trim the miter angle to a perfect fit.

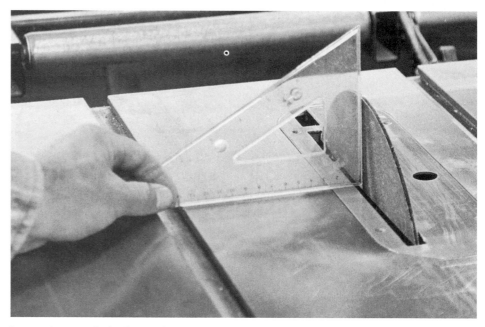

I square the tapered side of my sanding disc to the saw table by indexing it to a drafting triangle.

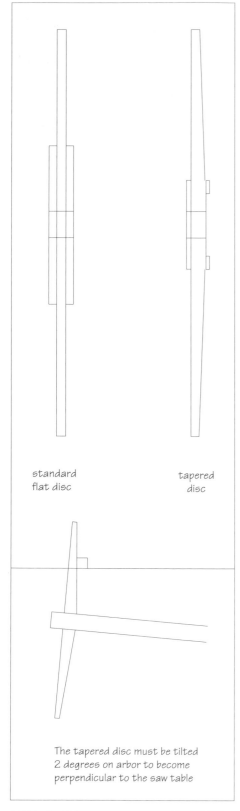

standard
flat disc

tapered
disc

The tapered disc must be tilted
2 degrees on arbor to become
perpendicular to the saw table

**DIFFERENCE BETWEEN TAPERED AND FLAT
SANDING DISCS**

fact, you will be freehanding the workpiece against the disc.

Begin by clearly marking the desired shape on the workpiece. Then turn on the saw and feed the workpiece into the spinning sandpaper on the flat side of the disc. Work only on the forward portion of the disc (in front of the arbor), where the sanding motion is down toward the saw table. This ensures the work is held to the table, for both safety and precision. If the

sanded surface is other than square to the underside face, adjust the arbor and thus the angle of the sanding disc accordingly. Keep the workpiece moving, turning it smoothly and steadily against the spin of the disc (counterclockwise if you are working on its left side) as you sand it to the desired shape. Use only a light amount of pressure against the disc. Most of your pressure should be to keep the workpiece flat to the table yet moving smoothly.

Maintenance of the Sanding Disc

A sanding disc gradually loses its effectiveness as shavings become trapped
between the abrasive particles. The problem is especially acute with resinous
woods, whose shavings become glazed
when heated. This, in turn, can lead to
overheating the wood and scorching. To
remove the particles, especially when I
notice they have accumulated to the point
where they are glazed, I spray the disc
with WD-40, wait about five minutes and
then rub the disc briskly with a stiff nylon
brush and wipe it off with a rag.

A worn sanding disc also increases the
chance of scorching the wood, as the particles lose their ability to cut the wood and
simply rub against it, heating it. The only
cure here is to take the time to replace
the disc when cleaning doesn't seem to
restore its cutting ability.

Careful to apply only light pressure, I freehand this workpiece against the flat side of the sanding disc to refine
the shape of the curved end cut. I work only on the front (downward-moving) portion of the disc and keep
the wood moving to avoid overcutting or scorching the wood.

Joinery

I have already shown many types of joints that can be cut on the table saw: housing joints, such as dadoes, grooves and rabbets; and simple butt and miter cuts, which, when fastened together with screws, dowels, biscuits or splines, create a joint. In this chapter, I will show you how to get fancy with these simple joints, offering tricks that increase the joints' surface areas or interlock structures to make them stronger (and often prettier). For example: Combine a tongue (a form of rabbet) with a groove to create a tongue-and-groove joint, join two grooved edges with a spline or cut grooves across the outside corner of a frame or box to create a feather-spline joint. I'll also show you how to utilize a version of the dado-spacing fixture (see chapter seven) to create a classic cigar-box-type joint and how to make lap- and bridle-type joints efficiently on the table saw. Then I'll present a variety of ways to use the table saw to make the most classic and ancient woodworking joint of all: the tenon. I'll conclude the chapter with a section on making a raised field along the perimeter of a panel—essential to making traditional-appearing frame and panel doors.

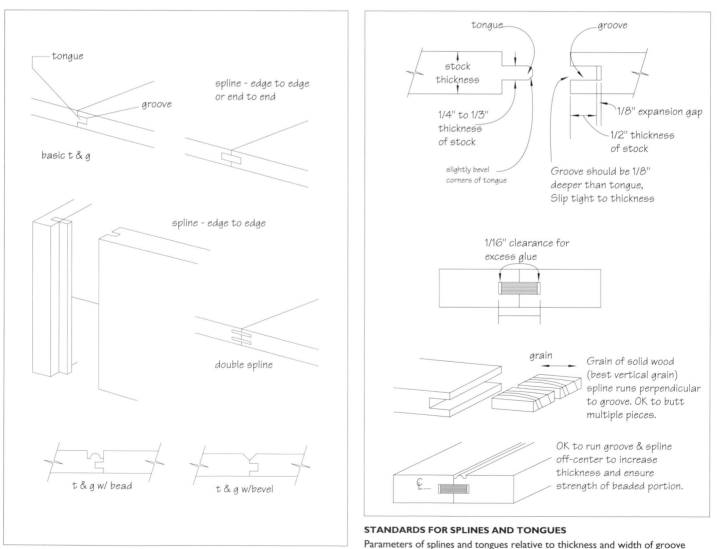

SPLINE JOINT AND TONGUE-AND-GROOVE OPTIONS

STANDARDS FOR SPLINES AND TONGUES
Parameters of splines and tongues relative to thickness and width of groove (note direction of grain for solid wood splines).

TONGUE-AND-GROOVE AND SPLINE JOINTS

When joining boards or panels edge to edge, you can mill a tongue along one edge of a board and an accepting groove into the adjacent board edge, or groove both edges and make a spline to act as a double tongue. I generally use a spline to glue-join plywood panels edge to edge or edge to face—the spline adds a huge amount of glue surface to the butt joint. I use the tongue-and-groove when dry-joining solid-wood boards—the tongue keeps the boards flush to one another yet allows movement due to shrinkage and expansion.

If I make the splines from hardwood plywood, generally one-fourth to one-third the thickness of the stock to be joined, I size the width of the groove to fit the plywood stock. As a general rule, I make the overall depth of the grooves equal to the thickness of the stock, adding ⅛" for glue clearance. If I decide to make the spline from solid stock, I orient the grain perpendicular to the joint to assure the spline won't break along the joint line. I make tongues ⅛" undersized in depth to provide room for expansion. I bevel the corners of both splines and tongues to ease assembly and prevent splinters from forming that might lift and obstruct the groove.

Unless I need to offset the groove—usually only if I'm cutting a bead or other profile in the face of the board—I center the groove along the edge of the board or panel. To do this with speed and precision, I set up the dado to make an undersized cut. I then run the stock twice: one face against the fence to create the first groove, and then the opposing face against the fence to make the second groove, which joins with the first to create a perfectly centered, full-width groove. As with any milling setup, I test the process first on scrap sized to the stock.

To keep the stock tight to the rip fence, I use the vertical featherboard fixture I designed for resaw work if the stock is greater than 6" wide. Otherwise I use the setup shown in the photo above. Notice that the featherboard on the outfeed side is set higher than the infeed board. This keeps the bearing pressure

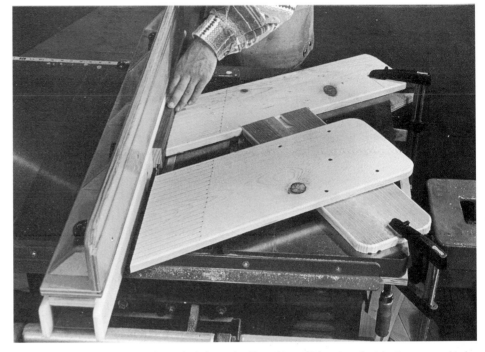

This arrangement of featherboards, in which the outfeed board is set higher than the infeed to prevent binding the outfeeding groove, keeps the stock tight to the rip fence, ensuring that the groove is milled parallel to the face of the board.

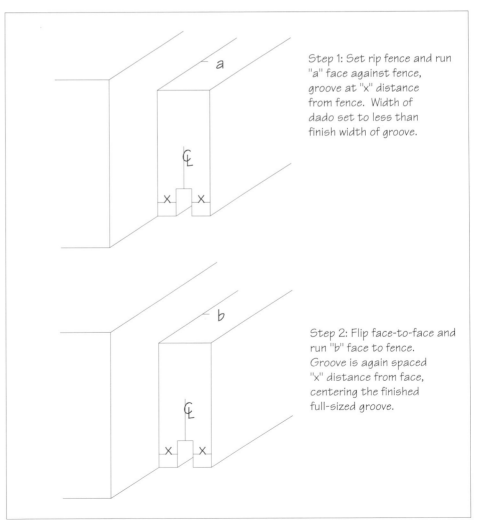

Step 1: Set rip fence and run "a" face against fence, groove at "x" distance from fence. Width of dado set to less than finish width of groove.

Step 2: Flip face-to-face and run "b" face to fence. Groove is again spaced "x" distance from face, centering the finished full-sized groove.

CENTERING A GROOVE

A dado blade cuts a tongue along the edge of a board in two passes. To ensure precision, I install shop-made featherboards to hold the stock tight to both the rip fence and to the saw table.

My setup for ripping an edge miter includes shop-made featherboards bolted to the universal fence fixture, a splitter set into the 45° kerf of a shop-made throat plate and the use of a shoe-type pusher (the overarm guard is removed for photo clarity).

above the newly milled groove so it doesn't collapse and bind on the blade. To prevent the outfeed board from shifting, I cut a shallow cross lap (⅜₆" deep) in the underlying diagonal board as well as screwing it in place.

To cut a tongue, I either use a tongue cutter on a molding head or make the cut in two passes over a dado blade. I set up the rip fence with my auxiliary rabbet fence and install ample hold-downs to keep the stock tight to the fence and saw table. Test cuts determine both the height of the blade and the setting of the rip fence. This dado method works well if the stock is uniform in thickness and you keep it under control through the cut. If your stock is uneven or is surfaced only on one side, use the molding head, which requires that you only index the finished, or "show," surface against the rip fence. This means the boards will be running on edge; you will definitely want to use the vertical featherboard and a tall auxiliary fence on the rip fence.

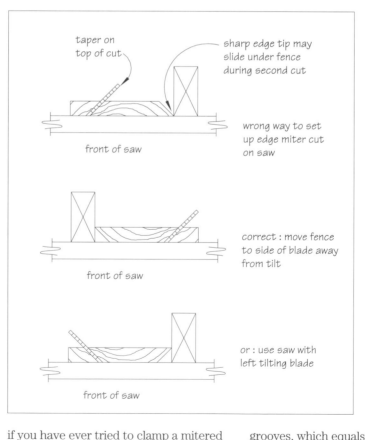

taper on top of cut

sharp edge tip may slide under fence during second cut

front of saw

wrong way to set up edge miter cut on saw

correct : move fence to side of blade away from tilt

front of saw

or : use saw with left tilting blade

front of saw

RIGHT AND WRONG ORIENTATION OF STOCK ON TABLE SAW FOR MITER CUT The first of these three diagrams shows the wrong way to set up an edge miter cut on the saw. The second diagram shows the correct way, while the bottom diagram illustrates an alternative method to set up the cut.

SPLINED MITER JOINT

Installing a spline into a miter joint adds a tremendous amount of strength and also helps hold the parts in position during assembly—something you will appreciate

if you have ever tried to clamp a mitered frame or box with only butted miters. I make the spline thickness about one-fourth the thickness of the stock (never more than one-third) and its width ⅛" less than the overall depth of the paired

grooves, which equals the thickness of the stock. I center the groove about one-third of the way up from the bottom of the miter to be sure that the groove doesn't cut through into the outside face of the stock. Again, I cut solid-wood splines so the grain direction runs perpendicular to the joint line.

When making the miter joint itself, I always orient the stock so the point of the miter comes out on the top side of the stock. This strategy prevents tear-out on the outside face of the stock and ensures more control when cutting the miter on the opposite edge, as I index the point to the side, rather than the bottom, of the rip fence. On right-tilt saws, this means placing the fence on the left of the blade when cutting an edge miter, an awkward position if you are not used to it—one of the reasons I opt for a left-tilt blade saw.

To cut an end miter, I guide the board through the blade with my miter gauge, setting it in the slot on the side of the blade away from the tilt. This keeps the pointed end of the miter at the top of the stock, ensuring a tear-free cut on the outside of the miter joint. The gauge's sturdy auxiliary fence and integral clamp help keep the board under control. If I'm cutting stock wider than about 8" or longer than 3', I use my crosscut box rather than the miter gauge.

To cut the spline groove in both edge and end miters, I run the miter joint through the blade (still tilted at 45°), indexing the tip of the miter against the rip fence. This ensures a safe and accurate cut. Never cut a spline groove into the edge of the stock away from the fence. Doing so is begging for kickback, not to mention an inaccurate cut. Be sure to set up the cut with scraps (sized to your stock) before committing the workpieces to the saw.

To cut a spline groove into the edge of a face miter, I use my rip fence sled fixture to carry the stock through the blade. I set the sled up by installing a backing board, with toggle clamp hold-downs, at a 45° angle to the table surface. A drafting square makes setup quick and easy. I position the rip fence-to-blade setting to cut one side of the miter joint on all the pieces. I then shift it slightly to cut the other side, placing the opposite side of the mating pieces against the sled face. I mark the outside face of the workpieces to keep all this straight, run test pieces and make a test fit with the spline.

If you don't want the spline to show on the outside corner of the miter joint, you

On my left-tilt blade saw, I cut an end miter (pointed side up to avoid tear-out) with the miter gauge set into the right-hand miter slot. The gauge's integral clamp holds the board flat to the table.

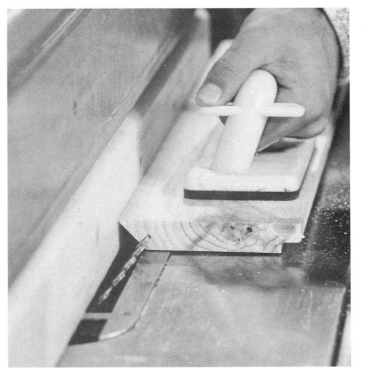

When cutting a groove for a spline into an edge miter, the rip fence acts as a safe precision guide. A shoe-type push stick keeps the board flat.

can make a blind groove instead of a through one. To do this, set up a stop block to limit the sled travel. This does mean, though, that you must shift the backing board to the opposite direction so the blade enters the back of the miter.

FEATHER-SPLINE JOINT

Feather joints are often created on the corners of a frame or box to add a decorative effect and more strength to an existing miter joint. I often make the feathers of a contrasting hardwood-grain running perpendicular to the miter line for strength—to make them stand out visually.

To make things easy, I make the spline the same thickness as the kerf of one of my combination blades. (You can, though, use a dado blade if you want to create a thicker feather.) In any case, I'm careful

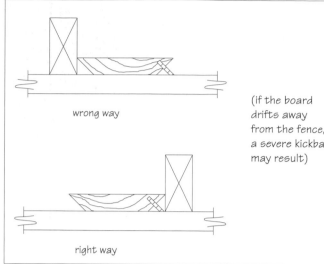

wrong way

(if the board drifts away from the fence, a severe kickback may result)

right way

THE RIGHT AND WRONG WAY TO CUT A SPLINE SLOT

USING MY RIP FENCE SLED TO CUT A BLIND GROOVE INTO A FACE MITER

to make splines thin enough to allow a little space for glue within the kerf. I test the fit by checking to see that the feather slips into the groove with almost no resistance yet does not go in so loose that it falls out of the slot.

To set up the feather joint fixture on the rip fence sled, place a drafting triangle on the side table and hold it to the underside of the infeed side workpiece support. Lock this support in place to the MiniTrack, and then align the second support perpendicular to the first by holding a framing square to both. To set the fence-to-blade position, I index a story stick laid out with the kerf positions for the feathers. A ⅛" hardboard plate on the infeed side support fixture creates a zero-clearance backing that prevents tear-out. I also use this backing plate to establish the blade height: I simply observe the kerf, raising the blade in increments to obtain the height, and thus the depth, of spline that I want.

FEATHER-SPLINE JOINTS

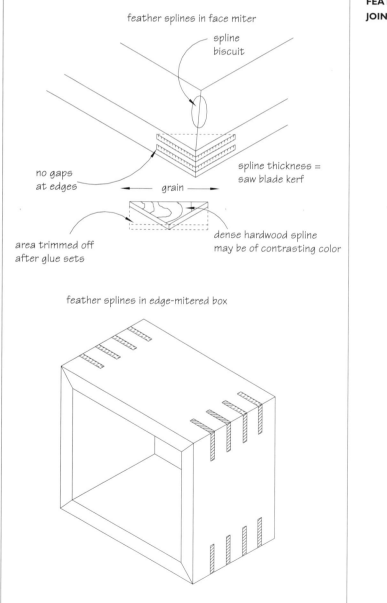

feather splines in face miter

spline biscuit

no gaps at edges

grain

spline thickness = saw blade kerf

area trimmed off after glue sets

dense hardwood spline may be of contrasting color

feather splines in edge-mitered box

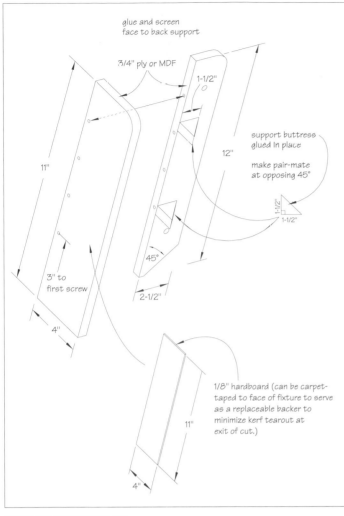

glue and screen
face to back support

3/4" ply or MDF

1-1/2"

support buttress
glued In place

make pair-mate
at opposing 45°

1-1/2"
1-1/2"

11"

12"

45°

3" to
first screw

2-1/2"

4"

1/8" hardboard (can be carpet-
taped to face of fixture to serve
as a replaceable backer to
minimize kerf tearout at
exit of cut.)

11"

4"

FEATHER JOINT FIXTURE

I set the second support square to the first support using a 24" framing square.

A drafting triangle set between the underside of the support fixture and the saw makes quick work of securing the workpiece support to the sliding rip fence fixture at a precise 45° to the table.

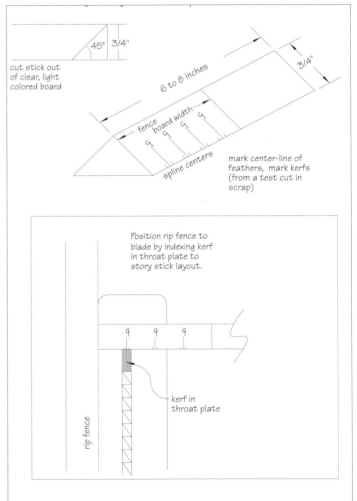

45°   3/4"

cut stick out
of clear, light
colored board

6 to 8 inches

3/4"

fence

board width

spline centers

mark center-line of
feathers, mark kerfs
(from a test cut in
scrap)

Position rip fence to
blade by indexing kerf
in throat plate to
story stick layout.

kerf in
throat plate

rip fence

STORY STICK LAYOUT FOR FEATHER SPLINES

A frame assembly sits in position on the feather joint fixture ready for spline cutting. The clamp pad bolted to the MiniTrack holds the frame tight to the side of the sled, ensuring an accurate spline kerf.

A box sits in its slotting position on the feather joint fixture. I use a guitar maker's padded clamp to hold the box to the support to prevent shifting.

I always preassemble frames and boxes before cutting the spline slots. Though you could theoretically cut the slots in the individual pieces, it's faster and more accurate to cut them into an assembly. I find that a glue joint is usually strong enough in small assemblies, though I often add spline biscuits with a biscuit joiner. Never use metal fasteners, as they could come in contact with the blade as you cut the corner splines.

To make the slot cut, I set the frame assembly into the crotch of the two supports, clamping it securely to the sled with a toggle clamp mounted to a pad, which is, in turn, bolted to the MiniTrack. I make the first slot cut, unclamp the assembly and then rotate it to make the second and subsequent slots in the other corners. I'm careful not to drag the assembly back through the blade as this can increase the width of the slot, causing a loose fit to the spline. Instead, I unclamp and remove the assembly after each forward pass through the blade.

Making kerfs for feather splines in the outside corners of a box is similar to slotting a frame assembly. In addition to the setup and procedures outlined previously, you must make multiple slot cuts. To do this, cut the outside spline kerfs at each corner by making the first slot and then turning the workpiece edge to edge to make the second. Now work your way in toward the center, cutting the next pair

Box joints add elegance to the drawers for my wall-hung toolbox. The groove in the side of the drawer surrounds a hardwood runner mounted inside the cabinet to create a drawer slide.

of slots from either edge. You can do one corner at a time or make one feather cut in all four corners before moving on to the next.

BOX JOINT

Another decorative joint that you can make on the table saw is the finger, or box, joint. This joint, though complex in appearance, is fast to make and produces an immensely strong corner connection. To make the joint, I use a dado-spacing fixture similar to the one shown in chapter seven—except I add a miniaturized version of this fence fixture to my small crosscut box. Again, a length of inlaid MiniTrack allows precision side-to-side movement of the fence to make it easy to set the key-to-blade distance.

After setting up the crosscut box with the sliding fence and key, follow this step-by-step procedure to make the box joint around the four corners of a box, such as a drawer.

1. Get out the box parts, cutting all sides from the same length of board, if possible, to ensure consistent width, thickness and appearance. Get out extra stock of the same dimension for test cuts.

2. Size the width of the key to equal the notch size determined from the layout. For ease of making this joint on the table saw, pin width equals notch width across the width of the board—and layout begins and ends with a full-width notch or pin. Set the dado blade to this width, and set the blade height equal to the stock thickness plus 1/32", which allows the pins

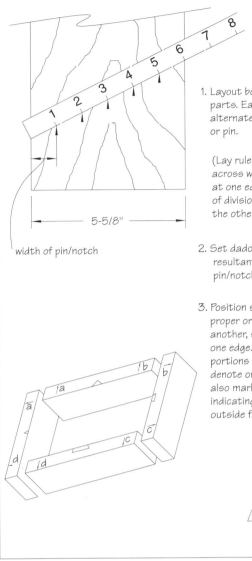

1. Layout board to even parts. Each part will be, alternately a notch or pin.

   (Lay ruler at angle across width of board—at one edge, the number of divisions wanted at the other edge.)

2. Set dado blade to resultant width of pin/notch.

3. Position sides of box in proper orientation to one another, standing up on one edge. Mark edge with portions pyramid to denote orientation and also mark each corner, indicating with arrow outside face.

5-5/8"

width of pin/notch

BOX JOINT LAYOUT

Having set the outside jaws of my caliper to the width of the key (to which the width of the dado blade has been set), I use the inside caliper jaws to index the distance from the edge of the blade to the key.

Using the side board as an index, I butt the front board against its edge to make the first notch.

With an auxiliary fence bolted to my small crosscut box, I position the side board of a box assembly over a key to index the second and subsequent notch cuts to create the pins of a box joint.

to protrude for flush-fitting with a plane when the joint is assembled.

3. Set the key-to-blade spacing equal to the width of the notch created by the dado blade. I use a set of calipers to index the spacing. Test cut two scrap pieces.

4. Begin cutting the box joint at the first corner by butting the top edge of the box's side board against the key and running the board through the dado to cut the first notch. Lift the board off the fixture (do not drag it back through the blade, as this can cause an oversize cut and tear-out), pull the fixture back, set the just-cut notch over the key and cut the second notch. Continue in this way to the last notch. What's left between the notches are the pins.

5. Now cut the receiving notches for these pins into the mating piece—the front board at this particular corner. To do this, reverse the side board (the board you just made the pins in) and set its first-cut notch over the key. Checking your pyramid and corner marks to keep yourself oriented, butt the top edge of the front board against the edge of the side board facing the blade and cut the first notch. (This strategy of using the last-cut board to index the cut guarantees that the last notch-to-pin fit at this corner will come out even.) Test cuts in scrap make this clear. Now remove the side board and continue cutting notches by setting the last-cut notch over the key until you reach the end of the board.

6. Repeat steps four and five at the next corner.

LAP AND BRIDLE JOINTS

While there are innumerable variations of the lap and bridle joints, the ones presented here represent versions that can be cut entirely on the table saw. I go with lap and bridle joints when I'm looking for easily made joints that offer exceptionally high structural strength without the need for additional fasteners.

Corner Half-Lap

Making the corner half-lap is easy. I start by setting a stop on the crosscut box (or miter gauge auxiliary fence) to index the shoulder cut. Instead of measuring, I hold the mating piece against the block and to the far edge of the saw-kerf in the table of

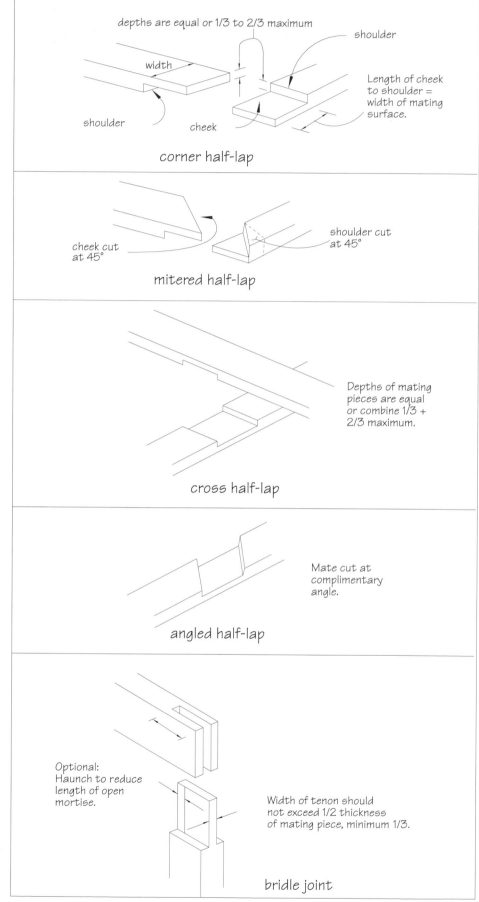

corner half-lap

mitered half-lap

cross half-lap

angled half-lap

bridle joint

CORNER HALF-LAP, MITERED HALF-LAP, CROSS HALF-LAP, ANGLED HALF-LAP, BRIDLE JOINT

the box. Don't index to the edge of the kerf closest to the stop—the shoulder would be overcut by the width of the saw blade. I set the height of the blade (testing on scrap) to cut to half the thickness of the stock and make the shoulder cut in both mating pieces, assuming both are of the same width; otherwise reset the stop.

Though I could just nibble away the waste from the shoulder cut to the end of the board by multiple passes over the blade—a dado blade would be even quicker—I can more quickly and accurately cut off the waste using my sliding rip fence fixture and running the workpiece vertically through the blade. After making test cuts on scrap to set the fence-to-blade position, I crank up the blade to the full length of cheek (to the top of the shoulder kerf) and mark the crank position on the face of the saw. I then back the blade down and proceed to cut the cheek of the joint in steps, never more than 1" at a time and even less in dense hardwood. If I'm cutting a number of these joints, I install a 24-tooth, thin-kerf rip blade, finding that this blade will run faster, cooler and thus more warp-free than a standard combination blade.

Mitered Half-Lap

A mitered half-lap joint gives you the look of a miter joint on one side with much more strength than a standard miter joint buffed up with a spline or a feather. That's because the broad cheek-to-cheek contact offers more glue surface area.

Begin cutting the mitered half-lap by cutting the shoulders on both pieces: Use a crosscut box set up with a stop to index the square shoulder cut. Use the miter sled to cut the mitered shoulder. Here you need only align the outside corner of the end of the board to the kerf in the sled table. To ensure accuracy, especially when doing several of these joints in sequence, I screw a stop block to the table to index the shoulder cut.

To complete the joint on the square-shouldered component, I cut off the cheek as described above for a standard half-lap, which is what this was up to now. Then I cut a miter across the cheek, from the end corner to the shoulder line. Cutting the cheek of the component with the mitered shoulder requires a modification to the rip

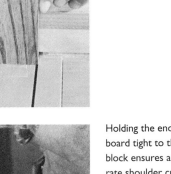

Hold the board to the far side of the kerf when indexing the crosscut box stop to the width of the mating piece.

Holding the end of the board tight to the stop block ensures an accurate shoulder cut on this cross lap. I keep the same stop setting if the mating piece is of the same width.

Cutting the cheek of the half-lap with the sliding rip fence fixture is a quick and accurate way to complete the joint. A backer board holds the workpiece perpendicular to table, prevents tear-out at the exit of the cut and clamps the workpiece flat to the sled.

I cut the 45° shoulder of a mitered half-lap with my miter box fixture. A stop screwed to the base indexes the cut to ensure precision—which is especially useful when I'm cutting a number of these joints.

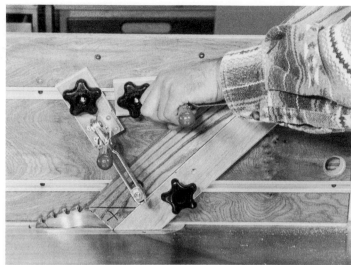

With the workpiece held to a backer board set at 45° on the sled, I cut off the cheek of the mitered-shoulder component. To cut the opposite end, I set up the backer at the opposing 45° angle.

fence sled: the installation of a backer board at a 45° angle to the saw table. I set the workpiece on the backer and use a clamp pad to hold it firmly to the sled. The offcut drops away from the blade. To cut the opposite end, I install a second backer at the opposing 45° angle.

Cross and Angled Cross Half-Lap

These lap joints allow two boards to securely interlock as they pass one another. In most cases, the laps are of equal depth so the faces of the boards come flush. To make cross laps on the table saw, I utilize a spacer system to automatically set the limits of the two shoulder cuts. The drawing at right shows how I set up this system on my crosscut box and stop system. I set the height of the dado blade to 1/16" less than half the thickness of the stock, figuring on trimming to the finished depth of lap with chisels and/or rabbet plane. In this way, the joint line will be straight and clean. To set the height accurately, I test cut on scrap.

I make the first cut with the spacer in place against the stop. I then remove the spacer and make a series of cuts, working my way toward the stop. At the stop, the cut establishes the other shoulder of the joint. I then make the receiving lap in the mating piece, shifting the stop and spacer on the crosscut box as necessary to align with the layout on the workpiece (the joint on the mating piece may not lie at the same distance away from the end of

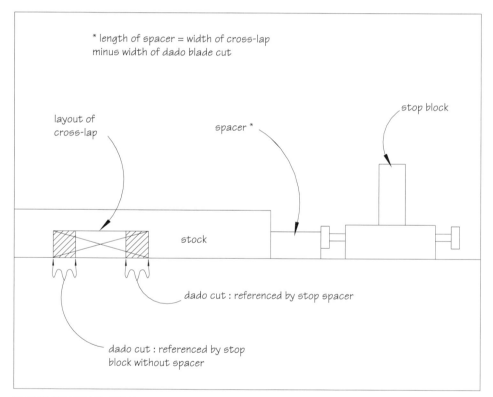

* length of spacer = width of cross-lap minus width of dado blade cut

layout of cross-lap

spacer *

stop block

stock

dado cut : referenced by stop spacer

dado cut : referenced by stop block without spacer

SIZING SPACER TO CUT CROSS LAP

the board). If both components are of the same width, I can use the same spacer to index the cut.

If I'm cutting an angled cross lap, I install an auxiliary fence with a stop-and-spacer system to a pair of miter gauges. After cutting scraps to fine-tune the cutting height, I cut the first angled lap in the same way I cut a standard cross lap. I cut the mating lap with the same setup at the same angle, though I may have to shift

the stop and spacer to meet the layout of the mate.

Bridle Joint

The bridle joint is both strong and decorative—you could call it a lazy man's mortise and tenon. It's lazy because the bridle is open and can thus be produced entirely on the table saw without the need for chiseling out the waste, as you do in a standard closed miter. Yet the shoulders and broad cheek surfaces make the joint amply strong, though not quite as structurally sound as a full mortise-and-tenon joint that features shoulders on all four sides. The length of the bridle, and thus the width of the tenon, is limited by how deep you can cut the bridle with your saw. If you are using a standard 8" blade, for example, your cut will be limited to about 2". You can, of course, haunch the tenon to fit the length of bridle.

I begin the bridle cut by laying out the joint on a story stick. To cut the bridle's open mortise, I set up a dado blade to the thickness of the tenon. Again using the story stick, I index the face of the sliding rip fence fixture to the outside edges of the blade, check the cut on scrap, and then saw out the bridle with a series of stepped passes through the blade. (See the chart in chapter seven to determine the amount to remove per width of blade per pass.) To provide adequate backing for the stock, I add a fresh removable backer strip to the vertical backstop.

To cut the tenon, I cut the shoulders on my crosscut box to a stop, and the cheeks with the rip fence sled indexed by the story stick to a thin-kerf rip blade. I make two passes, one for each cheek, keeping the same face of the stock to the sled. A spacer system ensures speed and accuracy. This eliminates errors from inconsistency in stock thickness, which can happen if I index one side and then the other against the fence, and allows me to cut the tenon off center if necessary. Alternatively, I may use the double-blade method to cut both cheeks at once.

TENONS

The classic mortise and tenon is the mainstay joint of woodworking. The side and end shoulders lend the joint tremendous mechanical strength while the cheeks offer a broad glue surface. This is the joint of choice for doorframes, bed frames, table aprons and anywhere else that strength is of primary importance. There are, however, some caveats: To ensure rigidity, the shoulders must fit tight to the mating surface and the cheeks must meet the sides of the mortise uniformly to give a good glue surface. But on your table saw set up with well-made fixtures, you have an excellent tool for creating the tenon

With a spacer sized to the width of the mating piece less the width of the dado blade cut, I index the workpiece to make the first cut of the cross lap.

Removing the spacer, I work my way toward the stop. The last cut with the end of the board indexed to the stop defines the finished width of the cross lap cut.

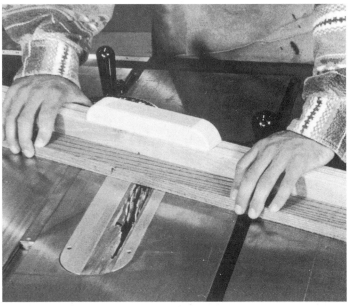

I use the spacer-and-stop system—here placed on a doubled miter gauge setup—to cut the seat of an angled cross lap.

With the stock held upright on my rip fence sled and snugged against a removable backing board to reduce tear-out, I make the first step cut of the bridle.

Using a story stick to index the face of the sliding rip fence fixture to the outside edges of the blade.

component of this joint.

In this section I describe two basic methods of producing tenons: the horizontal cut—a good choice if the board is longer than 3'—using a dado and a crosscut sled; and the vertical cut that employs the rip fence sled fixture. The vertical cut is best for shorter boards and for speed because you can use two blades to cut both cheek faces at once. I also show how to make specialized tenons, such as angled-shoulder and haunched.

Horizontal-Cut Tenon

To make a horizontal-cut tenon, first cut the shoulder with a standard combination or crosscut blade. I use the same setup employed for cutting the shoulders of the half-lap, except I add shoulder cuts to the other side and to one or both edges of the stock. (To keep millwork simple, I usually make the edge shoulder cuts the same depth setting as the cheek if possible.) Once the shoulders are cut, set up the dado blade to its maximum cutting width to speed the process, and set its cutting height to come to ¹⁄₃₂" of the cheek layout line. Before cutting with the dado, move the stop in slightly so the dado won't touch the shoulder kerf cut and throw it off. Then start dado cutting from the end of the board, working your way in until the board hits the stop. Turn the board

over and repeat the wasting process. Finally, clean down to the tenon line with the rabbet plane.

Vertical-Cut Tenon

Begin the vertical-cut tenon by making the shoulder cuts as shown for the horizontal cut. Then comes the vertical cut: Cut off the cheeks using the rip fence sled fixture. Here you have two choices: making two cuts with a single blade and spacer system or installing two identical blades to cut both tenon cheeks at once. I find the latter is more efficient for production work, but your saw must have sufficient power (2 hp minimum is recommended) to run two blades hard simultaneously. I also recommend going to a 24-tooth, thin-kerf rip blade—here you'll need two, of course—to ensure best results. If you do not have these blades, you could go with the two outer blades from a standard stacking dado set. Be aware, however, that they won't cut as efficiently as the thin-kerf rip blades and will require more step cuts.

Setting up the double blades requires a plywood washer (don't use solid wood, as its thickness can change with humidity) augmented by paper or plastic dado blade washers for fine-tuning the width. The washer width must be greater than the tenon width to account for the tip clear-

ance offset from the blade plate. Install a fresh throat plate and set the fence to a story stick.

Now test cut a scrap of stock. When satisfied, clamp the stock in place and begin making the cuts in steps, never more than 1" at a pass, less if dense hardwood. On the last cut in which the blades reach the shoulder cuts, push the sled all the way past the blade and turn off

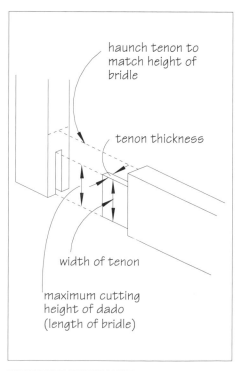

HAUNCHED BRIDLE JOINT

the saw. Then unclamp the stock and remove the offcut between the tenon and the sled face.

To cut the tenon with a single blade, I set up a stop-and-spacer system that automatically indexes the rip fence, and thus the sled fixture with the workpiece, to the blade for both sides of the cheek cut. I find the spacer system is a much better method than reversing the stock face-to-face to cut the second tenon. In the latter method, it is too easy to get the cut off the layout, especially if the stock thickness is inconsistent. The reversal method is also not usable if the tenon is offset.

To construct the spacing system, cut a spacer block to exactly equal the width of the tenon plus the width of the saw-kerf made by the blade you will be using. Install a stop to the right of the rip fence, clamping it to the saw and/or the extension table. My more permanent system uses a MiniTrack let into the extension table. To set the stop, I slide the stick side to side and lock it down with the two-handled bolts at the desired location.

After setting the rip fence to the stop and spacer—either to center the tenon or to offset it—make the first cheek cut with the spacer in place. Then remove the spacer, shift the fence against the stop and make the second cheek cut. Save the washer and story stick for the next time you want to cut this size tenon.

Angled Shoulder Tenon

If the shoulder of the tenon is to be at an angle, I first cut the end of the board to that angle. In this way, I can set the miter gauge to the end-cut angle and use the rip fence as a stop to index the length of the tenon and thus the shoulder cut. I use a mirror jig (see chapter seven) to set the mirror angle necessary to cut the shoulder on the opposite end. I cut the cheeks of the tenon with the workpiece upright in the rip fence sled, setting up supports at the cut angle, or I nibble away the waste with a dado blade.

Haunched Tenon

I use my crosscut box with a fixed stop to quickly cut the haunch of a tenon. I set the stop to index the length of the haunch, and the blade height to cut the

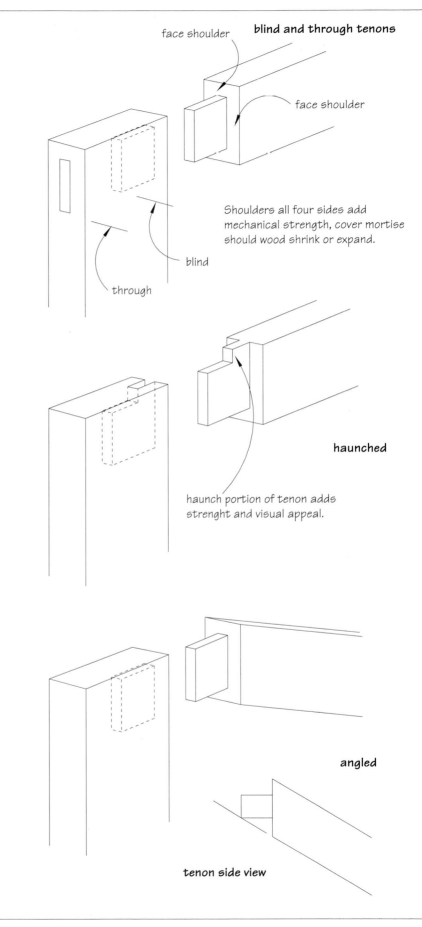

blind and through tenons

face shoulder

face shoulder

blind

through

Shoulders all four sides add mechanical strength, cover mortise should wood shrink or expand.

haunched

haunch portion of tenon adds strenght and visual appeal.

angled

tenon side view

TYPES OF TENON JOINTS

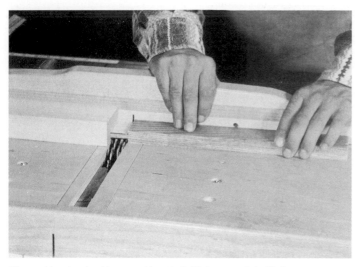

To make a smooth cheek that will adhere well to glue, use a rabbet plane to remove the rough surface left behind by the dado blade.

After making the shoulder cut with a single blade, use a dado blade to remove waste between the shoulder kerf cut and the end of the workpiece. The stop block prevents the dado from going into the shoulder.

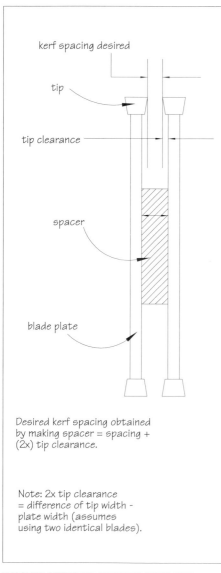

kerf spacing desired

tip

tip clearance

spacer

blade plate

Desired kerf spacing obtained by making spacer = spacing + (2x) tip clearance.

Note: 2x tip clearance = difference of tip width - plate width (assumes using two identical blades).

WASHER SETUP TO SPACE BLADES FOR DOUBLE CUT

A story stick makes quick work of setting the fence-to-blade position.

THE DOUBLE-BLADE CUT IN ACTION

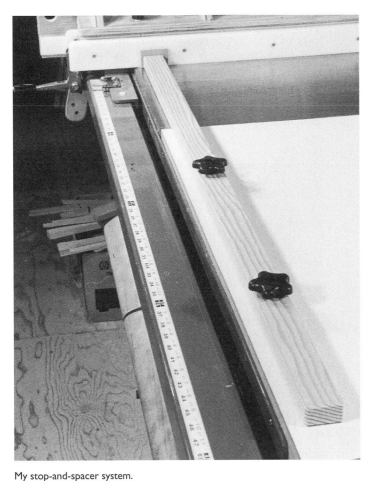

My stop-and-spacer system.

Here the sliding stop of my system is removed to reveal the MiniTrack that allows side-to-side adjustment and lockdown. I cut a groove with a router to let the track sit flush to the table surface.

haunch to width. To remove the waste I clamp the stock to the sliding rip fence sled fixture.

CUTTING A RAISED PANEL

Most cabinetmakers will use a shaper or router to cut raised panels, appreciating the wide variety of shapes and the ease of setup offered by this method. I often go this route also, but not always. There is a significant drawback to shaper-made raised panels: namely, the small size of the raised field. If I intend to make a traditional Shaker-style raised-panel door, which

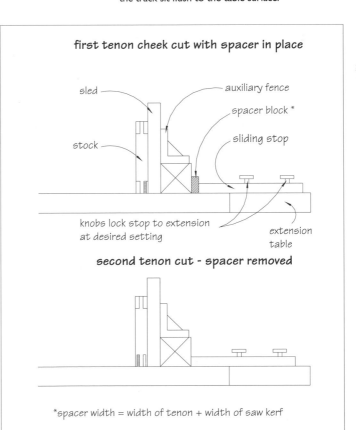

SPACER SYSTEM FOR INDEXING TENON CUTS

first tenon cheek cut with spacer in place

sled
auxiliary fence
spacer block *
stock
sliding stop
knobs lock stop to extension at desired setting
extension table

second tenon cut - spacer removed

*spacer width = width of tenon + width of saw kerf

SAFETY *tip*

Be sure to use a fresh throat plate to create zero clearance around each blade; otherwise, you lose support for the workpiece between the blades, which can result in the stock jamming in the throat opening.

By indexing the end of the stock to a stop, I quickly and accurately cut the shoulder of the haunch.

To make the waste cut, clamp the stock vertically to the sliding rip fence fixture.

typically boasts a raised field width of at least 2", I make the cut on my table saw. Depending on how I set up the cut, I can make either a shouldered or a flush raised panel. The secret to getting an accurate and consistent cut around all four sides of the panel is to use a fixture to carry the workpiece securely and predictably through the blade. Note that the carriage table can vary in angle to allow you to change the profile of the field.

Making the Cut

It's important to cut the angle of the raised field so that it fits snugly into the groove of the surrounding frame. If the angle is off, or you cut the field too shallow, the panel will rattle around—an especially noticeable and annoying trait in a door frame. Be certain the top and bottom of the panel fit tightly. At the sides it's OK to allow a little gap to accommodate expansion of the panel with humidity changes.

Set up the sled fixture to make the field cut by adjusting the angle of the panel carriage and the side-to-side position of the rip fence. I recommend that you use a combination blade to cut the field, finding it produces a smooth cut that requires only a little sanding. Set the blade height to cut to the kerf you've already made to define the shoulder. If there is no shoulder, the blade should be able to raise high enough to clear the face of the panel. Count on making a number

With the miter gauge set to the same angle as the end cut, I index the end of the board against the rip fence to cut the shoulder of this angled tenon joint.

of test cuts to get the cut just right, checking the field's fit (remember to sand off the rough blade marks) in the frame groove. Look from the end to observe the cross section of the fit.

When satisfied with your test cuts, place a presized and pre-shoulder-cut (unless flush type) panel in position on

the carriage, grain running vertically, with the bottom of the panel sitting on the hardboard guide and the front edge aligned against the front guide. Lock the panel down with one or more toggle clamps. If the panel is warped—that is, if it rocks on the panel carriage—use a back support with clamps instead of the front

MAKING A DEDICATED RAISED-PANEL FIXTURE

The carriage system of my raised-panel sled fixture (shown here) is adjustable to angles from perpendicular to about 15° relative to the blade—a range that covers most raised-panel field cuts. The heavy weight (inertia dampens vibration and jerky movement), snug-fitting guide system and clamp hold-downs reward me with fast, clean and accurate cuts.

Make all the primary parts of this fixture from a flat sheet of ¾" hardwood ply or MDF. Round all corners and edges, sand and finish. Use piano hinges at the junctures of the angle-adjustment plate and the panel-carriage hinge block. A strip of hardboard provides a reference surface for the bottom edge of panel stock while a pair of MiniTracks let into the panel carriage provides a grip for the hold-down/backer boards. Glue and screw the spacer and hinge block to the vertical base plate. Don't, however, glue the outer guide rail to the spacer; use screws so you can make fine adjustments in the sliding friction by inserting lengths of sandpaper strips.

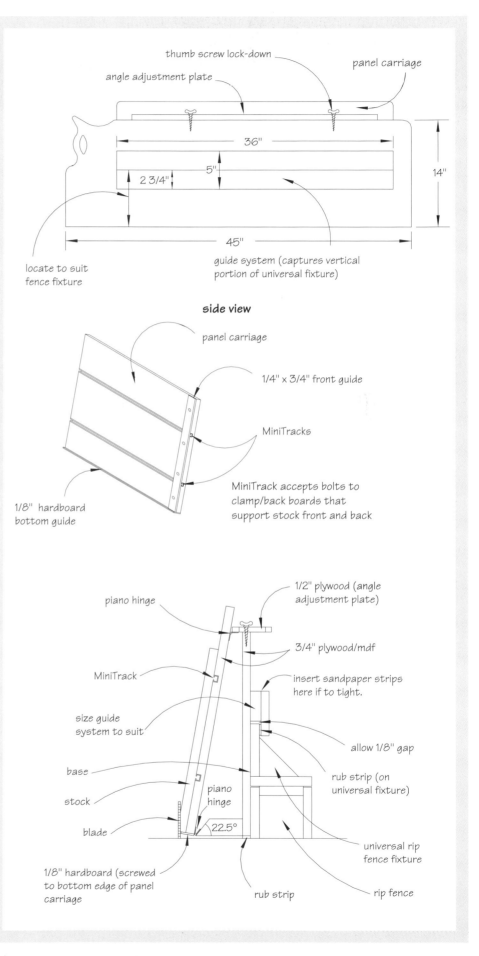

thumb screw lock-down

panel carriage

angle adjustment plate

36"

5"

2 3/4"

14"

45"

locate to suit fence fixture

guide system (captures vertical portion of universal fixture)

side view

panel carriage

1/4" x 3/4" front guide

MiniTracks

MiniTrack accepts bolts to clamp/back boards that support stock front and back

1/8" hardboard bottom guide

piano hinge

1/2" plywood (angle adjustment plate)

3/4" plywood/mdf

MiniTrack

insert sandpaper strips here if to tight.

size guide system to suit

allow 1/8" gap

base

rub strip (on universal fixture)

stock

piano hinge

blade

22.5°

1/8" hardboard (screwed to bottom edge of panel carriage

universal rip fence fixture

rub strip

rip fence

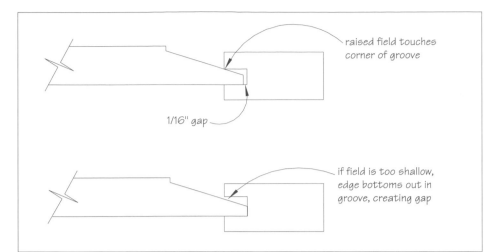

raised field touches
corner of groove

1/16" gap

if field is too shallow,
edge bottoms out in
groove, creating gap

RAISED-PANEL CROSS SECTION

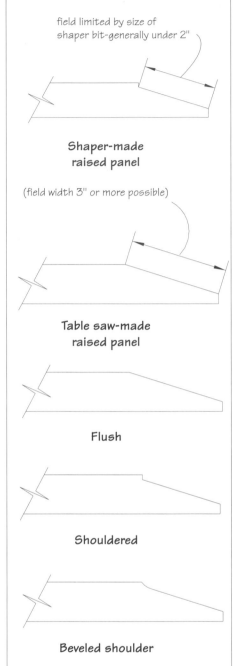

field limited by size of
shaper bit-generally under 2"

**Shaper-made
raised panel**

(field width 3" or more possible)

**Table saw-made
raised panel**

Flush

Shouldered

Beveled shoulder

RAISED PANEL PROFILES

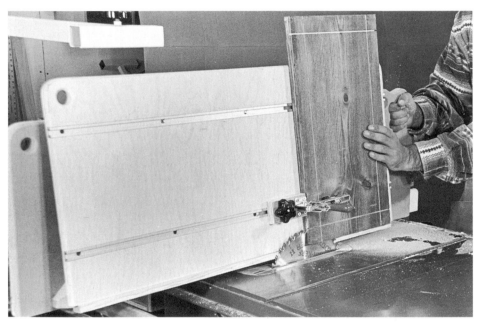

My sliding panel carriage, designed to work with the universal rip fence fixture, holds a panel flat and secure as I run it through the blade to create a raised field around its perimeter. The kerfs cut into the face of the panel define the shoulders of the field.

guide. Now turn on the saw and make the first field cut across the bottom end of the panel. Unclamp, rotate the panel counter-clockwise onto its side and make the second cut. Continue in this way until you've cut all four sides. If you are doing more than one panel, I let the blade run free for a half minute or so to cool. Clean the field surface with a sandpaper block. To prevent oversanding, check the fit of the field into the groove as you work.

APPENDIX A

Suppliers and Manufacturers of Tools That Appear in This Book

Saws
- Stationary saw, left tilt (by Jet)
- Contractor's saw (by Delta)
- Combination machine (by Robland from Laguna Tools)
- Combination machine (by Robland)
- Bench saw (by DeWalt)

Aftermarket Miter Gauges
- "Accu-Miter" (manufactured by JDS)
- "Deluxe Miter Gauge" (from Woodhaven)

Alignment and Setup Tools
- Arbor alignment bar (by Exact Cuts Tool Co., Inc.)
- Dial indicator and mounting bars (by In-Line Industries)
- "Gauge-It" angle and height adjustment tool (from Woodworker's Supply)
- Adjustable triangle (by AngleWright)
- "Mitermatic" table saw setup tool (from Garrett Wade Co. and Woodhaven)
- Table of cove cutting angles (by Klausz-Tech)

Safety and Dust Control Equipment
- Helmet with Forced-Air Dust System (from Airware America)
- Dust collector (main system by Jet; portable mini-collector by Woodtek from Woodworker's Supply)
- Remote switch system (from Woodworker's Supply)
- Antikickback rollers (from Woodworker's Supply)
- Shoe-type push sticks (from Jesada Tools)
- Panic stop switch (by Rei Tech)
- Magnetic feather board (by
- Safety glasses (by Industrial Safety Co.)

Jig-Making Materials
- "MiniTrack" extrusions (from Garrett Wade Co., Woodhaven)
- Stick-on rules (from Woodworker's Supply
- Miter gauge slot slide bars (the aluminum Miter Slider by Taylor Design Group, Inc. and solid steel bars from Woodhaven)
- High density plastic wear strips (from Woodhaven and Woodworker's Supply)
- Ball rollers (from Woodworker's Supply and Lee Valley)
- Knobs, toggle clamps, other hardware items (from Woodhaven, Woodworker's Supply and Reid Tool Supply)
- T-slot bolts and T-slot cutting router bit (from Woodworker's Supply)
- Steel cleats for hanging the blade box (from Woodworker's Supply)

Machine Accessories and Blades
- Saw blades and stiffeners (by Forrest Manufacturing Co.)
- Plastic throat insert (from Woodworker's Supply)
- Aluminum plate with replaceable wood insert (Wood Dynamics)
- Molding heads and cutters (by Delta and Sears)
- Belt and pully upgrade (by In-Line Industries)
- Adjustable stacking dado (by DMT and Sears)
- Mobile stands and drop-down outfeed roller table (by HTC Products)

Milling and Processing Accessories
- Sanding disc with one straight and one tapered side (from Woodworker's Supply)
- "Big Foot" roller stand (from Woodworker's Supply)

APPENDIX B

Manufacturer and Supplier Addresses

AIRWARE AMERICA
P.O. Box 975
Elbow Lake, MN 56531
(800-328-1792)

ANGLEWRIGHT TOOL CO.
P.O. Box 25632
Los Angeles, CA 90025
(310-471-7432)

DELTA
(800-438-2486)

DEWALT
(800-433-9258)

GARRETT WADE CO.
161 Avenue of the Americas
New York, NY 10013
(800-221-2942)

HTC PRODUCTS
Royal Oak, MI 48068
(800-624-2027)

INDUSTRIAL SAFETY CO.
1390 Nuebrecht Rd.
Lima, OH 45801
(419-227-6030)

IN-LINE INDUSTRIES
661 S. Main St.
Webster, MA 01570
(800-533-6709)

JET
(800-274-6848)

JDS COMPANY
800 Dutch Square Blvd., Suite 200,
Columbia, SC 29210
(800-382-2637)

FORREST MANUFACTURING CO.
457 River Road
Clifton, NJ 07014
(201-471-5236)

JESADA TOOLS
310 Mears Boulevard
Oldsmar, FL 34677
(813-891-6259)

KLAUSZ-TECH
Box 78
Pluckemin, NJ 07978

LAGUNA TOOLS (Robland saws)
2265 Laguna Canyon Road
Laguna Beach, CA 92651
(714-494-7006)

MESA VISTA DESIGN
804 Tulip Road
Rio Rancho, NM 87124
(505-892-0293)

MODULUS 2000 MACHINERY INC.
P.O. Box 206
Saint Hubert, Quebec J3Y5T3
(800-633-8587)

REID TOOL SUPPLY CO.
2265 Black Creek Road
Muskegon, MI 49444
(616-777-2951)

REI TECH
11965 12th Ave. South, Suite 200,
Burnsville, MN 55337
(800-385-6161)

TAYLOR DESIGN GROUP, INC.
P.O. Box 810262
Dallas, TX 75381
(972-243-7943)

WOOD DYNAMICS
15034 NE 172 Ave.
Brush Prairie, WA 985606
(253-896-9047)

WOODHAVEN
501 W. 1st Ave.
Durant, Iowa 52747
(800-344-6657)

WOODWORKER'S SUPPLY, INC.
1108 North Glenn Road
Casper, Wyoming 82601
(307-237-5528)

INDEX